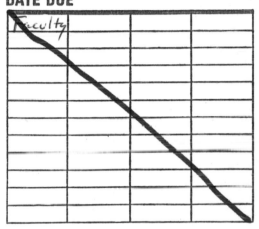

Evaluating Occupational Education and Training Programs

Evaluating Occupational Education and Training Programs

TIM L. WENTLING
University of Illinois

TOM E. LAWSON
3M Company

Allyn and Bacon, Inc.
BOSTON · LONDON · SYDNEY

Library of Congress Cataloging in Publication Data

Wentling, Tim L   1946–
    Evaluating occupational education and training
programs.

    Includes bibliographical references and index.
    1. Vocational education. 2. Occupational training.
3. Educational surveys. I. Lawson, Tom E., joint
author. II. Title.
LC1044.W37   375   74-32213

ISBN 0-205-05048-4

Contents

Foreword

Now, thanks to Wentling and Lawson, we have a vivid description of ways of evaluating programs in occupational education. Theirs is a "tried program" with real results. Developed in the armchair, and tested in the real world, *Evaluating Occupational Education and Training Programs* provides checklists and examples which have worked for others, and which no other book offers.

This is a book to be welcomed by those concerned with educational evaluation. In the past three years we have had several such books. *Handbook on Formative and Summative Evaluation of Student Learning,* by Bloom, Hastings, and Madaus, did well as a reference book on the single aspect of student learning. *School Evaluation: The Politics and the Process*, edited by Ernest R. House, tells us about many aspects beyond student learning. In *Evaluating Educational Performance: A Sourcebook of Methods, Instruments, and Examples*, Herbert Wahlbert (ed.) has shown us a variety of approaches to evaluation of innovations. Now there is *Evaluating Occupational Education and Training Programs*, by Wentling and Lawson.

Although most of the examples in this book deal with vocational-technical education (and career concerns), the methodologies suggested can be adapted to any area. Those concerned with evaluating *any* program—elementary school to university—should consider the methods and principles set forth in this book. Both Wentling and Lawson have had firsthand experience in this area. They know and appreciate the real problems of evaluating in the real world. I find the book informative, stimulating, and heuristic. The fact that the authors take us from a general overview of evaluation through managing a system, follow-up, the sources of judgments, the cost considerations, and the utilization of evaluation for planning makes this book distinctive.

Evaluation as a field is still in a state of flux. Methodologies are becoming more numerous and most people in the field are finding more problems with reporting. The sources of evaluation information have broadened over the past decade. You will find that this book helps with all these issues and problems.

J. Thomas Hastings, Director

Center for Instructional Research and Curriculum Evaluation
University of Illinois

Preface

The material presented in this book is directed toward meeting the need for improvement of occupational education and training programs within both public and private institutions. Specifically, it is designed to help teachers, administrators, and ancillary personnel of these institutions design and conduct evaluation activities. To practicing educators and trainers, the book can serve as a handbook and guide to the evaluative task. For prospective educators and trainers now enrolled in formal educational programs in colleges and universities, it can provide an orientation to evaluation and should help them develop the competencies necessary for effective evaluation of programs.

It may be beneficial to begin by defining what we will be referring to as occupational education and training programs. They will be those programs which provide career awareness information, career orientation, and career training for entrance, advancement, or upgrading in specific occupations or careers. The differentiation made here between education and training is a subtle one. Within this book, education usually refers to public educational programs offered in elementary, secondary, and post-secondary institutions. A training program is considered to be a private instructional program offered by an industrial or corporate firm for the purpose of upgrading its own internal personnel, or a similar program offered by an institution which is in the business of training personnel for a profit. While the material addressed in this book may be applied to all public and private occupational education and training programs, Chapters 4 and 5—the learner follow-up and the employer survey— are more applicable to the higher levels of these programs. The five other technique chapters describe activities which can be applied to any educational program level.

Major responsibility for Chapter 3 fell to T.E.L. along with contributions to Chapters 1 and 8. Responsibility for coordinating the manuscript and preparing the remaining chapters was assumed by T.L.W. Both authors wish to acknowledge the assistance provided by several individuals in the preparation of this book. First of all, to Marcia A. Langsjoen, for her critical analysis of content and her outstanding editorial revision of the manuscript, go the utmost appreciation and thanks. Also, Antoinette DeFalco deserves our most grateful appreciation for her preparation of the manuscript and the coordination of the many administrative details. In addition, thanks are due several individuals who reviewed segments of the manuscript and provided invaluable suggestions: John A. Klit, Joseph A. Borgen, and Richard Smock.

It would be nice to say that this book represents the culmination of our thoughts and ideas about evaluation. But it is nicer to think that our views and understanding of the process of evaluation will change from experience to experience, from day to day. That evaluation itself is a mutable and maximless field presents cause for both frustration and great excitement. At this printing, having written a book on evaluation, we know more than we did when we began. Having read our own book critically, we learned a great deal we had not known about evaluation. If there is any key we have found to understanding evaluation, it is evaluating, doing. It is our sincere hope that after reading this book you will know more about evaluation than you did before and that you will evaluate for yourself the ideas we have presented.

Tim L. Wentling

Tom E. Lawson

1

An Introduction to Evaluation

INTRODUCTION

Evaluation is an integral part of any decision-making process. While evaluation has been with us since any attempt at formal education was made, only recently has there been an organized effort to establish a strict and comprehensive evaluation methodology. It has come about as a natural consequence of our educational structure that occupational educators have led in the expansion of the role of formal evaluation. One reason has been that evaluation has heretofore been viewed in an extremely narrow light. The first formal evaluation activity in general education was limited to the assessment of student achievement. As this area of assessment received the most emphasis within university preparation programs, a great deal of attention was paid to the development of a methodology for testing and student measurement.

It was in the area of occupation-related education and training programs that the scope of formal evaluation was first broadened to include follow-up of graduates of programs. Although evaluation and follow-up are by no means synonymous, there has been a common misconception that they are. This has made it natural that occupational educators, to whom the relationship of success of graduates to quality of programs was extremely important, be prime movers in the development of both follow-up and evaluation programs.

In occupational education, the follow-up of graduates is more easily related to the quality of a particular program—especially if graduates have entered an occupation directly upon completion of that program. However, evaluation has also involved the follow-up of graduates who have entered more advanced occupational training programs. The methodology which we have presented in this text, both with regard to follow-up and with regard to the other evaluation activities, can be readily adapted to the evaluation of academic programs as well. The authors hold that evaluation methodology should not be limited to follow-up of students and hope that the practice of evaluation will be further developed and embellished in the broader areas of education. Be that as it may, this book has been designed primarily to give the occupational educator and trainer specific and practical advice on how to answer those questions most essential to successful evaluation and improvement of programs. Questions like: *Where are we? Where are we going? How are we doing in getting there? Have we made it?* are paramount in the development and improvement of programs. Evaluation has as simple a rationale as one can ever hope to find, but the contingencies encountered by the evaluator are as complex and variegated as those encountered by the educator in his everyday experience. Values held by the community, administrators, staff, students, and parents are important variables. These values will differ and oftentimes the evaluator is faced with a task not unlike dividing apples by oranges.

Nixon (1973) has identified two basic dimensions that are important to the consideration and conduct of evaluation: *methodology* and *people.* Of these two dimensions, *people* is without question the most demanding of our consideration. It is the people who determine values, who set standards. *Methodology* involves measurement against a standard. Selection of a methodology itself requires careful consideration. But, as it is the people who command the resources and make the decisions regarding which programs will be sustained and which will be terminated or changed, an acceptable methodology will, to a large degree, be one that reinforces the existing value system. The success of a methodology is ultimately measured against existing standards, as the success of an evaluation is measured mostly by the success of the changes that occur within education and training programs as a result of that evaluation—changes which are measured against a people-oriented value system.

An examination of the methodological and people influences in occupational education and training programs may help to clarify the rationale behind current evaluative approaches. A listing of influences that strongly affect evaluation includes: a divergence of viewpoints and needs, multiple units of programs, influence of funding, inherent conflict, lack of past evaluation activity, relationship to established programs, and assumptions about successful programs (Steele, 1973).

Divergence in Viewpoints and Needs

Needs for evaluative data regarding programs are different for different types of people. It is a difficult task to ensure that any evaluation methodology will provide the appropriate and necessary information to all those involved in the program being evaluated. Consequently, it is good to choose a method of evaluation that will involve representatives of each of these groups in the actual collection of data: program managers or administrators, advisory committees, the client, the management, program personnel, and program participants.

Multiple Units of Programs

An "occupational education or training program" may be managed and conducted by one instructor, or it may represent a joint effort on the part of all program personnel working for an education or training organization. Further, it can be a collective effort conducted in several locations between educational institutions or corporate training programs. There should be no vagueness about evaluation policies and procedures to be used at various educational and training levels. And attempts should be made to coordinate and articulate efforts.

Influence of Funding

When program development, maintenance, and implementation, as well as evaluation, are dependent upon outside funds, this funding may bring additional influence into evaluation. If an industrial plant is paying for the evaluation because they use a good proportion of the graduates, then their priorities will influence evaluation techniques. Funds will often be directed only toward priorities of decisions which must be made concerning program worthiness and appropriateness for their purposes. If a federal agency is evaluating, the standards will be heavily influenced by federal policies. This funding emphasis can pose a threat to program personnel and may precipitate unwanted consequences. Evaluation for improvement should not be overlooked if at all possible.

Inherent Conflict

The focus of occupational education programs will often conflict with that of academic departments in systems of public education. This poses additional needs for evaluation, as the majority of these conflicts involve reconciling opposing education or training values. Differences in ideas concerning what constitutes a "benefit" affect decisions concerning the selection of accountability models and the use of funding.

Lack of Past Evaluation Activity

Many occupational and training programs have been developed without a concern for a systematized evaluation. As a result, many problems have developed which have been solved in a hit-or-miss, intuitive fashion. Evaluation can provide information to help make these problem-solving decisions systematic and efficient.

Relationship to Established Programs

Most programs or course offerings are appended to a long-established education or training curriculum. New programs, as a result, may not relate well to existing offerings and frequently cause conflict which must be addressed by the evaluative approach. While new offerings sometimes appear to be more efficient, often an administrative or managerial bond to a conventional program will result in hindering the implementation of a new approach. For this reason, an evaluation approach should address attitudinal as well as content factors.

Assumptions about Successful Programs

A final type of influence on evaluation is the effect of technological progress and managerial science on attitudes regarding the effectiveness of occupational education and training programs. An evaluation approach must do more than analyze the extent to which a given program has adhered to an original plan or has attained its primary goals and objectives. Evaluation must assess the objectives themselves to determine if they are realistic and appropriate to the on-the-job situation encountered by the learner.

These are only a few of the conditions which can affect an approach to the evaluation of occupational education and training programs. The type of approach that is most needed is one that can cope with *both* people and methodology in real-world situations.

A BRIEF HISTORY OF EVALUATION

Formally documented systems of evaluation date back to 2200 B.C., to the elaborate system of competitive examinations used in the Civil Service Testing System of China. Under this system, the Chinese emperor examined his officials every third year to determine their fitness for continuing in office. After three examinations, officials were either promoted or dismissed—a practice curiously resembling current evaluation policies. Today, the granting of tenure in institutions of education and the maintenance and promotion of individuals within private training institutions are often conducted in a similar fashion.

In the early 1900's Robert Thorndike was instrumental in providing the impetus for early adoption of measuring techniques to assess or evaluate changes in learner behavior. This type of evaluation was predicated upon the use of content goals and objectives which characterized many educational programs in the early part of this century. The accreditation movement occurring in the early 1900's also had its impact on evaluation methodology. Accreditation evaluations, usually incorporating an external audit of educational programs for the purpose of establishing program credibility, were supported by numerous educational institutions throughout the United States. This accreditation movement has expanded to include literally hundreds of accrediting agencies in our contemporary educational realm.

Ralph Tyler's Eight Year Study, conducted in the 1930's, did much to emphasize the evaluation of student outcomes. This study involved the students of thirty high schools in the United States and assessed student performance on many different tests, scales, questionnaires, checklists, and student logs. The Coleman Study, conducted in the 1950's by James Coleman, focused on the opportunities available to minorities within the United States. A later study of similar magnitude was conducted in the 1960's. This study, entitled Project TALENT, was conducted by John Flanagan of the American Institute for Research and involved the measurement of abilities and characteristics exhibited by 440,000 individual students in a school situation. An attempt was made to associate these identified abilities and characteristics with success or failure in post-program jobs. In 1969, Ralph Tyler initiated The National Assessment Project. This project sampled student behavior at different grade levels in schools across the nation in an effort to chart student performance from institution to institution and from state to state.

Until 1963, most of these studies were the result of federally or foundation-funded projects and did not reflect evaluative action on the part of individual states or educational agencies. In 1963, with the passage of the Vocational Education Act, each state was required to establish a state advisory committee for vocational education which would be responsible for evaluation within each state. This act did precipitate the establishment of advisory committees within each of the fifty states. However, most of the state advisory committees did not assume the responsibility for evaluation as the legislation had intended. It was not until the passage of the Elementary and Secondary Education Act in 1965 that evaluation really became a prime concern of educators at the state and local level. In essence, ESEA legislation required that each project conducted under Titles I and III possess a specific evaluation component—to include a plan for the evaluation of process and product.

Until 1968, the approaches taken by various states to evaluate their own programs ranged from statewide follow-up surveys to activities that were focused on assessing the total programs of individual institutions by way of team visits similar to those utilized in accreditation evaluations. In 1968, the Vocational Education Amendments to the 1963 act were passed, and they reemphasized the requirement for evaluation on the part of individual states and on the part of advisory committees within each state. Specific references to evaluation within this act included the following:

1. The national council shall review the administration and operation of vocational education programs, including the effectiveness of such programs in meeting the purposes for which they were established.
2. The national council shall conduct independent evaluations of programs carried out under the 1968 amendments.
3. The national council shall review the possible duplication of programs at the post-secondary and adult levels within geographic areas.
4. The state advisory council shall evaluate vocational education programs, services, and activities assisted under this act.

In addition, all projects funded under Part D of the 1968 amendments—Exemplary Projects for Career Education—were required to incorporate a third-party evaluation which involved an evaluator external to both the funding agency and the project. Third-party evaluations included an outside agency or group of individuals who were responsible for evaluating project activities and outcomes, and reporting to both the funding agency and the project staff.

With the Vocational Education Act of 1963, its subsequent amendments in 1968, and the Elementary and Secondary Education Act of 1965, a considerable amount of pressure to evaluate was placed on state and local school systems. Even so, evaluation efforts seldom met with the intent of this legislation. One of the identified problems within local educational agencies as well as within state agencies was a failure to adequately define evaluation. Although the federal government had required that evaluation be conducted to assess the outcome and the return on investment for particular programs, it provided few guidelines on how to conduct an evaluation. With no definition of evaluation, and no guide to evaluative procedure, many people were confused about the requirement. Even if the federal government had more specifically defined the requirements and guidelines, local personnel did not have training that would enable them to actually design and implement evaluation systems and programs.

The many difficulties encountered by educators in meeting the requirements for evaluation led to discussion of the problem in many universities and school systems. The dialogue which resulted was an attempt to conceptualize the process of evaluation into models, frameworks, or theories. In many cases, the resultant models were applied to educational programs. However, little attention was paid to the actual institutionalization of these models or the actual formulation of local guidelines for conducting evaluations within the given frameworks. This text has been designed to provide guidance in the design and conduct of local evaluation activities by local school and training institution personnel. Hopefully, some of the traditional problems of evaluation can be overcome.

Emerging Evaluation Concepts

To help clarify what evaluation is, and to further explore the selection of evaluative approaches to be applied to occupational and training functions, we will next examine some of the various contemporary ideas about program evaluation. Steele (1973) summarized the literature and noted that the emerging characteristics, definitions and ideas about evaluation were changing significantly. While the various influences and historical developments cited earlier have, to a large extent, effected a change in conceptualization of evaluative approaches, evaluation theory and practice have not been sufficiently integrated to cope with present occupational and training assessment realities. There are, however, several emerging concepts which can help us formulate practical evaluative approaches. The following issues are among the more valuable new ideas concerning evaluation (Steele, 1973).

Program Evaluation Is a Process Rather Than a Procedure

There are many ways to approach occupational program evaluation; there is no single evaluation procedure to be followed in all cases. Evaluation is most useful when it is treated as a process—a way of decision making—and when it is applied as such. In the past several years, many evaluative strategies have emerged to assist in determining the worth of occupational programs and offerings. For instance, while specific assessment and measurement procedures will be applied to the evaluation of a particular sales training program, the decision-making approach itself is a generalizable process. Decision areas must be identified, sources for data specified, methods of analysis indicated, and evaluative decisions made. All of these steps would make up the evaluative process for the determination of sales training effectiveness.

Program Evaluation Is More Than Examining the Achievement of Objectives

It is important to differentiate between a description of the results of a program and an evaluation of those results. In the past, occupational and career evaluation was limited primarily to identifying and categorizing program results and determining to what extent they could be attributed to the program. The evaluation of results, however, involves the measurement of program outcomes against pre-specified program objectives. Assessment of the extent to which instructional programs attain their objectives is not the only dimension of program evaluation, however. The assessment of objectives as they relate to the needs of all those involved is of primary importance. We are starting to look beyond the accomplishment of stated program objectives to the worthiness of the objectives themselves. Unanticipated, undesirable program outcomes, which may occur as well as desirable and anticipated effects, are now being assessed. For example, a trainee may learn how to service a particular piece of technical equipment but while doing so will learn to hate diagnostic and problem-solving skills. A more comprehensive evaluation of the objectives-defining level might well have uncovered how this program was deficient. It is important because poor learner attitude will be reflected by poor on-the-job performance. A student may attain the objectives of an occupational program but be so disenchanted that he would not approach a similar occupational or training situation. A comprehensive approach would contrast the attained results with 1) the human, social, or institutional needs that caused the development of the program, 2) the minimum standards of success for retention of a program, 3) general occupational competency standards for the trade or profession, or 4) anticipated or expected program outcomes. Overall effectiveness is concerned not only with behavioral changes in trainees and students, but also with the utilization of student, organization, and manpower resources and the extent to which objectives are appropriate to real career development needs and the needs of individual learners.

Program Evaluation Is More Than Instructional Evaluation

Prior to 1960, "program" had rarely been used as a word in occupational and training evaluation, the focus before being on using objectives as a basis for data gathering on trainee and student performance. When occupational education and training development personnel began equating program evaluation with the evaluation of instruction—which was earlier advocated by Ralph Tyler in the 1950's—program evaluation became the assessment of student and trainee attainment of instructional objectives specified for the program. At present, the distinctions between program evaluation and instructional evaluation are becoming more obvious.

Instructional evaluation is focused essentially on a specific course or program activity, such as a case method approach utilized in management training. Program evaluation is concerned with the cumulative influence of a sequence of instructional components, such as the courses taken in a two-year food service apprentice program. The evaluation of instruction is, in most instances, directed toward changes in knowledge, skills, and attitudes, while program evaluation is concerned with the impact those changes have on an individual. Instructional evaluation should determine how a career or program satisfies the specific needs of the learners; program evaluation is more apt to concentrate on how the total program satisfies the occupational needs of the community or the training requirements of the corporate organization. Of course, program evaluation includes instructional evaluation at the same time it encompasses additional evaluative dimensions, including the establishment of priorities in instructional offerings. Further, program evaluation deals with the degree to which the instruction is accomplishing and promoting the organizational goals of the company or educational institution. It is also concerned with whether or not adequate resources are channeled to the appropriate programs.

Program Evaluation Is More Than Evaluating the
Results of a Program

Recently, there has been an impetus toward distinguishing the evaluation of occupational program *results* from the evaluation of occupational *programs*. Traditionally, evaluation has been considered essentially as a terminal endeavor wherein the results of an occupational program were assessed. However, formative evaluation, or the evaluation of a program in its developmental stages, is attracting attention, and such primary activities as planning, organizing, and managing are now being evaluated.

Occupational program evaluation includes activities that focus on both product and process. Process evaluation would include monitoring an instructor's performance, weighing the use of laboratory materials, or assessing the learning experiences found in the training or instructional setting. In contrast, product evaluation involves judging training outcomes and the costs incurred for a given program offering, relating these outcomes to prespecified objectives *and* considering both positive and negative unintended outcomes. Although both product and process evaluation are important, the emerging evaluation models vary in the way they describe the various components of an occupational or training program. For instance, several approaches focus on program processes, whereas others concentrate on product components.

This perspective of occupational or career evaluation encourages predevelopmental, developmental, and maintenance program evaluation. An approach which limits the analysis only to results is essentially interested in decisions about the continuance or completion of the program. Both approaches, however, are crucial for viable career program assessment. All training programs should be periodically reexamined to determine if they should be maintained. When new programs are unfolding, and when decisions have to be made regarding the continuance of existing programs, evaluation becomes essential.

EVALUATION DEFINED

From our historical review of evaluation and from the discussion of emerging evaluation concepts, it can be seen that the strategies, foci, and purposes of evaluation have been as varied as the situations to which evaluation has been applied. This variance has been reflected by the many definitions attached to the term "evaluation." To many public school administrators, evaluation has brought to mind accreditation visits or staff evaluation processes. To teachers, evaluation has meant the measurement and testing of student performance.

A traditional definition of evaluation limited evaluation to professional judgment such as the judging of a textbook or lesson plan by an expert. Another common definition held that evaluation was the comparison of student performance to clearly specified objectives or lists of desired competencies.

More recently, two less limiting definitions for evaluation have been more widely accepted. The most popular is one which considers evaluation in light of the decision-making process. Stated by the Phi Delta Kappa Commission on Evaluation: *Evaluation is the process of delineating, collecting, and providing information useful for judging decision alternatives* (Stufflebeam, et al., 1971). Evaluation activity in light of the decision-oriented definition involves the identification of decision situations, the determination of needed data, and the actual collection of the data to be used by decision making groups and individuals. Evaluation for decision making necessitates close communication and a working link between evaluator and decision maker to ensure relevance of provided evaluation.

The Phi Delta Kappa definition regards the evaluation role as distinct from that of the decision maker. The evaluator is not considered to make judgments, but is viewed more as an information gatherer. A second definition of evaluation which focuses more on evaluator judgment is offered by Worthen and Sanders (1973): *Evaluation is the determination of the worth of a thing. It includes obtaining information for use in judging the worth of a program, product, procedure, or objective or the potential utility of alternative approaches designed to attain specified objectives.* This definition of evaluation suggests that the major evaluation effort is addressed to not only the systematic identification and collection of data but to the analysis of data to ascertain the worth of both program processes and products. Under this definition for program-related processes, evaluation would include appraisal of activities and materials used in the instructional program. Program outcomes, both anticipated and unanticipated, would also be measured and a conclusion of merit or worth placed upon them. Upon analyzing and interpreting program information (of many types), the evaluator would appraise the value and worth of the program and, in the majority of instances, relate this appraisal in the form of conclusions and recommendations to the individual or group who has the responsibility for making decisions about the program.

Obviously, the Phi Delta Kappa definition and the Worthen and Sanders definition are not mutually exclusive. In fact, there is considerable overlap between the two. Both require the collection and reporting of evaluative data. The main difference occurs in how the results are presented to decision makers—as data alone or data accompanied by judgments of worth.

USING CHAPTERS 2 THROUGH 9

The remaining chapters of this book are addressed to improving the utilization of evaluation procedures with the end of improving decision making and, ultimately, of improving programs. Sound evaluation procedures exist for many situations but proper utilization of these procedures is necessary if evaluation results are to be useable. This means that evaluation procedures must be properly chosen, followed through, and followed up. The following chapters of this book may be categorized as they apply to one of three tasks. These tasks are enumerated below.

An Orientation to Evaluation

Chapter 2 gives the reader an orientation to the uses to which evaluation can be put, an overview of some of the shortcomings which evaluation has faced, and some general and specific advice on the design of an evaluation system. This chapter may be construed to be a sales promotion for evaluation—which it is. And, admittedly, many of those who have read this far will not need to be sold on evaluation. Nonetheless, Chapter 2 should help to reaffirm your reasons for picking up the book in the first place.

Guide to the Design and Implementation of an Evaluation System

Chapters 3 through 8 provide specific directions for designing and implementing specific evaluation procedures. Including student assessment, student follow-up, employer survey, consultative team evaluation, personnel evaluation, and cost analysis, these chapters provide practical suggestions and example forms and instruments to aid in evaluation.

Guide to the Utilization of Results

Chapter 9 presents a general overview of how changes occur within educational programs and continues to give an orientation on how evaluation results can be used to bring about educational change and improved program offerings.

REFERENCES

Elementary and Secondary Education Act of 1965, Public Law 89-10. Washington, D.C.: U.S. Government Printing Office, 1965.

Flanagan, J. C.; Davis, F. B.; Dailey, J. T.; Shaycroft, M. F.; Orr, D. B.; Goldberg, I.; and Neyman, C. A., Jr. *Project TALENT. The Identification, Development, and Utilization of Human Talents: The American High School Student.* Pittsburgh: University of Pittsburgh Press, 1964.

Vocational Education Act of 1963, Public Law 88-210. Washington, D.C.: U.S. Government Printing Office, 1963.

Vocational Education Amendments of 1968, Public Law 95-76. Washington, D.C.: U.S. Government Printing Office, 1968.

Nixon, G. *People, Evaluation, and Achievement: A Guide to Successful Human Resource Development.* Houston, Texas: Gulf Publishing Company, 1973.

Steele, Sara M. *Contemporary Approaches to Program Evaluation: Implications for Evaluating Programs for Disadvantaged Adults.* Washington, D.C.: Education Resources Division Capitol Publications, Inc., 1973.

Stufflebeam, D. L.; Foley, W. J.; Gephart, W. J.; Guba, E. G.; Hammond, R. L;

Merriman, H. O.; and Provus, M. M. *Educational Evaluation and Decision-making in Education.* Itasca, Ill.: Peacock, 1971.

Thorndike, R. L. and Hagen, E. *Measurement and Evaluation in Psychology and Education.* New York: Wiley, 1969.

Tyler, R. W. "Assessing the Progress of Education." *Phi Delta Kappan,* 1965, 47:13–16.

Worthen, B. R. and Sanders, J. R. *Educational Evaluation: Theory and Practice.* Worthington, Ohio: Charles A. Jones Publishing Company, 1973.

2

Designing an Evaluation System

WHY EVALUATE?

The Vocational Education Act of 1963 and its subsequent amendments of 1968, the Elementary and Secondary Education Act of 1965, and many more recent pieces of legislation have stressed evaluation of the public educational programs. Meanwhile, most state governments are more concerned than ever before about showing the worth of educational and training endeavors. Also of very great importance, the taxpaying public which supports public education and the students of educational programs are questioning the relevance and general worth of occupational programs. Recent concerns regarding private training programs have increased the need for reputable private institutions to evaluate their programs. Evaluation can assure clients (and investigative agencies) about the worth of private training programs as well as help them to produce the best possible product or trainee at the least possible cost. Corporate managers have always been concerned about the return on their investment in employee training programs. Each of these groups is becoming increasingly aware of the need to approach evaluation in a systematic and committed manner. Some of the reasons why evaluation is necessary and important will be presented in this chapter.

To Aid in Planning

Evaluative information which provides measures of resources, limitations, and possibilities, is essential to establishing and assessing objectives, and it can certainly be of use in developing plans. Also, such data can help instructors determine the worth of an existing scheme or plan and, in the long run, to determine if the overall plan has been reasonable and if goals have been achieved. So, the gathering of information as well as the determination of worth plays a very important role in planning.

To Aid in Decision Making

Decisions, regardless of their magnitude, must be based on a certain amount of information. Decisions regarding assignment of personnel to programs; selection of students; program changes, additions or deletions; and decisions regarding the selection of alternative proposals all require that objective information be gathered so that an individual or group of individuals can make a defensible decision. Decisions which are based on the intuition alone often lead to undesirable outcomes. Rational decisions, based upon evaluative information, are defensible and justifiable to program staff, the institution administrators, and the underwriters of public or private instructional programs. So, evaluation information can not only aid in making decisions, but its use will justify those decisions to others.

To Upgrade Program Personnel

Evaluation can also be of benefit to instructional or ancillary personnel. A comprehensive evaluation system is capable of identifying deficiencies and strengths of personnel performance, thus helping personnel to improve upon their performance. Many times the evaluation of faculty is conducted only to bestow tenure and promotions or to meet governing board mandates. However, staff performance is probably the most important contributor to the success of a program, and evaluation is invaluable to the improvement of staff performance. Not only will evaluation work to upgrade evaluated staff, but staff members who are involved in the evaluation and its procedures will gain a measure of evaluative expertise which should help them plan and evaluate their own activities. In this respect, participation in evaluation can be viewed as a professional development activity.

To Improve Programs for Students

Evaluation of programs will nearly always contribute to the better service of students. Obviously, if evaluation offers both value judgments regarding what is happening within the program and consultative suggestions for improvement, then ultimately this will have an effect on students. The improvement of programs and offerings is the most important goal that evaluation can assume. It is important that evaluation activities be integrated to supply information for planning and decision making and for assessing the merit of what currently exists. In addition to assessing the outcome of an activity, the evaluator must know what circumstances worked to bring about that outcome. If a program fails to promote desired outcomes, attention must turn to the identification of actions, components, or characteristics which have led to the ineffectiveness of the program. Once program deficiencies have been identified, corrective action may be taken. Processes or components which have been found to contribute to a program's success may be adapted to other programs or to other portions of the same program.

To Insure the Accountability of Expenditures

Both corporate and public hopes for evidence to indicate whether the outcomes of a program are worth the investment in it should be fully realized by evaluation. Just as a Wall Street broker assesses a return on his investment in the stock market, the taxpayers and the stockholders are seeking to justify their investment in public and private education. All this requires more than a financial audit of accounting records. Accountability requires a presentation of a program's results (e. g., placement of students in jobs, achievement scores, increased sales, more effective management) in relation to incurred costs and established objectives. Accountability can be considered from both an internal and an external perspective— internal program managers and administrators also need measures of accountability to help justify their decisions regarding the expansion, deletion, or revision of existing programs. A well-conceived evaluation program or system within an education or training institution can help to meet this accountability requirement.

WHAT HAS BEEN WRONG WITH OUR TRADITIONAL EVALUATION?

To any prospective evaluator, it is both important and worthwhile to understand what some of the problems with our traditional evaluations have been. Considering the two previously mentioned definitions of evaluation, one can reasonably say that educators and training personnel have been evaluating for a long time. Not only have these groups been evaluating, but others have evaluated as well. Learners, parents of learners, citizens of communities, employers and supervisors of former learners, and even the custodians of school and training facilities have done a considerable amount of evaluation. All of these individuals have formed opinions about education and training programs—some of which have been based on faulty evaluation.

Evaluation Has Been Informal

In many cases evaluation has been done informally without substantial planning of activities or the involvement of appropriate groups. This type of evaluation has certainly helped, but it has often proved difficult to justify resultant decisions to others—boards of education, the public, funding agencies, and corporate management—when conclusions have been based on informal evaluation. Also, the opinions formed by those who have evaluated programs informally in one way or another have, in most cases, been based on hearsay or very skimpy observation of the program and its operation.

Evaluation Has Been Fragmented

A common problem with traditional evaluation practices results from the failure to approach evaluation in a systematic manner. Even in cases where evaluation has been conducted on a formal basis, activities themselves have not been properly integrated. For example, although most education and training institutions incorporate some type of evaluation of their instructional staff, and most instructors evaluate the performance of their learners, this information is seldom combined to justify judgments or plans for improving the overall program. This is to say that evaluation has been conceived in terms of individual activities but these activities have not been tied into an overall evaluation system for a program or an institution.

Evaluation Results Have Seldom Been Used for Improvement

Another characteristic of our traditional evaluation practices has been that the results of evaluation activities have seldom been used formatively—to make changes in programs. Often, evaluation results have been used to show what or who was in error but without directing paths for future improvement. Students are evaluated to aid in assigning grades; teachers are evaluated so decisions on tenure can be made; and to meet governing board mandates. In addition, the results or reports of external team evaluations, such as those conducted by regional accrediting associations or state educational agencies, are many times shelved and not used to improve the educational or training program.

Evaluation Has Been Unrelated to Planning

Another problem common to evaluation has been the failure to tie evaluation efforts and planning into one activity. Integration of evaluation activities such as staff evaluation, resource evaluation, and student interest surveys, to name but a few, should facilitate the planning of new programs or the planning of changes in existing ones. Seldom, however, is any kind of evaluation incorporated in the formulation of program or institution plans. The identification of community, student, or corporate needs is a planning prerequisite and represents an evaluation effort. Also, evaluation of the attainment of program or institutional goals represents an important factor in the planning of new programs or the revision of existing ones. That is, if the evaluation results of a particular program indicate that the program was ineffective, then plans should be made either to change the program to overcome its deficiencies or to discontinue it.

Evaluation Has Lacked Commitment

In both private and public educational and training programs there has been a lack of real financial and personnel commitment to the task of evaluation. This has been contrary to the emphasis placed on quality control by our nation's production and service industries. These industries have paid a considerable amount of attention to maintaining certain quality levels in both the development and production of consumable products as well as the provision of services to the public. Industrial firms have spent up to 10 percent of production budgets to measure both quantity and quality of consumable products and to monitor the processes used in production for more effective resource utilization. Also, our service industries such as medically related institutions pay a considerable amount of attention to offering quality care and to monitoring this care (e.g., close scrutiny of reactions to certain drugs). To date, evaluation of education and training programs has been only token.

Evaluation Has Been Narrowly Focused

In many educational and training situations, evaluation has focused entirely on the assessment of student or learner performance. Certainly, this type of information has helped in the assignment of ratings or grades to individual learners and in many cases has contributed to the placement or further selection of individuals. However, in terms of evaluating an entire program, these results have been too limited. Evaluation has in most cases failed to consider the many other program aspects which have a great effect on the product of the program. Simply knowing the performance of graduates gives little aid to improving or changing the education or training program.

These have been just some of the things that have been wrong with our traditional evaluation. This list is by no means comprehensive, yet it does give an indication of some of our failures. Later sections of this chapter have been designed to advise the evaluator as he strives to overcome some of the traditional weaknesses of evaluation.

WHAT SHOULD BE EVALUATED?

Obviously, the goal of all education and training personnel, administrators as well as instructors, is to offer the highest quality program possible given the resources available. For program personnel to make maximum use of their opportunities, they must make sound decisions regarding available alternatives. To make these decisions, individuals need appropriate kinds of rational information in addition to intuition, hearsay evidence, personal experience, and informed management opinion. The following statements may help to clarify the relationship between planning, decision making, and evaluation.

1. The quality of programs depends upon the quality of decisions in and about the program.
2. The quality of decisions depends upon the abilities to identify the alternatives which comprise decision situations and to make sound judgment of these alternatives.
3. Making sound judgments requires timely access to valid and reliable information pertaining to the alternatives.
4. The availability of such information can be enhanced through a systematic means to provide it.
5. The processes necessary for providing the information for decision making collectively comprise the concept of evaluation.

Since the primary role of evaluation is to provide relevant information and informed judgments to key decision makers, evaluation activity should be initiated by finding out what decisions are to be made. To facilitate the classification of educational decisions in any type of educational or training program, one may initially choose to focus exclusively on the functions of decisions. The work of Stufflebeam and others has provided an excellent conceptual base for structuring evaluation and answering the question, *What should be evaluated?*

The types of decision situations in education or training may be classified as: 1) planning, 2) programming, 3) implementing, and

4) recycling. Planning decisions are those which focus on needed improvements by specifying the domain, major goals, and specific objectives to be served. Programming decisions specify procedures, personnel, facilities, resources, and time requirements for implementing the planned program. Implementing decisions include those which direct programmed activities. Recycling decisions include those necessary for terminating, sustaining, adjusting, or drastically modifying the educational program or its parts. Stufflebeam's evalua-

	Objective	Method
Context Evaluation	To define the educational environment, to identify student and other needs, to delineate problems, and to formulate goals.	By describing the context through data gathering and by specifying problems and goals.
Input Evaluation	To identify and assess alternative strategies for achieving goals or overcoming problems which are identified in context evaluation.	By analyzing existing resources, identifying possible solutions to problems, determining their feasibility and making comparisons.
Process Evaluation	To observe program oper-ation, attempting to ascertain procedural events and activities and to iden-tify problems in design and implementation.	By observing and otherwise monitoring program opera-tion to determine if hap-penings occur as they were planned to occur.
Product Evaluation	To assess program outcomes and to relate outcomes to objectives and to relate them to context, input, and process evaluation.	By measuring anticipated and unanticipated outcomes on students and on others associated with the pro-gram. And by relating outcomes to measures taken in the other evaluation areas.

FIGURE 2–1 *Description of CIPP Evaluation Components (adapted from Stufflebeam, 1971).*

tion model recognizes these four types of decision encountered in an educational or training program. This model introduced four forms of evaluation—context, input, process, and product (CIPP)—which are corollaries to the planning, programming, implementing, and recycling decision situations. Figure 2-1 presents a detailed description of each type of evaluation including its objective and method in relation to decision making in the change process.

Context Evaluation

Context evaluation is employed when a program or course is first being planned. Context evaluation is conducted to define the environment in which a program will take place, to discover the environment's unmet needs (student needs, community needs, and state needs), to identify some of the constraints and problems underlying those needs, and to discover the opportunities for meeting those needs which already exist in the community. For example, in public education a survey may be conducted to identify the need for trained individuals in specific occupations such as sheet metal work or stenography. This survey could include both contact with current or potential employers within the community and the identification of actual need or interest in the program on the part of prospective students. Also to be considered in the context evaluation are the financial constraints of the educational institution, personnel capabilities for conducting the program, and any possible "outside" sources or means of training individuals for that particular occupation. Basically, the questions answered by contextual evaluation are: *Where are you?* and *What are your needs?*

Within the realm of context evaluation is the formulation of goals and objectives for the particular program under consideration, and these should be rooted in the needs assessment for the program. So, with answers to: *What are your needs?* the focus of context evaluation will turn to the question, *Where are you going?* Context evaluation in a private training or corporate firm would be similar to that in public education but would be limited to the performance dynamics of the particular corporation under consideration. If a private training organization is preparing people for jobs in the public sector, then its needs assessment or context evaluation would be identical or close to identical to that of public education. In other cases the actual needs assessment would be an assessment of corporate needs for particular divisions, jobs, and positions. Regardless of the type of institution, the establishment and assignment of goals and objectives is still paramount within context evaluation.

Input Evaluation

The primary goal of input evaluation is to identify and assess capabilities of the instructional or training agency and alternative strategies to achieve identified goals and objectives. The primary question which input evaluation attempts to answer is: *How will you get there?* This is really the development of plans for achieving the desired goals. The end product of input evaluation is an analysis of alternative procedural designs in terms of potential costs and benefits. Alternatives are basically assessed in terms of their resource, time, and budget requirements, and consideration is given to potential barriers, the consequences of not overcoming these barriers, and possibilities and costs for overcoming them. For example, an aviation flight instructor may wish to design an instructional segment to acquaint students with the many controls of the control panel in a single engine aircraft. This goal could be achieved by several means: 1) designing a self-instructional package with many photographs and diagrams, 2) presenting a limited amount of verbal instruction and the experience of having each student spend fifteen minutes in a flight simulator to become acquainted with all the controls, or 3) giving each student actual flight experience with a qualified instructor. These alternatives need to be assessed in terms of their capabilities for achieving the intended goal and their costs with regard to accomplishing that goal. Evaluative information of an input type is needed to provide information for making judgments and decisions with regard to choice of alternatives.

Process Evaluation

The primary goal of process evaluation is to detect or predict defects in the procedural design of a program or course during the implementation or operational stages. In other words, process evaluation should determine if the program or course is being implemented as originally planned. The overall process evaluation strategy should identify and monitor on a continuous basis the potential sources of failure. These include interpersonal relationships among staff, the performance of teachers in a teaching situation, communication channels, logistics, the extent to which people involved in and affected by the program are in agreement with its intent, adequacy of the resources, the physical facilities, staff, and the time schedule. The real question to be answered by process evaluation is: *How are you doing in getting there?* Most external team evaluations such as those conducted by regional accrediting associations or state funding agencies are a form of process evaluation. This is because most external team evaluations monitor or assess a program while it is in operation, to determine how the staff is doing in meeting its goals. It is within the realm of process evaluation that the consultative purpose of evaluation is most clearly defined.

Product Evaluation

The primary objective of product evaluation is to determine the degree to which the intended objectives and goals have been met and to relate this to context, input, and process in the measurement and interpretation of the outcome. Product evaluation is used to determine the effectiveness of a program or course after it has been completed. The real question to be answered is: *Have you made it?* Traditionally, product evaluation has been accomplished solely through measuring learner accomplishment. However, there are several techniques which can be used to obtain a more realistic and ultimate measure of product. The follow-up survey and the employer survey, to be covered in later chapters of this text, are good examples. Product evaluation is extremely important to the local school system or the private training organization, and school or organizational personnel should do the evaluation because it is very difficult for any kind of external visiting team of experts or peers to identify the real products of the education or training program.

Therefore, an adequate evaluation design should incorporate a solid product evaluation in addition to considering context, input, and process evaluation measures. The interrelationship of these four types of evaluation cannot be emphasized enough. For example, if only product evaluation was conducted, the program manager might know if the program was successful or not successful, but if the program was not successful, he would have little or no idea why. On the other hand, if context, input, and process evaluation had been conducted, then the information gained from those types of evaluation could be scrutinized closely to identify the reasons for the ineffectiveness of the program in terms of product evaluation.

Context and input evaluation are necessary components in planning any new program, but it is best that the entire framework be utilized, from context through input, process, and product evaluation. This is the CIPP approach in its entirety. However, for operational programs, evaluative efforts may begin at the process or product evaluation stages. Starting at one of these two points, however, does not limit program personnel from cycling back to the context and input stages.

Also, many evaluation activities or information-gathering techniques can provide data that is useful for more than one type of evaluation (i. e., input and product evaluation). In cases which focus on process and product evaluation, another framework may be useful.

Focus of Program Evaluation

A considerable amount of research has been conducted to identify the components of a program which can contribute to its effectiveness. These areas of concern are: 1) administrative or management organization, 2) personnel, 3) objectives, 4) evaluation system, 5) content, 6) learners being served, 7) utilization of resources, and 8) guidance, personnel counseling, placement, and other ancillary services of the program. The specificity with which these eight components are considered will vary. For example, the evaluation of an institution or a multiprogram department could focus on the administrative, instructional, guidance and other supportive staff members, the goals of the organization, and so on. If, on the other hand, the evaluation is addressed to an individual program, the focus of the eight components will be much more specific. Such evaluation will assess the departmental structure, the instructional personnel, and, of course, the program objectives—continuing through all areas.

Focus of Course or Instructional Segment Evaluation

In a course evaluation, the eight areas of concern mentioned above can be slightly modified to: 1) students served, 2) goals and objectives, 3) organization, 4) personnel, 5) content, 6) teaching methods, 7) learning assessment, and 8) supplies, equipment, and facilities. In the evaluation of an overall course, each of these components or characteristics should be considered, though if the evaluation is addressed to an individual course segment, the scope will be more limited.

The specificity and scope of any evaluation of this sort is dictated by the type of primary questions formulated, questions which, in turn, are dictated by the exigencies of the situation. Primary evaluative questions should relate directly to the relationships among program or course characteristics. Displayed in Figure 2–2 is a method for conceptualizing the relationship of course characteristics. This matrix provides a fundamental source for formulating evaluative questions. Table 2–1 includes a list of sample questions that have been formulated by examining the relations of program characteristics. Letter designations from the table have been keyed to appropriate cells in the matrix. For example, if considering goals and objectives on the horizontal plane of the matrix and content on the vertical plane, the following questions will undoubtedly arise: *Are curriculum materials consistent with course objectives? Should curriculum materials "X" be adopted to facilitate attainment of objectives?* In addition, by considering the intersection of content with supplies, equipment, and facilities, this question can be formulated: *Is equipment capacity range within needs dictated by the instructional materials?* The point to be emphasized here is that evaluative questions should help to direct the evaluation to practical and realistic types of issues. When results of the evaluation have been achieved, they should help to throw light on the evaluator's original concerns. This question and answer relationship is the key to the utilization of evaluation results.

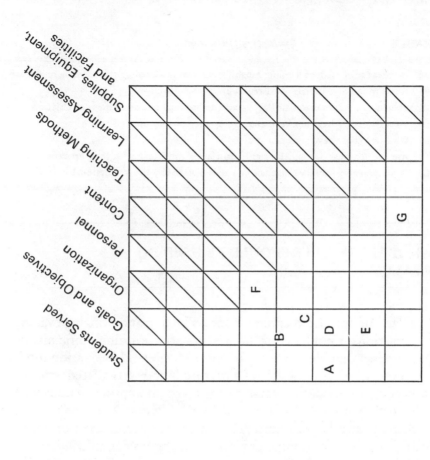

Program Characteristics

Students Served

Goals and Objectives

Organization

Personnel

Content

Teaching Methods

Learning Assessment

Supplies, Equipment, and Facilities

FIGURE 2–2   *Program Characteristics Matrix for Generating Evaluative Questions*

TABLE 2–1   *Example Evaluative Questions*

A) Is the range of student learning capabilities accommodated by the teaching methods?

B) Are curriculum materials consistent with course objectives?

C) Should curriculum materials "X" be adopted to facilitate attainment of objectives?

D) What objectives have not been attained by the teaching method used?

E) What objectives have not been attained?

F) Are instructional personnel assigned to classes consistent with their areas of expertise?

G) Is equipment capability range within needs dictated by the instructional materials?

WHAT TECHNIQUES SHOULD BE USED IN EVALUATION?

The lack of specific techniques for collecting and utilizing evaluative information in public educational and private training organizations has been a primary weakness of most theoretical evaluation models. An evaluation should be a structured and articulated endeavor, designed to provide information for program improvement as well as information to provide accountability indices. The design of the evaluation system, of course, should be specific to the needs of the local education or training organization, and no design will be universal for all situations. However, there are several techniques which can and should be combined to build a system of evaluation. These techniques include learner assessment, the follow-up of former learners, the employer survey, the consultative team evaluation, the evaluation of education and training personnel, and the cost-related evaluation.

Learner Assessment

Learner assessment—the measurement of learner performance—is probably the most widely used evaluative technique and can form the base for a total program evaluation. Student measurement should center around those competencies which have been specified as desirable by the objectives of the program or course. These competencies may fall within the cognitive, affective, psychomotor, or perceptual domains—or may constitute a mixture thereof. Many types of instruments may be utilized to measure student performance—paper and pencil achievement tests, attitude scales, project or product ratings, and presentation ratings. By combining a number of student measures on a number of individuals, a profile may be developed. A comparison of this profile to desired program or course outcomes will indicate areas which need improvement.

The Follow-up of Former Learners

Student follow-up studies can provide delayed measures of learner performance. A follow-up study involves contacting individuals subsequent to their participation in an education or training program. This contact, usually by way of a mail questionnaire, can provide placement information as well as other information relating to the post-program activities of the graduate or dropout. Simultaneously, the former learner may be asked for his perception of the education or training program's strengths and weaknesses. Most former learners are very capable of evaluating their job preparation and are willing to suggest ways in which the program might be improved.

The Employer Survey

An employer survey can provide yet another vantage point to learner performance. Performance ratings of former learners—and suggestions for improving the education or training program—may be obtained from employers via mail questionnaires or rating forms that are based on the actual on-the-job performance of graduates. The employer survey may be conducted concurrently with the follow-up of former students or it may be conducted independently at another time. It is evident that the information obtained for the same body of learners through the utilization of student measurement, student follow-up, and the employer survey can be integrated. The result of such integration could help determine the appropriateness of course and program objectives to the competencies desired by the employers in addition to identifying program strengths and weaknesses.

The Consultative Team Evaluation

A consultative team evaluation can also provide input to the assessment of a program or course. A team of external experts, internal personnel, community business and industrial personnel, and other types of individuals can be invited to review the organization, objectives, evaluative procedures, content, personnel, and other program and course components. In addition, the consultative team can make recommendations for bringing the program or course closer to meeting the combined needs of learners in the business and industrial community. Experience has shown that many business and industrial representatives are very willing to participate in such an activity, as are the peers of neighboring school districts and former learners. In addition, many experts in the field have discretionary time to work with local school districts and private training organizations on a consulting basis.

The Evaluation of Education and Training Personnel

The assessment of personnel performance is another important component of an evaluation system. Many times the evaluation of faculty is thought of only in terms of tenure, promotion, or meeting a governing board mandate. However, personnel performance is probably the most important contributor to the success of a program. Although the assessment of faculty and other personnel has traditionally been accomplished through observation and rating by a superior, evaluation through observation by peers, self-observation by way of video tape, rating by students, and the utilization of teacher performance tests can broaden the scope of faculty and ancillary personnel performance assessment. Such assessment can then be extended to the identification of specific deficiencies of staff members and recommendations for remediation can be made.

Cost Analysis Evaluation

A cost-related evaluation or assessment can also provide evaluative information which can be combined with that gathered through one or more of the foregoing techniques. A system of evaluation would not be complete unless it incorporated means for assessing costs in relation to program attributes and outcomes. Cost studies must attempt to correlate costs to outcomes, facilitating program decision making. Two courses having similar goals but different costs must be examined to determine the worth of the additional expenditure for one course over the other. Alternatives are considered by the individual shopping for a new automobile. He considers price in relation to passenger space, trunk space, convenience options, engine size, and many other features. Just as a car buyer cannot overlook the price tag when shopping, educators cannot afford to overlook costs when choosing or designing an occupational program.

WHO SHOULD BE INVOLVED IN EVALUATION?

Obviously, after a review of the possible approaches to be used in evaluation, it can be determined that no one individual can be responsible for accomplishing all of the evaluation requirements and their related tasks. It is important, therefore, to involve a number of program and nonprogram personnel in the task. Evaluation within a public or private education or training organization should represent a concerted effort on the part of the entire staff. The scope, of course, will generally determine who is to be involved, and specific recommendations will be given within each of the following technique chapters on possible participant groups. But as a rule, all individuals who share an interest in a course, program, or total program should be involved, and their degree of involvement should correspond to their interest. Personal involvement is probably the greatest factor contributing to the commitment to implement changes deemed necessary by the evaluation. Individuals who have participated in an evaluation will have seen first hand the need for improvement and will be in the best position to take remedial action.

Administrative Personnel

Administrative or management personnel should be involved in all types and levels of evaluation, even if they have not initiated the activity themselves. In some cases, administrators will not play a major administrative role in the evaluation itself. However, if they are not actually directing the evaluation they may be assigning aspects of the work, overseeing the activities, or conducting ongoing reviews of all parts of the work. Other roles open to administrative staff include acting as helper or counselor to the staff, liaison between an outside team and inside personnel, and so forth. Their support is necessary to insure adequate financial resources and released time, if required, to complete the evaluation activity. In addition, administrative support will be a major contributing factor in bringing changes which have been deemed necessary by an evaluation.

Instructional Personnel

Instructional personnel should also be involved in evaluation, judging their own endeavors as well as those of others. Self-evaluation may be the most accurate of any, if the proper atmosphere has been set. While direct observation often inhibits the real classroom behavior of students and teachers, instructional personnel are aware of the everyday problems they face in the classroom. To facilitate accurate and honest self-evaluation, evaluation goals must be carefully defined. This means that instructional personnel should be involved in the development of evaluation goals as well as the actual conduct of the evaluation. This will help reduce any apprehension on their part concerning the possible misuse of evaluation information.

Learners

For evaluation of instructional personnel and other program components, students are in the best position to observe those everyday problems that an outside observer is likely to miss. Students are also able to make important contributions to assessment of counseling and other student services. Who else experiences the results of these services so directly? Actually, there are very few evaluative activities (perhaps cost-benefit) to which students cannot contribute valuable input. The recent interest shown by them, and their increasing sensitivity toward the relevancy of their education, offer training personnel an excellent opportunity to incorporate student input into evaluation. This may be, in many instances, unique; and no other group or source may be capable of providing comparable information.

Ancillary Personnel

The opinion of individuals tangential to the course or program—counselors, academic teachers, placement personnel, personnel and divisional managers, and so on—can contribute greatly to the assessment of endeavors regardless of the level. These people can contribute primary or secondary opinions concerning program effectiveness and provide the base of consultative team evaluation. Ancillary personnel may have input in unexpected areas. Counselors may be in a position to give considerable advice to teachers conducting self-evaluations. They may have received comments by learners concerning individual courses or teachers. Placement personnel may have knowledge of program or course deficiencies that would be unavailable to other staff members. Likewise, academic teachers may be aware of attitudes, capabilities, and actual deficiencies of vocational students. All these individuals should be asked to supply any input they have, as there is a good chance they have access to information essential to a complete program or course evaluation.

Advisory Committee Members and Other Citizens

Advisory committee members can provide additional aid in the conduct and implementation of evaluation systems. Since they are normally local business people who have already made a commitment to education, they can provide an excellent source for consultation regarding some programs. Advisory committee members can encourage other local personnel to cooperate with interviewers in an employer follow-up situation. Furthermore, their expertise can be exploited when it comes to making recommendations for improvement after evaluative information has been gathered. Therefore, these individuals should not only be included in the conduct of evaluative activities but in the follow-up of those activities and the design of remedies as well.

External Experts

In addition to program personnel and community personnel, experts from private consulting firms, universities, or neighboring education or training organizations can also be most useful in evaluation efforts. External experts comprise the backbone of many consultative team evaluations. Because they may lack experience in the ins and outs of the institution, the expertise of these individuals can best be captured through team activities, which are discussed in greater detail in Chapter 6. If external experts are encouraged to work closely with existing personnel who are more familiar with the needs of the institution, their outside ideas can be of immense value to planners and evaluators.

Some general recommendations for involving personnel in evaluative efforts have been made. The actual component under consideration, as well as the activity or technique which is chosen, will dictate more closely those individuals who should participate in a particular activity.

WHAT ARE SOME GENERAL DESIGN FEATURES OF AN EVALUATION SYSTEM?

Before any activity to formulate an evaluation system is initiated, a number of features which are thought to be important to the design and implementation of such systems should be considered. Regardless of the scope of an evaluation, be it of an entire training organization or of an instructional segment, these design features are essential to its success. Some of what we have termed "features" resemble conditions and are more descriptive of a healthy environment for evaluation than of proper design. Nevertheless, the proper combination of tact, awareness, and personal commitment will help the evaluator achieve such an environment. Other features can be achieved by careful planning, intelligent choice of data, and flexibility.

Commitment

The most necessary feature of any evaluation system is a firm commitment on the part of all individuals at all levels of the educational training program or component under consideration. Commitment is not to be demanded, bought, or pried from those involved. The best way to insure commitment of all staff is to present the case for evaluation in a positive light. This means that the evaluation cannot threaten, but should focus on improvement. Goals of evaluation must be clearly delineated and they must be good goals. In a clinical sense, commitment can be facilitated by ego identification. This means that involvement of others must be encouraged, and the individuals whose commitment is essential should be involved in the initial development of plans for evaluation. This is not just an exercise in persuasion. A good evaluation is necessarily receptive to input from all sources.

Consultative Purpose

A second essential feature of any evaluation system is a consultative service to those who are instrumental to program operation. One of the shortcomings of evaluation up to now has been that the objectives have been limited to assessing the work and progress of the students and have seldom included a judgment of the quality of program content or instruction. Evaluation should help each individual improve existing conditions and programs offered to students. Without this, personnel evaluation activities are legitimately viewed as a threat by many instructional personnel. Many of these efforts have been directed at identifying personnel deficiencies for promotion, tenure, or salary decisions rather than at the consultative purpose of helping each individual staff member become more proficient at his or her particular job. If a public educational institution evaluates each of its departments by collecting information, comparing the results from department to department, and supplying departments with information regarding how they fared, in most cases this effort will have little impact on changing programs. However, if information relative to the strengths and weaknesses of *individual* programs and corresponding suggestions and *consultative input* regarding improvements is made, then results are far more likely to be put to constructive use.

Holistic Focus

The third necessary component of an evaluation system is a holistic focus. An accurate and useful evaluation of an institution, program, course, or course segment requires that it be observed as a whole, over and above observation of its individual components. It is misleading to assume that restricted observations and measurements of a program can detect or explain complex interactions between program methods, program staff, learners, and the environment in which the program operates. The point to be made concerning the holistic focus is that a program considered as a whole is greater than the sum of its individual parts. For example, in evaluating the Apollo space program, individual evaluations might be made of all its many components including the ground control system, the recovery system, and so on, identifying each of these systems as exceptional. Yet if each is not coordinated with the others, results would be disastrous. Therefore, it is necessary not only to consider each of the components but also to consider all of them in their relationship to one another.

Involvement

A fourth important feature an evaluation system should possess is the involvement of significant groups. It has been emphasized that evaluation should include everyone who is closely related to the educational segment under consideration, including the administrative staff, instructional staff, supportive staff, students, and community representatives, in addition to external experts in some cases. Evaluation must not be something that the administration does to departments nor should it be something that department chairmen do to teachers. The team approach is necessary in planning the evaluation system, implementing the evaluation, making the subsequent evaluation of how the system was carried out and how the results are being utilized, as well as in assessing the degree to which the results helped in improving offerings for students. Essential to any real involvement is personal identification. Experience has shown that individuals who can personally identify with planning and implementing an activity, whether it be an evaluation activity or any other, are most likely to follow through and use the results of that activity.

Broad Data Base

The fifth feature necessary to an evaluation system is a broad data base. Some systems focus entirely on the assessment of student learning. Certainly, learning is important and, in light of precisely presented performance objectives, is a useful input into evaluation. However, it is only one type. This has been a heavily disputed point among evaluation theorists—one group saying that only product measures are important, while the other group emphasizes measures of process or activity occurring within the educational program. It is the authors' contention that both should be considered. Evaluation systems which focus exclusively on student learning have many limitations. To begin with, measuring devices which are capable of assessing all student performances are usually not available. Also, student assessment more or less requires that every program being assessed be identical, focusing on identical objectives and goals. Another significant shortcoming is that many side effects—good ones and bad ones—are ignored. The pharmaceutical industry spends millions of dollars annually to study the side effects of certain drugs. It is possible that a student who can perform exceptionally well on a measure of cognitive achievement and psychomotor performance has acquired a negative attitude toward his career. This may be an overbearing side effect; the individual may not enter a specific career although he may possess the requisite skills. There are many more shortcomings of an evaluation system which focuses only on student learning, but the point to be stressed is that the system must have a much broader focus than simple student measurement. Ideally, it should focus on obtaining information and opinions from a number of all the individuals involved with and affected by the program, including present and former students, staff members, employers of students, parents of students, administrators of programs, and so forth. Information may also be gained from simple observation of the program and program characteristics. Certainly, there are many techniques, discussed in later chapters of this text, which can be utilized to gather this type of information on a broad data base—questionnaires, rating forms, observation by external personnel, and interviews of staff, for example.

Systematic Recording

The sixth major feature that an evaluation should contain is a means for complete, systematic, and comprehensive recording of all data which are collected regardless of the means by which they were collected. Careful construction of questionnaires will help to systematize evaluation findings, but in cases where open-ended items are utilized, data will be less easily systematized. The use of interview schedules and observation checklists will guide observation during interviews and will allow for consistent recording of findings. Regardless of the method utilized, some way of recording data in a consistent and systematic manner is a necessity. For example, if a team is charged with evaluating a particular program, each team member will make his own observations and analyses. Afterwards, however, the program manager and his staff may wish to gain an overview of the strengths and weaknesses of the program. Also, the program manager may want evidence to support the evaluative conclusions to others. If a systematic evaluation is performed in which data are carefully recorded, both these needs can be met even without a finalized evaluation report. There is more to be said for systematic recording. Depending on the method you choose to compile a summary report, your results may be quite different. A systematic recording system will keep more energetic, forceful team members from tipping the scales in favor of their own, possibly biased, opinions.

Judgment

The seventh feature of a good evaluation system is that of judgment. (If you recall the two definitions of evaluation that were presented in the first chapter, the first had to do with collecting information for making decisions and planning while the second had to do with determining worth.) The determination of worth requires that some type of judgment be made and, therefore, it cannot be left out of an evaluation system. Although a member of an evaluation team could simply gather and present educational program information, it must be synthesized into some type of judgment or opinion about the specific program. Otherwise, it may be very difficult to know the good and bad points of the program. Evaluation must be more than simply reporting information or describing programs.

Feedback

Clearly essential to the effectual changes in programs following an evaluation is an effective system of feedback. Feedback is the communication of judgment and data information regarding the evaluative focus (see page 30) back to the decision makers or the individuals who are responsible for making changes in programs. Possible mechanisms for feedback include reports, summary conferences, and planning meetings. Of course, this feature is the agent of the consultative purpose; for an evaluation to be of any use to improvement, the judgments and the information must be accurately fed back to those individuals who are in the position to utilize it.

Take the thermostat in our homes, for example. Its first role is the measuring of temperature in the home. It is fine that the thermostat reads this temperature, but there is little utility in such a system if it tells us only what we already know—that it's too hot or too cold for comfort. For the thermostat reading to be of any use, there must be a feedback system to emit signals to the furnace that cause it to stop producing heat.

An evaluation system must incorporate a similar feedback system. A system with a broad data base, a method for systematic recording of data, and the incorporation of sound judgments—all of these without an adequate feedback system would be ineffective. It is probably most important that this feedback be directed to the program personnel. However, information should also be sent back to the chief administrator or agencies responsible for the funding and supervision of the program or unit under consideration. To some this feedback process will appear to be threatening, and it is, if used improperly. But used properly, the evaluation results fed back to the administrators or funding agents should result in increased attention to problem areas. This could mean a change in priorities or additional funding of a particular deficient aspect.

Adaptability

The ninth feature that an evaluation system should have is adaptability—that is, that it can be applied to any and all occupational or training programs under the evaluating agency. If there are variations within programs, the system should be adaptable to each of them, even though the programs are not identical. An evaluation system could conceivably focus initially on specific aspects, causing all programs to conform to these specific requirements. However, this is not always helpful and diversification of offerings is more often advantageous. The type of community, type of institution, type of staff, and interest of the student body, in addition to the need of the corporation or the public employing sector, should be contributing factors in the design of individual programs. It is not only probable but desirable that programs will vary from department to department or institution to institution. The evaluation system should take into account these differences and should not penalize an individual program or institution, based on the results of its evaluation, for not living up to held standards or an accepted norm. This brings up an important point with regard to comparisons. It is the authors' contention that strict comparisons should not be made. It is more useful to know what the strengths and weaknesses of particular programs or institutions are than to know normative ranks and classes. This focus will lend more to the improvement of programs and will be less threatening to all who are involved.

Meta Evaluation

The tenth and last feature which an evaluation system should possess is a system for meta evaluation, which refers to the higher order evaluation or the evaluation of the evaluation system. It is very important that those involved with or affected by the evaluation monitor the purposes, processes, and outcomes of the evaluation system throughout its development and implementation stages. This is to say that all activities should undergo evaluation, including the system itself. The nine features that have been discussed are very good beginning points for monitoring a system. Keeping an eye on the commitment, involvement, focus, purpose, data base, systematic recording, type of judgment, feedback, and adaptability of an evaluation system is the beginning of overall assessment of the system. An added concern should be on what happens as a result of the evaluation system, whether or not the results are being used, for instance. If not, then possibly changes in the system itself should be made.

PROCEDURES FOR DESIGNING THE
EVALUATION SYSTEM

Chapters 3 through 8 give specific procedures for conducting individual evaluation activities. However, there is a need to develop an overall structure within which these activities can and should be conducted. Following are several procedures which should be followed in designing an overall evaluation system prior to the initiation of an individual activity.

Focusing the Evaluation

The first task that should be undertaken in designing the system should be focusing the evaluation—to spell out the objectives of the evaluation and to define policies which will govern the process of evaluation. The first concern should be the identification of levels at which decisions need to be made. The *audience* of the evaluation results should be identified prior to any activity or collection of information. For example, if a child care program is to be evaluated, there may be information needs or decision needs at more than one level. In this example the program operator or instructor may wish information to aid him in redesigning or restructuring the course or program and, in addition, the program administrator or supervisor may wish information dealing with the additional budget requests for either expanding programs, revising programs, or adding different instructional materials. Thus, two different levels of decision making have been identified, the instructional level, and the administrative or budgetary level.

Once decision levels have been identified, specific decisions that must be made should be detailed to aid in structuring the evaluation. In the case of the child care program, instructional level decision situations might include "choosing between alternative instructional techniques," "choosing between alternative instructional materials," "deciding to omit particular segments of a course," "determining whether the pace of a program should be accelerated," and so on. Such decisions should be projected prior to the design and conduct of any evaluation. In addition, decisions on the management or administrative level should also be projected. For example, *Should the program be continued or expanded?* or *Should additional or different personnel be assigned to the program?* These are just examples of management or administrative level decision situations which should also be projected when possible. The specificity of decision situations may vary considerably—the shortening of a particular instructional segment, for instance, may be the entire substance of a decision. In another case, the decision may be much broader, such as identifying changes to be made in the overall institutional program. In these cases, the evaluative technique as well as the detail of information to be gathered will, of course, vary with the specificity of the decision.

Once decision levels have been identified and decision situations projected, the next major step in focusing the evaluation system should be the formulation of evaluation questions. The CIPP model may be used, or a matrix of program characteristics (see Figure 2–2 on page 31) may help to generate many questions. Table 2–1 on page 32 shows questions which had been generated from the matrix shown in Figure 2–2. Evaluative questions can also be built directly

Decision Situation	Evaluative Question
1. Choosing between alternative instructional materials.	Should learning activity packages or textbooks be utilized in the child care program?
2. Omitting segments of a course or program.	Should the situational experience portion of the sales training program be deleted?
3. Determining the pace of a program.	Should the automotive technician program be accelerated?

FIGURE 2–3   *Example Decision Situations with Corresponding Questions*

from the decision situations which have been discussed in the preceding paragraphs. The questions merely pose the decisions in the format of a question thus aiding in the collecting of information. For example, several of the decision situations mentioned above are presented in Figure 2–3 with their corresponding question.

Obviously the development of evaluative questions is simply the rewriting of the decision situations. This step may seem somewhat superfluous; however, it will prove to be useful at later stages when designing the evaluation system and in using the evaluation results. To summarize then, evaluative questions can be generated from specific decision situations at hand, from a program intercorrelation matrix, or from the CIPP evaluation model. The matrix will be most useful when general evaluations are being made or at least initial attempts at evaluation are being made of programs or courses. Following the initial evaluation, more precise questions can be generated which will focus the subsequent evaluation efforts more specifically.

Selecting Appropriate Evaluation Activities

Once decision situations and levels have been identified and evaluation questions specifically delineated, techniques or activities must be selected which enable program personnel to obtain information for answering the questions so as to provide information for making the necessary decisions. The first step in the selection of evaluation activities should be to isolate the information needed for answering the posed questions. This can be accomplished by analyzing each question and asking, *What type of data or information will help me answer the question?* For example, consider the following list of evaluation questions as just questions to begin with.

1. Where should we address our efforts for improving our institution?
2. Should the wood technology program be discontinued?
3. Are the objectives of our wood technology program congruent with necessary on-the-job competencies?
4. Is our in-plant sales training program cheaper to run than paying another institution for training our employees?
5. What can we do to upgrade our health care program instructional staff?
6. Are the graduates of our automotive technology program being placed in appropriate jobs?
7. Is the instructional equipment in the machine trades program obsolete?
8. Which textbook should be used in our child care program?
9. Have the graduates of the electronics technician program achieved the course and program objectives?

This list of questions represents a broad range of educational decisions. A particular institution or department may have only one of these questions to guide an evaluation while another may have an extensive list. Once questions have been stated there is a need to identify activities which will help to answer these questions. The first section of Chapters 3 through 8 contains a list of reasons for conducting that particular activity, which are given in the form of objectives. Table 2–2 lists these objectives under the individual activities or evaluative techniques. A first step in identifying activities once questions have been stated is to review Table 2–2 to identify objectives which correspond to questions (see pages 50 and 51).

By comparing the nine evaluative questions given above with Table 2–2, it can be seen that some of the questions relate to objectives within the activities or chapters listed. For example, question 3, on the congruence of objectives with competencies, can be assessed through the activity described in Chapter 5, the employer survey. And question 4, regarding the feasibility and costs of alternative programs, can be assessed through the technique and activity described in Chapter 8, the cost analysis evaluation. Also, for question 5, on upgrading the health care program instructional staff, Chapter 7 can provide information to aid in making this decision and answering this question. Question 6 can be answered through the use of the follow-up study to determine if the graduates of the automotive technology program are being placed in appropriate jobs. Likewise, other questions can be answered with specific activities. However, in considering question 1, *Where should we address our efforts for improving our institution?* all of the activities or techniques included in Chapters 3 through 8 can provide helpful information. Question 2 is a similar yet more specific question, and a number of techniques may be needed to answer it. In approaching these types of questions, it is apparent that it would be impossible to conduct all evaluation activities within a time period of, say, one year. Therefore, it is necessary to identify activities which can provide the most information yet cost the least in terms of time and resources allocated. In the case of question 1, use of the consultative team evaluation described in Chapter 6 would probably be the most efficient use of resources considering the breadth of the question. For question 2, regarding the discontinuance of a program, the consultative team evaluation in combination with the cost analysis evaluation would probably be most appropriate for an initial attempt. In cases such as in the first two questions, where specific evaluation activities are not readily identifiable, an attempt should be made to define the information needs. For example, in question 2, *Should the wood technology program be discontinued?* the analysis would include listing such information as student flow data, student outcome data, personnel performance data, identification of strengths and weaknesses of the program, cost of the program, and so on. Once the data have been identified, then the most important should have priority in terms of selecting the evaluation activities or techniques. In the case of the information needs just given, identification of strengths and weaknesses of the program and identification of costs are probably the most important. Therefore, the selection of the consultative team evaluation and the cost analysis evaluation would be justified.

Structuring Evaluation Activities

Review Complete Chapter

Before any activity begins, every chapter which describes a specific technique to be used should be reviewed thoroughly. Not everyone

TABLE 2-2   *Evaluation Activities Included in This Text with Corresponding Purposes*

Chapter 3 — The Measurement of Learner Performance

To assess competency attainment of learners

To assign grades to learners

To enable learners to make wise career choices

To aid in the placement of learners in programs consonant with their interests and abilities

To assist in the assessment of occupational instruction, course or program

To provide input for instructor appraisal

Chapter 4 — The Follow-up as an Evaluative Tool: The Student Follow-up

To determine the adequacy of the educational or training program in preparing individuals for job entry

To determine the adequacy of ancillary services such as guidance counseling and placement

To determine the adequacy of preparation for entry into advanced training such as community college, industrial training programs, university, or adult education program

To emphasize the primary objective of career education to staff and students

To determine realistic job descriptions for positions obtained by former students or trainees

To determine the immediate demand for positions within the community

To determine the career patterns of former participants of various programs

To determine the mobility of program graduates

Chapter 5 — The Follow-up as an Evaluative Tool: The Employer Survey

To assess the competency list of specific course or program

To assess the performance of former students

To determine how specific program graduates compare with graduates of other training programs

To elicit employer recommendations for improving the occupational program

To estimate supply and demand for individuals in particular occupations

To determine the recruitment practices of employing agencies

To aid in the public relations of the education or training agency or institution

TABLE 2-2 *(Continued)*

Chapter 6 — The Consultative Team Evaluation

To provide an outside view of the program and its components
To help update and insure the relevance of programs and their components
To provide expertise otherwise unavailable to the program or institution
To inform community personnel of program character
To facilitate working relations between instructional and ancillary personnel
To provide in-service training for team members
To identify program components which are deficient
To reinforce aspects of the program which are beneficial and outstanding

Chapter 7 — The Evaluation of Education and Training Personnel

To help insure the accountability of education and training programs
To help improve the effectiveness of personnel
To aid in decision making regarding tenure and salary
To help make decisions regarding promotions
To aid in selecting education and training personnel
To certify practicing and prospective instructional personnel

Chapter 8 — The Cost Related Study

To determine optimum load for a particular program
To determine the advisability of financing the development of a new program
To justify resource allocation decisions
To promote better utilization of facilities
To compare alternative programs
To decrease costs of high cost low incidence programs
To determine optimum staff assignments
To provide fiscal accountability
To determine optimum scheduling/sequencing

involved with the particular activity needs to do this, but should each person involved be asked to read the activity, many benefits can be realized. To begin with, none of these activities will apply strictly to your institution's needs. Joint reading of the chapters, followed by discussion by all those participating in the study, will increase a sense of involvement which, as we suggested previously, contributes greatly to commitment on the part of those persons doing the work.

Redefine Focus

After the chapter review, the focus for each evaluation activity, based upon the capabilities of the particular activity, should be redefined. Familiarity with the activity may lead to either broadening the focus of the evaluative questions or to further specification. In some cases, the activity will provide information in much greater detail than anticipated and refocusing the evaluation will lead to more efficient activity.

Determine Who Should Be Involved

Each of the "working" chapters, 3 through 8, suggests who should be involved in a particular activity. This ranges from program personnel—administrators, instructors, and ancillary personnel—through students, community representatives, and external experts, to name but a few. In planning any activity, this section of each chapter should be consulted to aid in the identification of individuals within your particular institution or program who should be involved.

Identify Activity Subtasks

Subtasks of an evaluation activity under consideration should be described and explained in full detail. This will help in later distribution of staff and projection of necessary resources and will insure the continuation of administrative support. It is important that the evaluation team know exactly what must be done to insure that they can indeed handle problems that arise unexpectedly and roles which have been unrehearsed. In each chapter, these subtasks are usually identified by major subheadings and will represent the body of work that must be completed in order that the evaluation activity be a success.

Inform Personnel

Program personnel and all others who will be involved should be oriented to the purposes and the procedures of the evaluation activity. It will not be enough to merely assign personnel to a given task. These people should have a good feel for the thrust of the evaluation to allow them to make good decisions as the need arises, to adequately explain evaluation goals to others, and to comprehend the difficulties that might be met by other personnel. If all members are properly informed they will be in a position to help one another. This is essential to the success of the evaluation itself.

Assign Personnel Responsibilities

Staff assignments should, of course, be made for each of the sub-tasks. The scope and extensiveness of the evaluation activity will dictate the number of individuals needed. The director of the evaluation should probably assume overall leadership of all subtasks, though with very large activities it may be advantageous to also identify individual leaders for each of the subtasks. The director can ask for volunteers in situations where no special knowledge is needed, or he can select the individuals, when expertise is required to complete the job.

Sequence Subtasks

The next step involves the sequencing of individual subtasks in a configuration which is most efficient in terms of resource and time utilization, i. e., the development of an evaluation schedule. Many

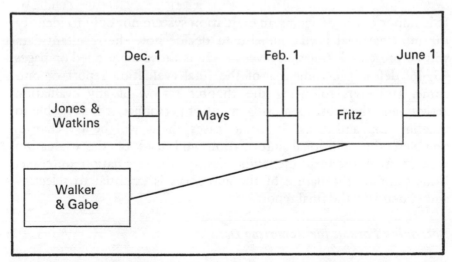

FIGURE 2–4   *Graphic Portrayal of Evaluation Activity Sequencing*

activities can be conducted simultaneously, but others will have to be conducted subsequent to each other. To initiate this sequencing step, one should list all of the subtasks and identify those which are dependent on preceding tasks. Then the activities can be placed into a pictorial schedule or PERT-type chart such as the one in Figure 2–4, where subtask 1 and 3 must be completed before subtask 4 is begun, and work on subtask 2 can be started concurrently with work on subtask 1.

Determine Time Estimates

Once activities have been scheduled and sequenced, estimates of time should be attached to each subtask. The example of sequence scheduling presented in Figure 2–4 shows personnel assigned to each of the four activities and completion dates. It is often useful to include the names of those involved. Each of the subtasks may require more than one individual, and the name of at least the leader of the particular activity, or the person responsible for its completion, should be attached to the schedule.

Structuring the Evaluation Outcomes

It is important in designing an evaluation system not only to identify the informational needs but also to decide how the resultant data will be presented. Decision levels, such as those mentioned on pages 45–46, define the audiences of the final evaluation report or outcome. However, following the chapter review of any evaluation activity and the subsequent assignment of personnel, it is advisable to redefine the audiences. In some cases there will be no change; however, the additional information and uses of the evaluation activity may broaden the audiences of the evaluation outcome. Understanding the nature of the audiences is essential to selecting and structuring the final report.

Determine Format for Reporting Data

Data can be reported in a number of ways depending on the sources of the information. Some examples of reporting format include

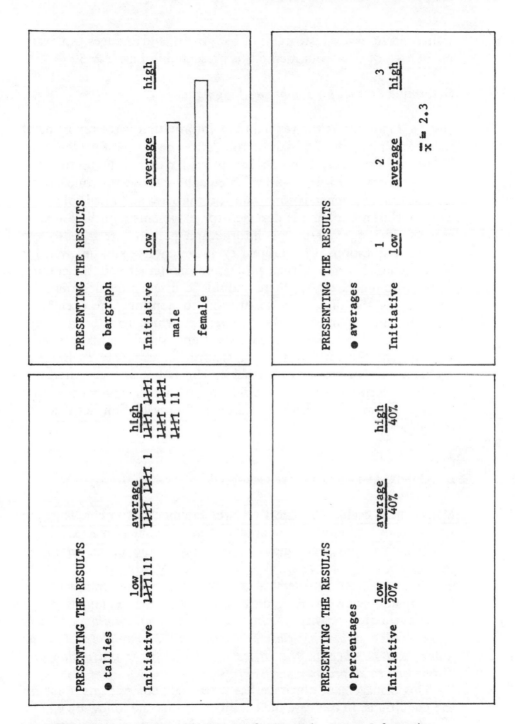

FIGURE 2–5   *Four Example Formats for Reporting Survey Information*

tallies, percentages, histograms or bar graphs, and averages. An example of each of these four methods is presented in Figure 2–5.

Determine Format for Reporting Judgments

Just as important as the reporting of information is the reporting of judgments made on the basis of the data. The format for presenting judgments can vary, but one has proved particularly useful. The format shown in Figure 2–6 has three columns, one for conclusions, another for recommendations, and the third for suggested solutions. The conclusions column is designed for judgments regarding specific aspects of the program, or information gathered relative to the evaluative questions. Conclusions or judgments should be given for both exemplary and deficient program characteristics. In the column under recommendations, there should be listed general statements encouraging the district or institution to continue the exemplary characteristics or improve the deficiencies which have been identified. The third column—suggested solutions—should contain specific actions that the local district or institution can take to improve program components or deficiencies. This is but one suggested format for presenting evaluation judgments. (Chapter 6 presents several others that may be adapted to any of the evaluation activities or techniques.

Developing Management Evaluation Objectives

Management evaluation objectives are statements of intent. They are useful in communicating the activities of an evaluation endeavor to all individuals involved and are, essentially, the verbalization by management of the overall evaluation plan. Management objectives can be constructed at several levels. For example, the following is a very broad objective which indicates the plan for the completion of a broad evaluation activity: *By May 1 of next year, a follow-up study of last year's graduating class of nursing will be completed and the report will be filed in the office of the dean of instruction and distributed to all program staff.*

This management objective has three main components. First are the conditions. In this case the condition is that the follow-up will be completed by May 1. The second part of the objective indicates the

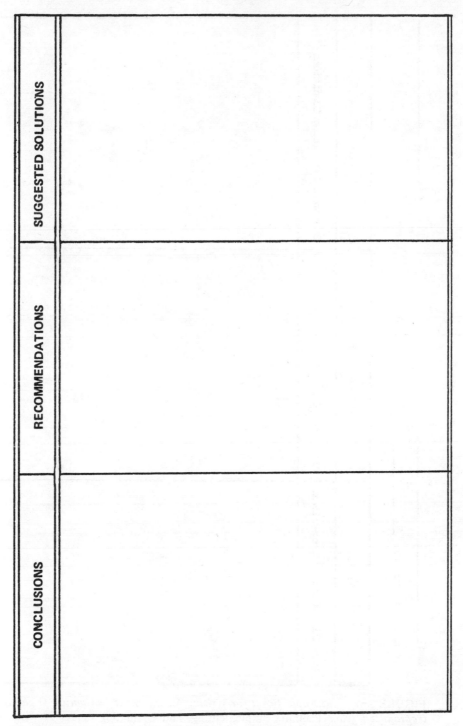

FIGURE 2–6   *Example Format for Reporting Evaluative Conclusions,*
Recommendations, and Suggested Solutions

58

Name

Title and/or Position

CONDITIONS	OUTCOME STATEMENT	CRITERIA
Time Period and/or Target Date	Plans for Evaluation	Statement Describing Conditions That Will Exist

FIGURE 2—7   *Example Form for Writing Management Evaluation Objectives* (*reproduced from* Planning, Implementing, and Evaluating Career Preparation Programs, *with permission of J. A. Borgen, D. E. Davis and McKnight Publishers*).

outcome of the activity—a follow-up study of last year's graduating class will be completed. The third part of the objective is the criterion for completion—in this case the criterion for completion is that the report will be filed in the office of the dean of instruction and distributed to all program staff.

In addition to management evaluation objectives of this broad nature, such objectives can be prepared for each of the subtasks within an evaluation activity. The following objective covers the development of an instrument: *By October 15, a follow-up survey instrument will be developed and tested and will be placed in the hands of the program manager.* These more specific management objectives which cover subtasks are very useful in communicating exactly what is required of the program personnel and their leader. In a sense, these subtask objectives tie in with the PERT or scheduling chart mentioned earlier. To aid in the formulation of management evaluation objectives, the form presented in Figure 2–7 can be utilized. This form allows each management objective to be written separately.

Incorporating a Means of Meta Evaluation

Meta evaluation is of the second order and is the evaluation of the evaluation system. It should focus on monitoring each activity as it is completed and on searching for constraints or limiting factors within each of the activities. This is especially necessary when multiple activities or subtasks are being conducted simultaneously and their outcomes are to be combined later. In addition to specific monitoring, a broader meta evaluation should be conducted to assess the ten general design features described on pp. 38–45, including commitment, consultative purpose, holistic focus, involvement, broad data base, systematic recording, judgment, feedback, adaptability, and meta evaluation itself.

REFERENCES

Stufflebeam, D. L.; Foley, W. J.; Gephart, W. J.; Guba, E. G.; Hammond, R. L.; Merriman, H. O.; and Provus, M. M. *Educational Evaluation and Decision-making in Education.* Itasca, Ill.: Peacock, 1971.

3

The Measurement of Learner Performance

WHY MEASURE LEARNER PERFORMANCE?

Of all the evaluative techniques used in occupational education and training, learner performance tests have been most widely emphasized. However, use of these tests and other measuring instruments has traditionally been limited to assigning grades or placing individuals into special classes or occupational programs. Learner performance measures can provide additional information to program managers, instructors, evaluators, and, most important, the learners themselves. Once data has been gathered, the results may be used in a number of ways.

To Provide Information to Help Learners Make Wise Career Choices

Results from ability tests, aptitude tests, achievement tests, attitude inventories, and interest surveys can be very useful in helping a learner select an occupation which is most congruent with his aptitudes, interests, and abilities. It is best that the learner begin in an occupation for which he is well suited, even if it does not measure up to his expectations. If performance indicates, for example, that he should start in an apprentice-type situation, this information may avoid a situation where he will accumulate records of poor performance on the job. Similarly, if the learner's performance is exceptional, it is important that he does not begin in a career for which he is over-qualified. Frustration can result from boredom or lack of adequate challenge as well as incompetence. Of course, trained personnel such as counselors or advisors should monitor test results and present this information to learners in useful and understandable form.

To Aid in Placing Learners in Programs Consonant with Their Interests and Abilities

Once learners have made tentative career choices, programs must be established to fulfill their occupational needs. Test results can be employed to identify the competencies currently held by the individual, and he can thus be placed at the appropriate level within the occupational program. Also, deficiencies in the learner's repertoire of skills can be identified, and remedial instructional sequences or courses may be prescribed to compensate for these deficiencies. Here again, improper placement can have devastating effects on motivation. Performance testing can avoid a situation where early disillusionment estranges the learner from a career for which he would otherwise be well suited.

To Assist in Assessing the Instruction, Course, or Program Objectives

Learner performance results can provide excellent indices for assessing the effectiveness of an occupational program. Once the *objectives* (desired learner outcomes) have been stated for each course or program, deviations from these standards may suggest that: 1) the program was ineffective, 2) some objectives were unrealistic or unattainable, 3) the learners were not motivated, 4) the measuring instruments were invalid, or 5) the learners were not challenged. In this way learner measures can be used to assess the quality of instructional objectives.

To Provide Input for Instructor Appraisal

Increases in learner knowledge or skills may be utilized on a criterion-referenced scale as one of the means by which to assess instructor proficiency or competence. In some cases, changes between initial and end-of-instruction occupational competence can be attributed to teaching expertise, providing valuable data for assessing instructional performance. Ultimately, the proficiency of any instructor and the quality of instructional methods can be observed in the results of learner proficiency examinations. More attention is paid to this purpose in Chapter 7.

To Assess Competency Attainment of Learners

Learner performance or achievement measures can be used to assess characteristics and properties of competency attainment for given occupational tasks. Performance criterion levels can be established at any point in instruction where it is necessary to ascertain the extent of the learner's attainment of performance goals.

To Assign Grades to Learners

Test scores, work incidents, projects, class participation, and many other instructional occurrences can be used to obtain comparisons among learners for grading purposes. Ordinarily, arbitrary cutoff points are set for the distribution of each grade—that is, 90 percent for A's, 75 percent for B's, and so on. Grade assignment in this traditional sense has both advantages and disadvantages. The most outstanding disadvantage lies in the inherent assumption that only a few learners deserve the top marks. An advantage is that grade assignment facilitates the selection of the best qualified learners for advanced education or training programs and indicates which learners are best suited for advancement in job placement and career paths.

CLASSIFICATIONS OF MEASUREMENT

General Mental Ability

General mental ability (GMA) tests are probably the most highly developed of all performance measures and are standardized by publishing companies who usually handle all scoring and reporting for the instruments. Consequently, practicing educators and human resource developers will seldom need to be concerned with develop-ing their own measures of GMA, but they should be versed in the interpretation of published tests. Individual mental ability tests re-quire a one-to-one relationship between the examinee and the test administrator and for this reason are used only in special cases.

General mental ability tests can be verbal or manipulative. Verbal tests rely totally on written or spoken responses to items which have been heard or read. Manipulative measures, on the other hand, rely entirely on the use or manipulation of objects such as peg or form boards, picture puzzles, or blocks. Many individual tests include both verbal and manipulative components; however, most group tests of GMA rely only on verbal items.

Numerous business and industrial test-screening programs employ verbal general ability tests which have been validated by follow-up of career success. Other companies, who wish to ensure that they gain an accurate estimate of the potential capability of employees with disadvantaged backgrounds, use GMA test scores that are believed to work independently of language skills or reading abilities. A com-plementary basic skills survey is often employed along with the nonverbal GMA test. When combined, these two tests can provide an index for initial career placement, placement in continuing education programs, or transfer to organizational training programs. Science Research Associates offers an array of excellent general mental ability and basic skills tests (SRA, 1973).

Aptitude Tests

Aptitude tests measure capabilities or skills that are considered important to achievement in a given career or occupational field and can suggest the possibility of an individual's success in a particular course or program or his success in a specific career or occupation. Examples of aptitude tests used in occupational education include tests of clerical aptitude, mechanical aptitude, verbal aptitude, math-ematical aptitude, and so on. Being based only on an individual's current capabilities, aptitude measures do not take into account such variables as learner motivation or further training, which may offset the indications of measurable "aptitude." However, the tests do provide counselors and advisors with information with which they can design appropriate occupational experiences for individuals and help them plan careers.

In business and industry, initial placement or career advancement is often facilitated by the employment of an aptitude test. Either a general aptitude battery, assessing the combination of traits or attributes essential for competent job performance, or a special set of measures formulated for a specific occupational or career area may be employed.

Achievement Tests

Achievement tests differ from aptitude measures in intent. If we desire to predict certain job competencies that a learner might achieve, an aptitude test will be appropriate. In contrast, if our intent is to ascertain competencies that the learner has attained as a result of previous training or instruction, an achievement test should be employed as the measuring instrument. Basically, there are two versions of achievement tests—standardized and instructor-designed. Standardized versions are used by career guidance counselors to assist learners in making more viable career choices. School administrators often utilize standardized versions to evaluate instructional programs and section classes, using the results to interpret to the community the influence of the occupational or career program. However, the most significant function of achievement testing is that of measuring classroom or laboratory performance, and while both standardized and instructor-designed tests are used, the instructor-made test is most commonly employed.

Interest Inventories

Interest inventories are measures to determine the learner's domain of career interests and aversions as well as his preferences for job activities and work-related environments. These tests are widely employed by industry and business and are commonly referred to as vocational interest surveys. Although scores on these tests are not indicative of the learner's ability to perform in any given career area, they frequently provide a point of departure in predicting future occupational success and job satisfaction. Recent investigation into the formulation of "interest survey scores" for specific careers suggests that interest inventories be used for career program selection, placement, development, or counseling. A total occupational profile or individual scales can be obtained through the use of the Strong Vocational Interest Blank (Strong, 1943), Kuder Preference Record—Occupational (1957), or Kuder Occupational Interest Survey (1962). Moreover, all of these scales assess interests in activities related to various occupational areas as well as precise "career interest definition" which is relevant to career choice.

Attitude Surveys

Attitude surveys may determine: 1) the way learners feel about their occupational programs, 2) learner attitude toward instructor effectiveness, and 3) anticipatory work attitudes on the part of learners. Career education places emphasis on work attitude development, and so learners are constantly being exposed to information about the world of work. Once attitudes are formed, however, questions remain concerning the way in which schools can most effectively assist students in the career assimilation process. Students are likely to have developed attitudes toward the world of work by the time they enter the fifth grade. An attitude measure for high school age youth has been developed and validated by Graen and Davis (1971) covering such topics as attitudes toward work, expectations about working, and basic preferences or occupational needs.

In business and industry, attitude surveys and questionnaires are employed to determine employees' feelings about their job environment, job supervision, and management. This type of assessment is of particular importance in business, as operating efficiency and production are highly contingent upon the employee's work attitude, and surveys can provide information for isolating indices of production and servicing morale. Such data may also be used for identifying the way employees feel about management, career development opportunities, working conditions, pay benefits, and other areas of concern that can influence job execution and profits.

Personality Measures

Personality measures, when used by qualified personnel and interpreted on the basis of empirical validation, can contribute effectively to learner and employee placement programs for numerous careers. It should be noted, however, that scores from personality measures should not be used to categorize individuals in terms of career potential. Their purpose is to provide data as to plausible career areas to be investigated further.

In business, several personality tests have been specifically formulated for such occupational groups as sales, supervision, and management, and focus on the particular values, traits, and attitudes indicative of successful performance in these areas (SRA, 1973).

The concept of "career interests" has been viewed by experts in psychometrics as independent of personality. However, definitions of measured occupational needs, orientations, values, and interests indicate a considerable amount of overlap. Research strongly indicates that interests and needs, and career orientation, are probably independent elements comprising *career personality* (Salomone and Muthard, 1972). Since needs and interests may be considered independent facets of career personality, it would be desirable for an occupational or personnel counselor to differentiate one from the other, and relate them to the student's or employee's potential career adjustment and occupational satisfaction.

INTRODUCTION TO ACHIEVEMENT MEASURES

The courts and the Equal Employment Opportunity Commission have ruled that examinations, given as a prerequisite for employment, which are not job-related and which have a discriminatory impact are in violation of the law.* For this reason alone, it is imperative that examinations given both actual and prospective employees be job related. Moreover, carefully developed job-related examinations can

---

*Refer to the 1971 opinion of the Supreme Court of the United States in the case of Griggs vs. Duke Power Company.

ensure the selection of personnel most appropriate to given tasks in a given organization.

Written tests have received increasingly heavy criticism as discriminatory and, consequently, inaccurate predictions of employee competence. Intrinsically, these tests are highly accurate, although they are sometimes employed or interpreted incorrectly. The written test is but one of numerous measures which can be used in examining job applicants. In many cases, the use of additional indicators—work samples, critical incidents, performance or simulation test results, oral interviews, and review and analysis of educational and employment experiences—is more appropriate. Employment examinations formulated in accordance with the foregoing procedures better represent job relatedness and effectiveness in selecting high quality employees.

Measurement of learner achievement should be based on well-specified instructional objectives that reflect clearly defined competencies that will be needed by the program graduate. Through close analysis of specific occupations, the required tasks, attitudes, and skills can be identified. Once identified, necessary competencies can be translated into learner performance objectives. For example, analysis of the work of a materials technologist yielded a long list of tasks in which an effective person would demonstrate proficiency at materials analysis. One task was to perform tension, compression, and shear tests on given materials. This competency is easily converted to a learner performance objective by adding both a condition and a criterion for measurement.

EXAMPLE PERFORMANCE OBJECTIVE

Given four test materials, set up a materials tester and perform a tension, compression, and shear test on each material, correctly recording the resulting data.

Once objectives have been stated to encompass all desired competencies, measurement strategies can be designed to assess the attainment of the objectives.

Many occupational and training personnel identify competencies, state objectives, and implement appropriate instructional strategies. However, the process must be carried further—to the development of measuring instruments that are capable of sampling learner behavior, and to the interpretation of the results.

Taxonomical Considerations for Measurement

To formulate measurement instruments suitable for assessing occupational tasks, one must first identify the nature of the learning outcomes desired. The type of objectives selected for a given classroom or laboratory course will, however, depend upon the subject matter, the philosophy of the institution, the occupational needs of the learners, the career outcomes attained in related previous courses, and the large number of other factors affecting the occupational program.

A classification system may be used for identifying varying *levels* of competence so as to provide a conceptual framework of behaviors deemed most critical for career preparation or advancement. The Taxonomy of Educational Objectives (Bloom, et al., 1956 and Krathwohl, et al., 1964) and the taxonomies developed by Simpson (1966) and Moore (1971) can be employed in approaching this task. These are comprehensive schemes for classifying objectives, competencies, and measures within one of four domains: 1) cognitive, 2) affective, 3) psychomotor, and 4) perceptual.

The taxonomy of the cognitive domain encompasses the intellectual outcomes of occupational learning. The affective domain covers attitudinal and interest-based learning tasks. The psychomotor domain includes both simple and complex motor skills. The perceptual domain relates to attentive behaviors. The classification schemes for the cognitive, psychomotor, and affective domains have been developed and tested extensively (Bloom, et al., 1956; Harrow, 1972; Krathwohl, et al., 1964; Simpson, 1966). Development of and research on the taxonomy for the perceptual domain is now underway. Measurement of work-related behaviors is necessarily concerned with all the domains, and in this section we shall focus on identifying objectives for measurement purposes within the four. It should also be noted that a close relationship exists between the cognitive and affective domains and the perceptual and psychomotor domains, respectively. This relationship is apparent in both instructional and measurement situations.

Cognitive Domain

Measurable outcomes in the cognitive domain are divided into two major classifications: knowledge and intellectual abilities, and skills. These are further subdivided into six levels of increasing complexity (Bloom, et al., 1956). The hierarchy ranges from simple recall of factual information through the increasingly complex levels of comprehension, application, analysis, synthesis, and evaluation.

In developing an occupational achievement test to assess cognitive processes, using Bloom's taxonomy would be helpful. It not only provides a standard vocabulary for analyzing, classifying, and defining occupational outcomes, but also provides examples of behavioral objectives upon which measuring instruments can be formulated. Within the cognitive domain some common methods for measuring include recognition items (multiple choice, true-false, or matching) and constructed response items (completion, short answer, definition, and essay). These item types are of a very "clean" nature and appear to have high face validity.*

Affective Domain

The *Taxonomy of Educational Objectives, Handbook II, Affective Domain* (Krathwohl, et al., 1956) provides an excellent guide to operationalizing and classifying occupational objectives that represent attitudinal factors such as feeling, emotion, or indications of acceptance or rejection. As was suggested earlier, attitudinal qualities may be assessed indirectly through many of the methods of measurement commonly employed for cognitive abilities.

Measurable outcomes in the affective taxonomy are also arranged from simple to more complex qualities. At the lowest level of this hierarchy the learner is simply attending to or perceiving occupational content. At the second level, the learner responds to the content with feeling or emotion. At the third level, the learner

*Face validity refers to the judgment that a test or measurement technique will measure "so and so" simply because it looks like it should.

intentionally responds to career information in a value-oriented way. Next, the learner organizes his attitudes and feelings and further conceptualizes these into an attitudinal structure. Finally, the learner characterizes his attitudinal structure in terms of consistent occupational and career behavior patterns.

For measurement purposes, attitudinal outcomes in the affective domain are structured into five major categories: 1) receiving (attending), 2) responding, 3) valuing, 4) organization, and 5) characterization. Corresponding to identified levels are objectives that exemplify various occupational areas. Thus, the objectives serve as a formative means for structuring measuring instruments.

The significant effect of occupational instruction on attitudinal or affective behavior is widely acknowledged but often overlooked from a measurement standpoint. Without receptive attitudes toward occupational content or career-oriented tasks, learners may have difficulty acquiring knowledge in the cognitive domain, as research has shown that attitudes are deeply involved in retention. When instruction is incompatible with the learner's attitudes and values, learning is weakened significantly. An earnest attempt must be made to weigh attitudinal qualities important to the competent performance of cognitive objectives. Techniques for constructing attitude measures will be discussed in a later section of this chapter. They include rating scales, questionnaires, and Q-sort techniques.

Psychomotor Domain

The third behavior classification scheme, important for measuring competencies in occupational education, is termed the psychomotor domain (Simpson, 1966) and includes competencies in the physical performance of an occupational skill or task. Many technical and occupational tasks require a high degree of ability and skill competencies and these can be derived and assessed through the employment of the psychomotor taxonomy. As is characteristic of the two preceding domains, the psychomotor taxonomy is hierarchical or sequential in nature. The five major levels, beginning with the most basic elements involved in the execution of a physical skill are as follows: 1) perception, 2) guided response, 3) set, 4) mechanism, and 5) complex overt response. These levels, along with descriptions and representative occupational objectives, can be found in Simpson, 1966.

Use of this classification system not only allows the instructor to clarify his instructional intentions regarding motor or skill development, but it also helps him in formulating appropriate instruments for measuring varying levels of skill development. Psychomotor behaviors can be measured by several techniques. These techniques are discussed later in this chapter.

Perceptual Domain

The final taxonomy relevant to measurement criteria for occupational instruction is that of the perceptual domain (Moore, 1967). Essentially, this domain is characterized by sensory-dependent activity executed by the learner in the presence of a given occupational stimulus, and performances range from simple to highly complex behavior. A "perceptive" learner may be characterized as one highly capable of encoding, storing, and retrieving information transmitted during instruction.

Competencies in the perceptual taxonomy are sequential behaviors ordered on the basis of increased information extraction by the learners. Performance is affected principally by factors such as age, personality, and emotional qualities rather than learner background and ability. Because learner background and ability cannot be precisely estimated or controlled, tests based on the perceptual domain will never achieve optimum reliability* indices.

The major levels of the perceptual taxonomy are as follows: 1) sensation, 2) figure perception, 3) symbol perception, 4) perception of meaning, and 5) perception of performance. Collectively, the categories have been conceived as a series of ongoing, perceptual transactions made by the learner in instructional situations. A beginning typing student, for example, initially becomes visually aware of the keyboard structure, selectively discriminates key position, perceives the symbolic relationship between keys and letters, indicates an awareness of correct sequencing for key (character) execution, and, finally, diagnoses the resulting typed image. It should be noted that there is a high degree of dependency between the psychomotor and perceptual taxonomies. Many physical tasks depend initially on accurate and complete perception for subsequent execution. For instance, a welder must first perceive the adequacy and appropriate-

---

*Reliability refers to the consistency of measurement.

ness of the welding flame before he actually performs a fusion welding task. Also, as in the aforementioned taxonomies, occupational competencies in the higher categories are more difficult to classify for measurement purposes than those in lower categories.

In this section, four behaviorally oriented taxonomies have been discussed as relevant to the classification of occupational competencies for measurement purposes. These are the cognitive, affective, psychomotor, and perceptual domains. The major categories of each taxonomy are given, as are representative specific objectives upon which viable testing items can be formulated. Further, it has been indicated that higher categories within each taxonomy are instrumentally dependent upon lower categories and thus constitute hierarchical strategies for classifying occupational tasks. Effective employment of the taxonomies in designing measurement techniques will ensure that the objectives of instruction are made both explicit and specific.

The Point of Reference for Measurement

The measurement of competency attainment can be considered from two points—the norm-reference and the criterion-reference—the former being the most common. Most instructors, managers, counselors, personnel directors, and administrators are well acquainted with the use of the normal curve, comparing the learners with the norm for an immediate or external norm group. The focus is not on what competencies each individual learner manifests.

In a survey conducted by the National Education Association, it was discovered that over 85 percent of the occupational and academic instructors surveyed used some technique which compared learners. Comparative measurement uses test items which are designed to discriminate among individuals and spread out the group in terms of achievement scores. Mental ability tests, aptitude tests, and most achievement tests are usually norm-referenced. Norm-referencing provides an ordering or comparison of learners to other learners; the focus is not on what competencies each individual learner manifests.

The focus of *criterion-referencing* is on explicit learner competencies and gives us information regarding a learner's present behavior as compared to a standard. Almost everyone has been exposed to criterion-referenced measurement, possibly without being aware of it. A good example is the driver's license examination required by most states. It makes no difference how a person compares to others taking the test either at a particular time or in the norm group as a whole. The person must meet a predetermined standard—a criterion number of correct items on the written portion and the exhibition of the correct behaviors, or lack of incorrect behaviors, on a driving portion of the test—before a license is granted.

The choice of referencing by educators and trainers in meeting their measurement goals should be constantly evaluated. The question to be raised before any measure is made is: *Is our task really to "sort out" learners (i. e., is variability our goal), or is our goal to determine when everyone has attained a specific competency?* As can be readily seen, in industrial training and public education programs it is better to assess what competencies the learner possesses at the end of instruction than to know how he compares to other learners. However, norm-referencing still has many uses, which will be described in the following section.

The Role of Measurement

Formative

The *time* at which measurement occurs influences the *role* of measurement, which includes the following: formative, summative, and ultimate. Measurement is *formative* when it is employed to improve performance and, when used prior to or during a lesson, can indicate deficiencies a learner may possess or express, illuminating these inadequacies to both the instructor and learner and, when structured appropriately, aiding in the selection of alternatives that will eliminate them. Used at the end of a unit or sequence of instruction, formative measurement not only shows the learner his strengths and weaknesses but may also alert the instructor to possible deficiencies in the instructional sequence. When a learner does very well in the area measured by a test, this will give him confidence that his present mode of learning and approach to study is adequate. This sort of reinforcement will help decrease the learner's anxiety toward learning. For this reason, formative tests are often given at short intervals during instruction to indicate progress or competency attainment. In this role, formative measurement would be of a criterion-referenced type and would indicate the learner's progress with regard to predetermined standards. It would be of relatively little educational and training value to compare learners on these measures in a norm-referenced mode.

Summative

The second use or role of measurement in instruction is termed *summative measurement* and, as the term implies, is an end-of-instruction or terminal appraisal. Attitudinal, cognitive, psychomotor, or perceptual competencies could be assessed to determine the extent to which the learner had achieved the overall predetermined course or program objectives. Attitudes, for instance, might be tested to determine whether a learner possesses the desired attitude or to find out if a change in attitude has occurred as a result of instruction. The same is true of the other competency classifications.

Summative measurement may be criterion-referenced (comparing the individual to a proficiency continuum) or norm-referenced (determining the learner's rank or relative location among a group of individuals). For example, a group of ten college graduates in a company may be tested to aid in selecting one who will receive managerial training. Because *selection* is involved, norm-referencing would be appropriate.

Ultimate

Ultimate measurement is a third role which achievement measures may assume and in occupational and career education is used to evaluate what the learner was taught with actual performance on the job. It is made following the completion of instruction and after an individual has begun employment (week, month, year, or more), and is the most valuable type of measurement for assessing the overall success of the learner and the educational or training program. Used as an evaluative technique, a criterion-referenced type would provide the most useful information, although circumstances could dictate the use of norm-referencing. Ultimate measurement is probably the most difficult of the three types to operationalize and employ for assessment purposes. The employer survey described in Chapter 5 and the follow-up study described in Chapter 4 are two means by which educational personnel can obtain ultimate measures. Informal contacts with employers can also be used. Subsequently, this information can be utilized to improve various facets of the educational or training program.

CONSTRUCTING MEASURES OF COGNITIVE ACHIEVEMENT

The Taxonomy of Educational Objectives provides an excellent framework for classifying behaviors (competencies), instructional objectives, and measures of cognitive skills. Essentially, the cognitive domain may be broken into two sections: knowledge or intellectual abilities and skills. Within these two broad classifications exists a more detailed breakdown of behaviors. These subordinate categories are hierarchical in terms of complexity of behavior. For example, intellectual abilities and skills are broken down to five subcategories. Ranging from least to most complex, they include comprehension, application, analysis, synthesis, and evaluation. The taxonomy depicts the major sections of the cognitive domain with corresponding examples of general and specific objectives. For further instruction in the development of behavioral objectives, the reader is referred to Mager and Beach (1967) or Borgen and Davis (1974).

Items for eliciting and measuring cognitive achievement fall into two categories: *recognition items*, which include the multiple choice item, true-false item, and matching item, and *constructed response items*, including the completion item, short answer item, definition item, and essay item.

There are two major considerations in selecting the type of item to use in measuring a specific occupational skill or knowledge. The first should be the type or complexity of behavior to be measured, as determined through the use of the taxonomy (e. g., knowledge, comprehension, and so on). The second consideration should be the quality of the item which can be constructed to most directly measure the behavior.

Recognition Items

The *multiple choice item* has been the most popular of all those used within occupational education and organizational training programs. Each consists of a stimulus statement, usually referred to as a stem, and a list of possible responses or alternatives. The stem may be an incomplete sentence or a direct question followed by a listing of alternative answers. Only one alternative should be correct; the remaining alternatives should be incorrect and are often referred to as "distractors" or "foils."

Examples of an incomplete-statement item and question-statement item are shown below.

EXAMPLE ITEM 1

Teflon pans should be used with:
    a. nylon utensils.
    b. plastic utensils.
    c. steel utensils.
    d. aluminum utensils.

EXAMPLE ITEM 2

Which one of the following types of utensils should be used with teflon pans?
    a. Nylon
    b. Plastic
    c. Steel
    d. Aluminum

Both items pose the same problem. However, the question-statement form is probably the easiest to construct since the writer must simply write a question. Each example has four alternative answers, but five or six are often desirable since the chances of guessing the correct one are decreased. There is no set rule, however, for the number of alternatives—even within a specific test. One technique of obtaining effective distractors for multiple choice items is to administer the item stems to learners as constructed response items, then using the incorrect responses as the distractors for later tests.

Basically, construction of multiple choice items requires adherence to the rules of punctuation and grammar, a little work, and some common sense. The following types of guidelines have been emphasized repeatedly by testing specialists.

1. State the stem of the item in simple and correct language.
2. Make all alternatives grammatically consistent with the stem.
3. Make alternatives short and unambiguous.
4. Word the stem positively, if at all possible.
5. Underscore negative wording when the stem is stated negatively.
6. Avoid systematic construction that will enable learners to select the correct answer on the basis of grammatical clues, stereotyped language, length, or position in a series.
7. Make distracters plausible but include only one clearly correct answer.

The form of multiple choice items can be varied according to the type or complexity of behavior to be measured. Below are examples which correspond to the various levels of complexity within the cognitive domain. Items have been written to correspond to one objective within each of four levels shown in Table 3—1.

A second type of recognition item which can be applied to the measurement of cognition is the *true-false item*. A great difficulty in constructing such items lies in the fact that statements must be unequivocally true or clearly false. Many times it is necessary to incorporate conditioners such as *in general, always,* or *never.* These words or phrases can cue the learner to the correctness of the statement. However, respondents may react to these key phrases rather than the intended content. Thus, the desired behavior is not being assessed. Rather simple modifications of true-false items can be made to overcome some of their apparent shortcomings. For example, consider Example Item 3.

EXAMPLE ITEM 3

T   F   Generally, occupational education is not appropriate for college-bound students.

TABLE 3–1   *Example Objectives and Corresponding Test Items for Four Levels of the Cognitive Domain*

TAXONOMY CATEGORY	OBJECTIVE	TEST ITEM
1. KNOWLEDGE	Without the use of references, define technical terms commonly used in nursing by matching the term with the correct definition.	Which one of the following best defines the term _____? a. _____ b. _____ c. _____ d. _____
2. COMPREHENSION	Distinguish between subassembly, assembly, isometric and working drawings by pointing to the correct name when shown examples of each.	The following drawing is an example of a/an a. Assembly b. Subassembly c. Working d. Isometric
3. APPLICATION	Presented with the cost price and sale price of an article, determine both the markup and margin of the article by applying costing principles.	The given automotive article costs $1.00 and sold for $1.50. What is the markup and margin of the article at selling price? a. Markup is 50% margin is 33% b. Markup is 33% margin is 50% c. Markup is 200% margin is 50% d. Markup is 50% margin is 200%
4. ANALYSIS	Presented with information used in comparing two given jobs, distinguish between that information related to the duties of the job and data relevant to the amount and kind of benefits.	Present two different job descriptions and ask the following: Which one of the following statements best compares the benefits of a job "A" versus those of job "B"? a. Job A provides more medical benefits than job B. b. Job B provides more medical benefits than job A. c. Both job A and job B yield identical or similar benefits.

It is a good guess that this T-F item would be true. Not only will the respondent recognize that any statement is more likely to be "generally true" than "true," but he will know instinctively that the test maker would be less likely to qualify a false statement. In addition to responding *true* or *false,* the respondent might be instructed to state why the item is false or to rewrite the item to make it true. For example, the previous item could be accompanied by the following directions: *Read the following items and circle the correct answer, either true or false. If they are not true, explain in the space below why each item is not true, or correct the item.* As with the multiple choice item, construction of an effective true-false item should take into account rules of clarity, punctuation, and grammar. With the true-false item, it is particularly important to avoid the use of negative wording (or double negatives), and the test maker should take careful thought to balancing true and false answers, and should attempt to randomly assign items to the test so that a pattern is not established.

A third type of recognition item is the *matching item,* a modification of multiple choice, and includes multiple stems as well as multiple alternatives:

EXAMPLE ITEM 4

Directions: Column A contains a list of advantages of varied shopping outlets. Choose from column B the outlet which best fits each advantage in column A and insert the identifying letter in the space provided. Responses in column B may be used more than once.

Column A		Column B
___ 1) "One stop" shopping	a)	Mail order
___ 2) Offers 24-hour service	b)	Door-to-door
___ 3) Armchair shopping	c)	Vending machine
___ 4) All prices may be lower	d)	Department store
___ 5) Product demonstrated at home	e)	Specialty
___ 6) Open counter display	f)	Used clothing

___ 7) Sold at low price often   g) Discount

___ 8) Many services provided   h) Variety

___ 9) A greater variety in specific area

___10) Stores are usually open for night shopping

It can be seen that the matching item can be economical in terms of paper space and in terms of responding time. It is very important that all alternatives in the right column match with one or another of the premises presented in the left column. Standard procedure for constructing matching items is to put brief responses on the right. Lists of items should not be excessively long. If directions clearly indicate that this is the case, responses may be included which are correct for more than one premise.

Constructed Response Items

Constructed response items, as the name implies, require the learner to respond by forming his own answer. They can be classified as completion, short answer, and essay. The *completion* item is simply the presentation of an incomplete statement, usually lacking one or two key words. Example Item 5 is a completion item.

EXAMPLE ITEM 5

The mixing of air and gasoline in various ratios for an internal combustion engine is a function of the _____.

It is important to make the statement as unambiguous as possible. One problem with the completion item occurs in the scoring of answers. For example, feasible answers to Example Item 5 might be *carburetor* or *fuel injector*. Both may be correct since a *fuel injector* is a special type of carburetor. Therefore, it may be difficult to judge all responses equally.

A second type of constructed response item is the *short answer item* and it can assume several forms. The first simply asks a question and expects a one- or two-word response or a listing, as in Example Items 6 and 7:

EXAMPLE ITEM 6

What is the term for converting messages into code? _____

EXAMPLE ITEM 7

List the four necessary steps in cleaning an IBM Executive typewriter.

1)_____

2)_____

3)_____

4)_____

A second form of short answer involves the presentation of a written stimulus, with the response being a word or short phrase. This form is presented in Example Item 8.

Examples of other special stimulus items include the presentation of several odors of medical solutions such as rubbing alcohol, ether, or formaldehyde, with instructions for the learner to write the names of the substances in the order of presentation. Similarly, malfunctions of an automobile engine could be presented via a tape recording to assess the learner's ability to diagnose problems by auditory stimuli.

A third type of short answer item is the *definition item*. As the name implies, this item incorporates a request for the respondent to write the definition of a word or series of words.

The final type of constructed response item, and probably the

---

EXAMPLE ITEM 8

Identify the following tools:

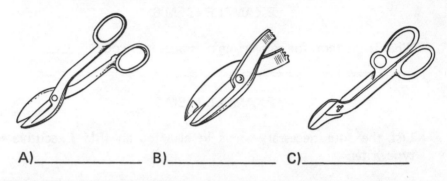

A)_____   B)_____   C)_____

---

most difficult to score, is the *essay item*. Objective tests can be scored by clerical help and, in many cases, by machine. Essay items are time consuming when compared to objective items and require that an instructor or similarly qualified individual read and score each test. Even when the essay item is scored and graded by one individual, it is difficult to ensure consistent grading. However, the essay item has the advantage of allowing the learner to express his responses in his own words, allowing him to organize and synthesize his own knowledge. Yet this is not an advantage for some types of learners. It has been demonstrated that an individual naive to a particular subject, yet proficient in English and rhetoric, can score very high on many kinds of essay tests. This means that knowledge-able learners who lack writing skill may be faultily judged in terms of their actual achievement.

A definite advantage of the essay item is its utility in assessing the higher levels of behavior within the cognitive taxonomy. These levels include application, analysis, synthesis, and evaluation. Below is an example of an essay item:

EXAMPLE ITEM 9

Explain three (3) nonmonetary benefits that workers often receive for performing their jobs.

Obviously, essay items may need to be limited in scope, as in the above item that asks the respondent to explain only three benefits. The work *nonmonetary* has limited it even further. This item could be considered a restricted essay item. An unrestricted or extended item might simply ask the learner to explain all or any benefits of performance on a job, or within a career structure.

CONSTRUCTING MEASURES OF PSYCHOMOTOR AND PERCEPTUAL PERFORMANCE

This section is intended primarily for the occupational or training evaluator who is involved in formulating and administering test instruments for the assessment of either psychomotor or perceptual competencies. However, the content should prove useful to anyone concerned with the measurement of performances which closely approximate some type of job situation a post-learning career or occupational setting in which the performances are to be applied. Unlike the measurement of either cognitive or attitudinal competencies, the measurement of performance requires that a given job situation be simulated both in terms of the testing conditions (stimuli to which the examinee must respond) and operations performed (responses elicited from the examinee by the testing conditions). A performance measure should be comparatively *realistic* in characterizing or approximating actual occupational or training stimuli and desired job responses.

Objective-setting

Basically, objective-setting involves the identification and selection of either psychomotor or perceptual occupational competencies to provide the basis for the design of the performance measure. The following points should be considered in setting the objectives:

1. Objective Domain and Level—the category and relative difficulty of the objective.
2. Representation—the degree to which selected objectives are relevant to the criterion or job activity.

Dimensions

	Domain and Level	Representativeness	Means
Definition	The performance taxonomy domain(s) and its (their) appropriate level for the criterion or job situation.	The degree to which selected occupational objectives are relevant and correspond to the actual criterion or job situation.	Product—a measure used when the examinee's performance results in product or record of what was done and how well. Process—examinee's performance recorded as the behavior actually occurs. A checklist or rating scale is used for this purpose.
Examples	Psychomotor Level 2 Perceptual Level 3 Psychomotor/Perceptual levels	Criterion situation objective Criterion situation objective	Product—typed letters, bid specifications, combination salad, etc. Process—timing an engine, closing a sale in role-playing situation.

FIGURE 3–1   *Objective-setting Dimensions for Performance Measures*

3. Operations Performed—the means, either product or process, by which objective performance is to be measured.

Examples of these dimensions belonging to the objective-setting process for designing performance measures are shown in Figure 3–1.

Types of Performance Measures

The design of performance measures should reflect performance circumstances—and these circumstances are quite variable. As was suggested in Figure 3–1, *process performances* are best assessed through the employment of either checklists or rating scales. In contrast, *product performances* lend themselves more readily to a measurement strategy that relies on *critical incidents* as measurement criteria. Bell, et al. (1963) recently compared three approaches to measurement of job competencies in sixteen occupations. Behavior-oriented approaches proved to be more useful than trait-oriented indices. In order of increasing relevance to actual occupational and organizational performance, the types of performance measures were: work samples, ratings, and critical incidents.

Work Samples

The work sample performance measure is the most prevalent type of assessment instrument for evaluating psychomotor and perceptual performance in occupational education and human resource development. Essentially, the work sample requires the examinee to perform a career-related task, and his performance is then assessed through either process or product measurement. This type of instrument:

> ... is based on tasks, job segments, evolutions, or any portion of the total work load that makes up a job and which might be judged to be important. Tests based on these samples may either be conducted in the context of the job using regular ... equipment and space, or they may be based on simulators or test situations specially constructed to duplicate the task (Wilson, 1962, p. 361).

As previously mentioned, the work sample measure may be employed to assess either the process or product of performance. In any event, the measure must closely represent an actual job situation that the examinee will be expected to encounter at the conclusion of his educational or training experience.

The formulation of a work sample measure requires a thorough analysis of the specific occupation. In most instances, this information can be obtained during several interview sessions with job experts or observation episodes with job incumbents. Since information of a specific type is to be collected, these sessions should be systematized and broken down into five stages. The five suggested stages are listed and described below.

Stage 1. Experts are requested to list all tasks that compose the given job or occupation and, for each task, to indicate the frequency of performance and evaluate its importance relative to the job.

Stage 2. Experts are requested to provide another task listing based upon previous work experiences or incidents of job applicants.

Stage 3. To delineate the critical dimensions of work performance for the given occupation, the group of experts should first list the major facets of work between effective and ineffective behavior on the job. Second, each expert should independently write behavioral incidents to illustrate performance on each dimension. The experts should then pool their information, discuss differences, and determine the critical dimensions of work performance—for example, use of tools, and work accuracy.

Stage 4. Experts are requested to assemble tasks as possible work sample measures. It is important that the tasks selected be representative of the tasks performed by the incumbent under actual job circumstances and appropriate to the job applications. Further, each task must provide ample opportunity for the examinee to demonstrate performances relevant to the critical dimensions. Also, the performances elicited by the work sample measure must be easily observed and recorded by the administrator. The tasks should then be selected based upon the above criteria.

Stage 5. Experts break the selected tasks into logical steps required to master them. In order to ascertain the various approaches a job applicant might pursue, each step is analyzed in detail. Next, the recordable performances corresponding to the approaches are specified and *weights* assigned to them on the basis of their viability as evaluated by job experts. This results in a list of possible performances associated with each step in task behavior, with all performances assigned a weight for scoring purposes. Thus, in most instances, the recording form is in a checklist format which requires that the test administrator *identify* rather than evaluate the job applicant's behavior. Figure 3–2 illustrates an example item and corresponding weights.

Installing and Aligning a part	
1. Measures radial misalignment with	Weight
_____ Dial indicator	10
_____ Straight edge	3
_____ Feel	1
_____ Visual or other	0

FIGURE 3–2   *Example Work Sample Item with Corresponding Weights*

OBSERVER'S RATING FORM FOR A PERFORMANCE TEST

THE START CIRCUIT OF A 5-KW GENERATOR SET   (PART III)

Student_____Time Started_____Time Completed_____

Possible Score_120_   Critical Score__84_Student Score_____

	Score if Task Properly Accomplished	Student Score
1. ATTEMPT TO START ENGINE ELECTRICALLY		
a. Place fuel valve in tank position	1	
b. Place oil pan baffle rod in proper position	1	
c. Place air cleaner intake shutter in proper position	1	
d. Place governor control in start position	2	
e. Place remote/local switch in local position	1	
f. Place emergency run/stop switch in normal position	1	
g. Hold start switch in start position (no more than 15 second intervals)	3	
TOTALS	10	

FIGURE 3–3   *Observer Rating Form for a Performance Test (reproduced from Boyd and Shimberg, 1971).*

Another example of a work sample measure is exemplified in Figure 3–3. In addition, the following documents are needed to satisfactorily formalize the work sample measure (Boyd and Shimberg, 1971).

1. *Instructions to the test administrator or observer.* These outline the procedures to be adhered to: needed equipment, tools, or materials, and safety precautions. Setup procedures should also be included.
2. *Instructions to the examinees.* These written or oral directions advise the examinee of the test purpose, time limitations for completion,

INSTRUCTIONS

1. The purpose of the test is to provide you with an opportunity to demonstrate your ability in troubleshooting the start
circuit of the 5 KW generator. Using the prescribed procedure
you have been taught, you are to find any incomplete circuitry.

2. You will be allowed 30 minutes in which to complete the
test. A satisfactory grade cannot be achieved unless the correct
procedure is followed.

3. During a field exercise you are required to furnish power
for lighting the area. The output power is 120 volts, single phase,
60 cycle alternating current. You have already performed the
required Preventive Maintenance Services and you found no
deficiencies.

4. The following equipment will be provided:

   5 KW generator
   Load bank
   Load cables
   Multimeter
   Hydrometer
   Tool kit
   Schematic
   Grease pencil

5. Requirements:

   a. Attempt to start engine electrically (10 points)
   b. Check battery voltage with multimeter and specific
       gravity with hydrometer and orally report to
       instructor (16 points)
   c. Disconnect battery (5 points)
   d. Trace the engine start circuit on the schematic
       diagram using a grease pencil, starting at (-) side
       of battery (22 points)
   e. Make a complete continuity check of the first part of
       the start circuit to make sure that K4 coil can become
       energized, with a multimeter (47 points)
   f. Point out the defect to the instructor on both the
       equipment and schematic (20 points)

6. On completion of troubleshooting the circuit, move to the
next station.

FIGURE 3–4   *Example Instructions to Students for a Performance Test
(reproduced from Boyd and Shimberg, 1971).*

RATING SHEET	DATE: _____						
GENERAL MANICURING	60 POINTS 45 PASSING						
IDENT. NUMBERS							
1. TABLE SETUP							
a. Required labelled supplies _____							
b. Implements in wet sterilizer_____							
c. Disposal unit available _____							
d. Polish removed _____							
2. FILING AND SHAPING							
a. File held at proper angle _____							
b. Moved from corner to center_____							
c. Shaped nails improved (as model's hands permit)____							
d. Ragged scarf beveled_____							
3. USE OF ORANGEWOOD STICK AND PUSHER							
a. Cotton tipped orangewood stick used_____							
b. Flat side of pusher follows curve of cuticle __							
c. Only spade end used, with light pressure ____							
d. Nail kept moist with solvent or bath ____							
e. Nail plate not scratched _____							
f. Dead cuticle removed from nail plate ____							
4. USE OF NIPPERS							
a. Adjusted and held so not pointed into flesh __							
b. Cuticle improved (as hands permit)_____							
c. Skin unbroken after nipping _____							
5. APPLICATION OF LIQUID POLISH							
a. Applicable consistency_____							
b. Smoothly applied _____							
c. None left on skin_____							
6. MAINTENANCE OF SANITATION							
a. Table kept orderly_____							
b. Instruments in sterilizer when not in use____							
c. Disposal unit used _____							
	Total Possible Score	60	60	60	60	60	60
	Minus Penalty Points						
	Applicant's Score						
Examiner's Signature _____							

FIGURE 3-5 *Example of a Work Sample Performance Measure (reproduced from Boyd and Shimberg, 1971).*

equipment or tools provided, criterion requirements underlying the performance task, and safety precautions to be exercised.

3. *Scoring, checklist, or rating form.* For each performance task some standardized method of scoring must be developed to systematically record the examinee's responses. This will help to ensure both reliability and validity as to the measurement of either performance processes or products.

To illustrate the above supplementary documentation, Figure 3–4 provides an example of instructions to learners for a performance *process* test.

A final example of a work sample performance measure appears in Figure 3–5.

Ratings

Another systematic approach to the criterion problem of adequately measuring either performance processes or products is the use of rating scales for the evaluation of occupational or training performances. Chapter 7 specifically discusses the various types of rating scales and their structure and format. However, the formulation of either graphic or Likert-type rating scales should proceed through the following stages:

Stage 1. A list of descriptive statements, specifically applicable to the execution of the given job, must be collected. These statements can be obtained through observation or interview of the job incumbent. Supervisory or managerial personnel should also be requested to provide this information, and they should base their responses on the actual observation of personnel executing these tasks on the job.

Stage 2. Descriptive statements must then be submitted to either supervisory or managerial personnel in industrial or career-based organizations to be rated on a scale from 1 to 7 (least important to most important).

Stage 3. For the above, mean importance rating and standard deviations are calculated for each of the statements. Only those statements with means above 3.75 and standard deviations below 1.75 should be used as criterion variables.

Stage 4. For Likert-type rating scales, the final evaluation form

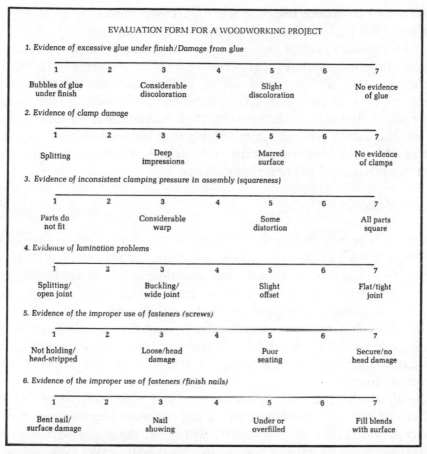

FIGURE 3–6   *Example Graphic Performance Rating Scale for Woodworking* (*reproduced from* Handbook on Formative and Summative Evaluation of Student Learning *with the permission of Thomas S. Baldwin, Benjamin S. Bloom and McGraw-Hill, Inc., 1221 Avenue of the Americas, New York, New York.)*

consists of n statements meeting the statistical criteria suggested in Stage 3 and appears something like this:

Statement

1	2	3	4	5
rarely	seldom	frequently	often	always

In addition, the order of the rating scale values should be randomly alternated to reduce response set. Figure 3–6 illustrates an example of a graphic performance rating scale for woodworking.

In summary, performance rating scales must be used to evaluate work functions actually performed or to be performed. This will provide more accurate and useful information than a rating of general work characteristics. To determine relative validity, ratings of the job incumbents can be made by their immediate supervisors using two alternative sets of scales (odd-even numbered statements, for example) and checked against independent assessments made by work associates of the same incumbents.

Critical Incidents

A third type of job-oriented performance criterion measure employs what is known as the critical incident approach. This method (Flanagan, 1954) defines a specific job assignment which an employee executes either very effectively or very ineffectively. In organizational situations, the supervisor of the examinee is questioned, usually through structured interview, regarding the job elements considered essential to successful performance. After these elements are listed and defined, the supervisor is asked to rate the examinee on each performance element.

Obviously, the process is laborious and time consuming. It has the disadvantage, moreover, of rating individual examinees in an occupation against varying criteria. However, the major advantage is that the resulting ratings correspond to specific tasks assignable to examinees. Since prospective employees with similar job titles often perform different work tasks, this is an important advantage. Flanagan and Burns (1955) suggest that the following developmental stages be completed in utilizing critical incidents as performance measurement criteria.

Stage 1. Develop interview forms to be used by the test administrator.

Stage 2. Collect critical incidents from job supervisors which describe specific deeds they have seen job incumbents perform—deeds that represent either outstanding or marginal contributions to organizational effectiveness or morale.

PERFORMANCE RECORD

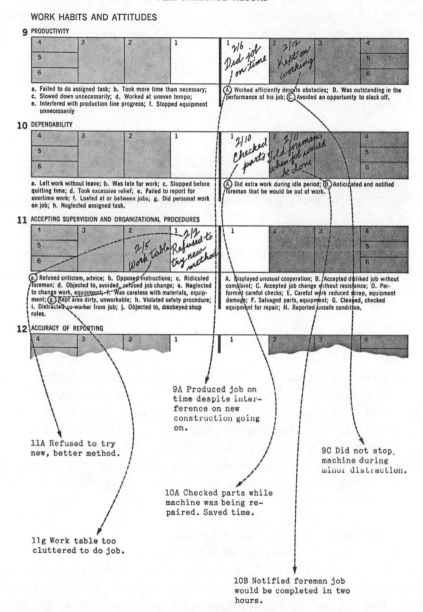

FIGURE 3–7 *Example Format for a Performance Record Sheet (reproduced from* Harvard Business Review *with the permission of John Flanagan and* Harvard Business Review, *Boston, Massachusetts).*

Stage 3. Analyze and classify incidents according to categories of critical job performances and requirements. These should be reduced to between twelve and twenty critical job performance areas. Here are three examples:

> Checking and inspecting
> Coordination
> Recalling

Stage 4. Several critical behaviors should be listed within each major job performance area. One group should indicate ineffective incidents while the other should indicate outstanding performances.

Stage 5. Formalize a *performance record sheet* for recording examinee performance within specific job performance areas. Figure 3–7 presents an example format. Note that the left side is for recording ineffective performance incidents while the right side is for recording outstanding behaviors. On this sheet, the examiner can record each incident, *effective* or *ineffective,* for the examinee involved.

Designing the Performance Measure

Plans for a performance test should include an outline of the competencies to be evaluated and should include a detailed description of the tools and equipment, materials, and directions for both the examinee and test administrator. Essentially, this plan must indicate what perceptual or psychomotor competencies the examinee is expected to exhibit and under what testing conditions he is expected to exhibit them. Once a specific competency is identified, the procedure and equipment necessary to attain that competency should also be specified. Figure 3–8 illustrates the process through which the performance test plan can be generated.

Once relevant testing conditions have been identified, the next step is to formulate a tentative test document which will ensure that the instrument will be administered in a systematic and objective way. Instructions to the administrator and examinees, and rating and scoring procedures should also be developed. Once complete, the performance test measure should be pilot tested to ascertain the validity of its appraisal of the job incumbent's proficiency in the task

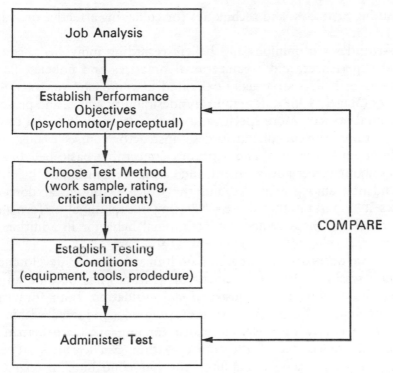

FIGURE 3–8   *Sequence of Steps in Designing a Work Sample, Rating, or Critical Incident Performance Measure*

or tasks assigned. All tasks, however, must be completed to ensure that accurate observations can be made on all performances and to make certain that the procedures and directions are clear and unambiguous.

CONSTRUCTING MEASURES OF ATTITUDE

Each of the four classes of competencies—cognitive, affective, psychomotor, and perceptual—requires unique measurement procedures. This section introduces the final domain—attitudinal assessment. Included are relevant attitudinal concepts, why attitude measurement is important, some of the problems and issues of measuring attitudes, and techniques for collecting affective or attitudinal data.

Attitudes are opinions and beliefs regarding individuals, educational experiences, and organizational practices and policies. These opinions or beliefs are usually exhibited in approach/avoidance tendencies (Mager, 1968), desirability/undesirability scales, and pro/con or neutral stances. More specifically, they may include initial career expectations, on-the-job attitudes, instructor/course evaluations, world-of-work opinions, and attitudes concerning basic beliefs and values about career advancement. Increasing recognition of the interdependency among attitudes and the other taxonomical domains makes it important that those evaluating occupational performance attend to the measurement of attitudinal behavior in addition to cognitive, psychomotor, and perceptual abilities.

Within occupational programs or human resource development training sessions, the measurement of attitudes has become an increasingly critical facet of instructional evaluation, both formative and summative. Formative attitude appraisal conducted within or prior to a course can help the instructor improve learner attitude during the remainder of the course. Although a learner's attitude toward a given occupational program can contribute to cognitive achievement, the enhancement of a more positive attitude toward the experience is a desirable outcome in itself. An example of the importance of attitude measurement is in the instruction of sales representative complaint handling, where the instructor desires to facilitate favorable attitudes on the part of the sales trainee toward handling customer complaints in an earnest and purposeful manner. Even a sales trainee who demonstrates a relatively low level of proficiency in completing a complaint form may have developed a strong, positive attitude toward handling and coping with customer complaints. Often, however, this attitude goes unnoticed.

Fundamentally, attitude measurement is the assessment of positive and negative opinions associated with some occupational event, statement, circumstance, or value (Thurstone, 1946). Results should represent directions—either positive or negative, favorable or unfavorable, approach or avoidance—of an individual's feeling toward an occupational task, including the extensiveness or degree of that attitude. If a learner refers to his instructor as *exceptionally boring*, however, what is observed is a statement made by the learner with respect to another person; the statement is not the attitude. Certainly, we may conclude that the learner has an unfavorable attitude toward his instructor, but we have not witnessed the feeling or the negative feeling.

In measuring attitudes, the first step is to ascertain the behavior to be observed which is relevant to the occupational topic or variable in which one is interested. It is possible, in some cases, to identify occupational situations in which immediate behavior would provide an indication of the underlying attitudes. Sensitivity or T-group training is certainly an issue which evokes emotional reaction in many training personnel. What is said about sensitivity training can be recorded and will, in this context, represent spontaneous behavior.

The use of group membership as an index of attitude toward occupational events, concepts, and objects is another approach to attitudinal assessment. Groups are sometimes formed on the basis of specific factors—unionization, promotion of business safety laws, or industrial pollution. Unfortunately, group membership as an indicator of expressed attitudes affords only a gross classification of individuals into identifiable groups.

Survey and Questionnaire Techniques

The majority of occupational evaluation strategies must depend on some form of verbal response. One technique often used is that of the survey or interview; individuals are asked questions concerning whether they like or dislike, are for or against, or approve or disapprove a certain issue, event, and so on. Sometimes the evaluator will want to measure the attitude of a group such as a class, school, or district. Here, care must be taken in the choice of a sample. Numerous strategies have been formulated for identifying a stratified sample of the population that will be truly representative of the target group. Scott and Wertheimer (1966) provide an excellent discussion of sampling methods. Also, Chapter 4 of this text includes a brief discussion of sampling.

Survey questions may be either closed or open-ended. A closed question provides the individual with a set of response categories and requires that he indicate the alternative most closely paralleling his own attitudes, as in Example Item 9. The open-ended item requires that the respondent respond in his own words while the interviewer writes the answer word for word. Item 10 is open-ended.

EXAMPLE ITEM 9

SA   A   D   SD   I would like to begin a career in the construction industry.

EXAMPLE ITEM 10

How do you feel about construction work as a career?

Figure 3–9 illustrates the advantages and disadvantages of both types of survey questions. It is possible, of course, to combine the two types of questions, incorporating the strengths of each. Open-ended questions may be employed in a small pilot study to determine plausible response patterns. Closed questions may then be developed for use in the main attitudinal investigation.

Survey questioning often creates reluctance on the part of the respondent to express his attitude honestly and without anxiety. Complete honesty or freedom of attitude concerning an employee's opinion about his employer cannot be expected if the employer asks the questions or is present as they are asked. Likewise, an instructor who attempts to measure how learners feel about numerous facets of his own instruction cannot expect complete objectivity and frankness if the learners think that their expressed attitudes will have an effect on the grade they receive.

Respondents can be encouraged to express their attitudes more candidly through the employment of a written questionnaire. Essentially the same questions can be asked as with an interview, although the respondent retains his anonymity. Moreover, written questionnaires are less time consuming and costly than interviews and can be administered to large groups of individuals. Because of the standardized format, there is greater reliability from one measurement

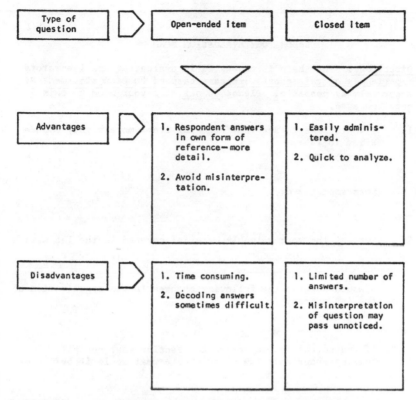

FIGURE 3–9   *Advantages and Disadvantages of Survey Questions*

setting to another. However, when a questionnaire is used, there is little opportunity to identify an ambiguous response. Thus, an interview might yield more attitudinal information and greater opinion-based data than the structured questionnaire.

Questionnaire items should be organized and presented in a standardized format, thus limiting the opportunity for the biases of the evaluator to affect responses. A learner attitude questionnaire as shown in Figure 3–10 allows for open-ended responses. In designing a questionnaire, a balanced format should be maintained, i. e., an individual with an overall favorable feeling about his training laboratory experience would presumably find sufficient space on the questionnaire to record his responses as would the respondent with the contrary view.

```
                        LABORATORY EVALUATION FORM

Directions:  Your help is requested in evaluating the laboratory
experiences of this course.  Please respond to each statement as
accurately as possible.  Please do not sign your name to this
questionnaire.

1.    I would like to see the following items more highly empha-
      sized in lab:



      Less emphasized:



2.    For me, the most valuable material covered in the lab was:



3.    I would suggest the following changes in the organization of
      the lab course:



4.    If you select one adjective to describe your overall
      feeling about your lab experience - what would it be?



                              - etc. -
```

FIGURE 3–10   *Example Learner Attitude Questionnaire*

Scaling Techniques for Attitude Assessment

When large groups of individuals are involved in attitudinal assessment, attitude scales may be used to provide a more quantifiable and systematic approach to measuring a respondent's feelings. An individual's attitude may be represented by a single score which can be measured in reference to a series of occupational items, each of which is relevant to a single issue, career item, or job concept. Both the intensity (*strongly* agree, *somewhat* agree) and the direction (good, bad) can be evaluated. The purpose of an attitude scale is to discriminate among varying intensities of attitudes.

Like achievement tests in the cognitive domain, attitude scales should be administered under controlled, standardized conditions. Items should be carefully selected and edited in accordance with the classifications of the affective taxonomy.

Individuals responding to an attitude scale answer by defining their feelings about statements underlying the occupational object or career concept. The beliefs, feelings, and opinions of an individual provide the standards by which a judgment is made regarding the *correct* response.

Statements incorporated within attitude scales should be unambiguous and succinct, encompassing only one thought and stated in simple sentence structure. Items must be included that represent the entire spectrum of feelings from strongly positive through neutral, to strongly negative toward the concept or object being assessed. Edwards (1957) suggests editorial criteria for writing statements. Shaw and Wright (1967) have assembled an extensive collection of attitude scales designed to measure and reflect a variety of concepts and objectives. In addition, they provide scoring procedures and other technical information in some detail on construction procedures. The reader is directed to these sources for detailed examples and further instruction. Three basic types of attitude scales will be discussed here: Likert, Thurstone, and Q-sort.

Likert-type Items or Scales

A Likert scale contains a group of items, usually directional statements or questions with a corresponding scale. In most instances, the scale for this type of item incorporates five major divisions or rating points. Likert-type items can possess differing descriptors for the ratings. Example Items 11 and 12 range from *excellent* to *poor* while Items 13 and 14 each have more detailed descriptors.

The stages in constructing a Likert-type scale are as follows:

Stage 1. Collect or write a large number of items, which are clearly favorable or unfavorable in tone, referring to the concept being assessed.

Stage 2. Administer these items to a pilot group of individuals who are representative of the population with which the final scale will be utilized. Request that each individual indicate the degree to which he

---

EXAMPLE ITEMS 11 and 12

Please circle the appropriate response characteristic.

	Excellent					Poor
1) Organization and presentation of course materials	5	4	3	2	1	0
2) Clarity and thoroughness of explanations	5	4	3	2	1	0

EXAMPLE ITEMS 13 and 14

How would you describe the organization of your department?

5	4	3	2	1
well organized		moderately well		poorly planned

Does your supervisor encourage you to seek his help when necessary?

5	4	3	2	1
I feel welcome to seek help		I feel hesitant to seek help		I avoid seeking help

---

agrees with the item on (usually) a five-point scale ranging from *strongly disagree* to *disagree, uncertain, agree* and *strongly agree*.

Stage 3. Assign scores of 1–5 to the answer categories for each statement in such a way that 5 will reflect a strongly favorable attitude. The direction of the scoring weights assigned to the answer categories will depend on whether a given item is favorable or unfavorable. For example, if an item is thought to be favorable, scoring weights assigned to the five categories would be 5 for *strongly agree*, 4 for *agree*, 3 for *uncertain*, 2 for *disagree*, and 1 for *strongly disagree*. In contrast, if an item is regarded as being unfavorable, the direction of the weights is reversed.

Stage 4. For each respondent, complete a total score by adding the separate weights assigned to his answers over all statements.

Stage 5. Determine high and low scorers, that is, those individuals whose scores fall in the lower and upper 25 percent of all scores.

Stage 6. Contrast the answers of the high and low scores to each statement. Compute the difference between the means of the high and low scoring groups for each statement and keep those items for which this difference is largest.

Stage 7. Compile the final scale, deriving this from the original statements which differentiate between individuals manifesting a positive feeling and those holding an unfavorable attitude. A respondent's total score is computed to be the sum of the weights assigned to responses to individual statements. This score constitutes the degree of favorableness of attitude and ranks the summated answers in reference to others responding on the scale. Example items 11 to 14 indicate examples of Likert-type attitude measures. The Likert scale is based on the assumption that each item assesses a common concept or objective. A scale which challenges this assumption is discussed next.

Thurstone-type Scales

This attitude-measuring technique not only places the respondent somewhere along an agreement/disagreement continuum for a given occupational or career concept but at the same time scales the attitudinal statements themselves. Thus, each statement is attributed a *scale value* which represents the intensity of attitude for, say, a favorable response to the statement. Rather than being equal, the statements in the scale are assumed to be differentially sequenced or arranged and weighted. Although a Thurstone-type scale yields similar results to the Likert scale, it is somewhat more difficult to formulate. Example items 15 through 18 provide several examples of Thurstone items.

In constructing a Thurstone-type scale, the following stages are suggested:

Stage 1. Select and write a series of short, concise statements which reflect varying degrees of attitudes concerning a particular occupational object or concept.

Stage 2. Identify a group of individuals who are representative of the population for which the scale is intended. Have each individual

---

EXAMPLE ITEMS 15 THROUGH 18

My instructor presents his subject matter better than any
other instructor.   (8.2)*

If this course was an elective, I'd still enroll.   (6.3)

This company treats its employees better than any
other company.   (10.3)

Doing it all over again, I'd still work for this company.   (7.2)

---

categorize the statements into a series of eleven stacks, A–K, in accordance with the statement's relative degree of favorableness or unfavorableness.

Stage 3. For each statement, determine the distribution of assigned values—1 through 11—as judged by the various individuals and locate the midpoint or medium of the distribution's scaled value.

Stage 4. Do not use statements that indicate a significant discrepancy among individuals.

Stage 5. To check for internal consistency, present the remaining items to a group of representative respondents and ask them to mark those items with which they agree.

Stage 6. From the remaining statements, select those whose scale values are equally spaced along the attitude continuum.

In most instances, the chosen items are printed in random sequence without their scale values, and individuals are simply asked to indicate, through checking, those items with which they agree. Seemingly, respondents holding unfavorable attitudes will agree with statements that have unfavorable scale values and individuals with favorable attitudes will agree with statements that have favorable scale values. Scores for each respondent are computed as the mean of the scale values of statements with which there is agreement. Then an

---

*Indicates the scaled value for each statement. An individual responding to these statements checks the items with which there is agreement; the values of each of the checked items are totaled and divided by the number of answered items to give a mean scaled value held by the individual.

interpretation is made which indicates the respondent's position on a scale of favorable-unfavorable attitude toward the occupational or career topic under study.

Q-sort Technique

Another method developed by Stephenson (1953) to assess attitudes is the Q-sort technique. The Q-sort method has several attractive advantages, including the elimination of response or answer sets such as denial, hedging, or lack of consentience. Since its introduction, the technique has been used in the attitude analysis of many types of occupational and career problems. The objective of the Q-sort method is to *map* a respondent's opinion of a concept or object by asking that he sort a given number of attitudinal statements about the concept into piles representing a range of attitudes. Q-sorts may be employed to assess any changes in attitude that may result over time, perhaps as a function of instruction given between measures. For example, an evaluator may use the Q-sort to ascertain a respondent's attitudes toward managerial or supervisory training prior to and upon completion of the training seminar. Or an instructor might utilize Q-sorts with his students several times during the semester to determine their dynamic feelings and attitudes toward numerous occupational or career learning experiences.

The stages for developing and administering a Q-sort are as follows:

Stage 1. Decide on the standard on which the scoring will be based (e. g., the agreement or disagreement with a statement).

Stage 2. Assemble attitudinal statements (words, phrases, sentences) relevant to the attitude or task being assessed—usually thirty to fifty statements are used.

Stage 3. Determine the number of intervals or response categories into which statements will be sorted.

Stage 4. Decide on the number of statements to be placed in each category to ensure that the final distribution of responses conforms to a normal curve. For example, if twenty statements are to be sorted into seven intervals, the number of statements assignable to each category would be as follows:

	Strongly Disagree					Strongly Agree	
Category	1	2	3	4	5	6	7
Number of items	1	2	4	6	4	2	1

Stage 5. Present cards containing one statement each (or use form such as illustrated in Figure 3–11) to the respondent, with directions for sorting according to: 1) the criterion, 2) the number of piles, and 3) the number of cards to be sorted into each pile.

The individual statements are scored by the scores assigned to the successive categories according to the degree of favorableness. For example, if seven categories are used, the one containing *strongly disagree* would be assigned a score of 1 and so on to a score of 7 for the most agreeable. Measures of relationship may be used for Q-sort administration both before and after instruction to study the change in a respondent's sorting preferences.

PLANNING AND ORGANIZING THE ACHIEVEMENT MEASURE

An occupational performance instrument can assume any of several formats. However, the following list of steps has been found to be most effective in planning and organizing any of these tests.

1. Identify and categorize performance or competencies to be assessed.
2. State the competencies in terms of explicit, observable performances.
3. Formalize and outline the content area to be assessed.
4. Prepare a test matrix.
5. Employ the test matrix as a basis for organizing and constructing the performance measure.

From the foregoing list of steps it should be noted that the major factor in test planning and organization is to ascertain *what* is to be assessed. Further, content must be described in a precise way, so as to facilitate the construction of test items or assessment instruments that elicit the predefined career performances.

Directions: Forty-five statements concerning managerial preferences and self-evaluation are presented in this booklet. Read these statements, and then classify them according to the degree to which you agree or disagree with each one.

Each statement is to be assigned to one of seven categories indicated below. The categories, their definitions, and the number of statements to be assigned to each are as follows:

Category	Definition	Number of Statements to be designed
A	The statements with which you agree most fully.	3
B	The statements with which you agree most strongly.	5
etc.	etc.	
G	The statements with which you most strongly disagree.	3

Recording: Space for recording your sorting of the 95 statements is provided on the inside. As you assign a statement to a category, write the number of the statement in one of the boxes located above the designation for that category (A, B, C, etc.); then cross out the statement so that you do not make the mistake of classifying it again.

PLEASE FOLLOW THE PRESCRIBED FREQUENCIES (3-5-8-13-8-5-3) EXACTLY, AS THIS IS AN ESSENTIAL FEATURE OF THIS METHOD.

Statements

1. I would not like to work under the supervision of a woman.
2. It is easy for me to accept criticism of my work.
    :
    .
45. Even if I don't like someone, I don't show it.

Recording Section: Write statement numbers in boxes provided.

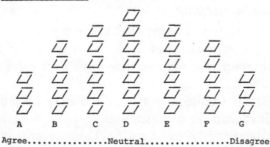

| A | B | C | D | E | F | G |

Agree................Neutral.................Disagree

FIGURE 3-11   *Example of Q-sort Deck Presented in Booklet Form*

Identifying the Desired Performances

The performance outcomes assessed by an achievement test must credibly represent the occupational competencies of the instructional lesson, unit, or course. Therefore, the first step is to identify them; the second is to state the competencies in a manner that will be effective for measurement purposes.

Four conceptual schemes useful for identifying and categorizing occupational objectives are the Taxonomies of Educational Objectives (Bloom, 1956; Krathwohl, 1964) and the taxonomies developed by Simpson (1967) and Moore (1971). As previously mentioned, these are comprehensive frameworks for identifying and classifying career objectives within each of four domains: cognitive, affective, psychomotor, and perceptual.

To be most effective for test and instrument planning, the performance outcomes must be stated in terms of *terminal behavior* that is explicit and observable. That is, the objectives should indicate learner behaviors to be demonstrated at the termination of the occupational learning or training experience. The following list, stated as general intents for a unit in business law, illustrates this type of performance outcome. Prior to test or instrument planning and organization, each would demand further refinement in terms of specific performance behaviors.

EXAMPLE ITEM 19

Broad Performance Outcomes—At the termination of this unit in contracts, the learner will:

1. Know the common terms used in contracts.
2. Know the various types of components of an enforceable contract and methods by which an offer may be terminated.
3. Understand exclusive rights which may be granted to specific individuals or businesses.
4. Understand the types of contract assignments unique to a given transaction.
5. Recognize the alternative ways which best describe the type of agreement for contract termination.

6. Be able to determine whether or not a minor is exercising his proper rights under the law involving a contract.

Explicating the Competencies

Upon satisfactorily listing and clearly stating the general occupational outcomes, the next step is to identify and name the specific behaviors which are to be accepted as evidence that the performances have been attained. For instance, what exact behaviors indicate that 1) a learner knows the common terms used in business contracts or 2) understands the exclusive rights granted to specific individuals? Specific behaviors for these two areas have been explicated and appear as follows:

EXAMPLE ITEMS 20 and 21

1) Knows the common terms used in business contracts.
   1.1 Identifies the correct definitions of terminology.
   1.2 Recognizes the meaning of terms when used in contract context.
   1.3 Differentiates among contract terms on the basis of meaning.
   1.4 Indicates the most relevant terms when describing business contracts.
2) Understands exclusive rights which may be granted to specific individuals or businesses.
   2.1 Identifies the types of exclusive rights.
   2.2 Determines the respective parties involved.
   2.3 States the rights or privileges of the parties involved.
   2.4 Isolates any legal limitations placed on the parties.

The terms employed to describe the explicit performances constitute behaviors which can be demonstrated to another individual, and the characteristics of the overt behaviors can be agreed upon. Further, these can be evoked explicitly by either test items or measuring instruments. To illustrate what is meant by defining occupational or career competencies in *explicit behavioral terms* the following list is provided:

categorize	develop	identify	name
classify	determine	isolate	order
construct	differentiate	list	troubleshoot
describe	distinguish	match	state

These terms indicate accurately and without ambiguity what the learner is capable of performing in demonstrating his achievement. Imprecise and vague terms such as *know, understand, appreciate, feel,* and *really understand* should not be used.

Formalizing the Performance Content

The occupational competencies indicate the ways in which the examinees are expected to respond to performance content of a lesson, unit, or course. It is recommended that the learner behaviors and performance content be listed separately. In this way, the evaluator can ascertain and prescribe multiple ways of reacting to performance content. Consider the following illustrations:

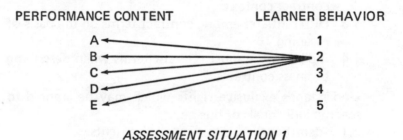

ASSESSMENT SITUATION 1

In the above diagram, the learner is reacting in the same way (behavior 2) to five facets of performance content.

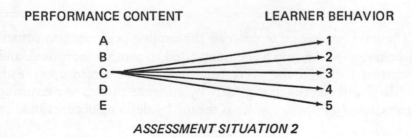

ASSESSMENT SITUATION 2

In assessment situation **2**, the learner is reacting in five different ways to the same aspect of performance content.

Obviously, learner behaviors can overlap a variety of performance content areas; similarly, performance content areas can correspond to numerous learner behaviors. This could be shown as:

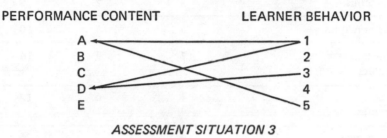

PERFORMANCE CONTENT   LEARNER BEHAVIOR

ASSESSMENT SITUATION 3

Since this is often prevalent, it is more expeditious to list each separately and to relate them in an outline form.

Though the performance content of a lesson, unit, or course may be outlined in detail for instructional purposes, for test or instrument planning and organization only the salient categories should be listed, as shown in the following outline:

A. Automotive tune-up and repair
   1. Battery cell electrolyte level
   2. Testing an ignition coil
   3. Testing engine compression
   4. Replacing generator brushes
      etc.

B. Secretarial Skills
   1. Typing/corrections
   2. Office machines/copying machines
   3. Office practices/telephone skills
      etc.

Preparing a Test Matrix

After defining the performance competencies (behaviors) and content of the occupational lesson, unit, or course, the evaluator should prepare a test matrix, a two-dimensional diagram which interrelates the two and provides a representative sampling plan to assure measurement coverage of both.

TABLE 3–2   *Example Test Matrix for General Metals*

Outcomes / Content	Properties of metal	Operations and functions	Soldering	Total no. of test situations
Knows terms	4	3	2	9
Knows principles		5	5	10
Demonstrates procedures		7	9	16
Applies procedures	2	4	6	12
Can recognize properly executed procedures	1	4	5	10
Total no. of test situations	7	23	27	57

Table 3–2 illustrates a test matrix for general metals. In each cell, the numbers indicate the number of test situations (items, attitudinal statements, and so forth) to be generated for that respective area.

Factors to consider in assigning relative weights to performance content and career behaviors include:

1. Importance of performance content in total career, occupational, or training experience.
2. Relative on-the-job *applicability* of performances.
3. Time devoted to each cell during instructions.

In summary, the preparation of a test matrix includes the following steps:

1. Identify and categorize the performance content and occupational or career behaviors to be assessed by the evaluation test or instrument.
2. Determine the relative weights of importance to be assigned to the performance content and behavior cells.
3. Construct the test matrix in correspondence with these relative weights by distributing the test situations in proportion to the relevant cells of the matrix.

The two-dimensional test matrix indicates the type of assessment instrument necessary to measure the performance content and career behaviors in a proportional format.

Employing the Test Matrix in Test Formulation

The test matrix specifies the performance characterization test or instrument. Indeed, the quality of the performance measure will be largely contingent upon how effectively the evaluator constructs test situations which match the specifications representing the classes of behaviors and performance content described in the matrix. Below are three examples. Mager (1973) also provides an excellent discussion of matching criterion test items with objectives.

Performance Outcome: Defines contract terminology in own words.

Instructions: In no more than two sentences, define each of the following terms:

1. Fraud
2. Validity
3. Offers
4. Liability

Performance Outcome: Identifies the procedural steps for soldering a seam or joint with a soldering copper.

Instructions: Which one of the following steps should be completed first in soldering a seam?

1. Apply a flux.
2. Clean the areas of the metal to be joined.
3. Coat the pieces to be soldered with flux.
4. Place the surfaces together with soldered sides in contact.

Performance Outcome: Lay off a specific distance on a given piece of wood stock according to specifications.

Test Situation: The learner is given a piece of hardwood, 8" X 4" X 3/4", and asked to lay off a distance of 6 inches.

Criteria: The process may be evaluated in terms of the criteria established in the objective. The product must reveal the exact laid-off distance as stated in the specifications.

Additional Characteristics Inherent in Test Formulation

In formalizing occupational or career test situations, the following additional characteristics must be present:

1. The levels of competencies (knowledge, comprehension, and so on, from the cognitive domain) are stated as explicitly as possible.
2. Each performance level is characterized by a set of test situations through which the performance can be portrayed in reference to all critical incidents.
3. A sampling plan (test matrix) must be employed to select the test situations that will be utilized on any form of the occupational test or instrument.
4. The examinee's score must express objectively and meaningfully his performance capabilities in each level of occupational or training tasks.

UTILIZATION OF RESULTS

Because learner performance measures may be used for a great number of different purposes, we will discuss utilization of results in relation to specific purposes.

To Facilitate Learning

Results of measures from any of the four domains, when used effectively, can facilitate student growth and learning. This can occur by way of several avenues. First, the distribution of graded or scored instruments to students and their discussion of each item can obviously help those students who missed certain items. Also, this can help reinforce the learning of those who responded correctly. A second means involves the careful analysis of objective achievement by instructors and can focus on either individual students or classes of students. If on the individual student, the results can be used to design remedial instruction to overcome the individual's deficiency. The following example objectives were not met by an individual:

Objective 16:   Each student will be able to type 60 words per minute.

Objective 17:   Each student will demonstrate familiarity with the output function of the Magnetic Card Selectric Typewriter (MCST) by scoring 90 percent on an identification test.

Since these objectives were not met by the student—and they are assumed to be important for job performance—the instructor can prescribe certain practice and tutorial sessions or some other action to aid the student in achieving the objectives.

Analysis of a total class's or class section's achievement of objectives can similarly facilitate learning. Consideration of the above-mentioned objectives on a class focus might look like the following:

		Percentage of class achievement
Objective 16:	Each student will be able to type 60 words per minute.	95
Objective 17:	Each student will demonstrate familiarity with the output function of the Magnetic Card Selectric Typewriter (MCST) by scoring 90 percent on an identification test.	51

The test results for the two objectives show that Objective 16 was successfully achieved but only about half the class achieved Objective 17. This indicates a definite deficiency and since such a great percentage of students is involved, the instructor may wish to return to the instruction pertaining to this particular objective.

To Assess Instruction

Analysis of objective achievement and other student outcome information can contribute to the evaluation of courses, programs, and the total education or training program. By displaying course and program objectives with the percentages of learners achieving the respective objectives, program personnel and evaluators can obtain a good indication of the degree to which intended goals are being met. The display shown in the preceding section is one example of how an objective/achievement result can be portrayed. From such a display, conclusions can be drawn regarding instructional success in bringing about desired learning or change. Likewise, suggestions for improving the course or program can be made by the evaluator.

In using the results of learner performance measures for assessing instruction or programs, more than the achievement of objectives should be considered. A very basic question which should be raised by the evaluator is "Are the objectives appropriate to necessary job success?" By relating the results of student performance measures to the results of follow-up studies and employer surveys (discussed in the following chapters), program personnel and evaluators can begin to judge the appropriateness of objectives by observing the relatedness of objective achievement to various measures of job performance.

Another point which should not be overlooked is the measurement and consideration of unintended student outcomes. Attitude and interest are two consequences of instruction that are often overlooked by program personnel. For example, an individual may be a content expert following a program but possess no interest in pursuing a job in a related field. Instruction, in this case, might have been successful in performance achievement but lacking in fostering the proper attitude on the part of the learner.

To Facilitate Placement and Guidance

The use of standardized aptitude, achievement, interest, attitude, and performance measures is normally a responsibility belonging to the counseling and placement staff of an educational institution who are most often well trained in the use of these scores. However, a word of caution is not without its place here concerning the use of these sorts of measures. Aptitude scores are perhaps best utilized as supplementary information to be applied to other more reliable indices. An individual who has achieved high scores or grades, but scores poorly on standardized aptitude tests should not be discouraged from pursuit of his chosen field. Likewise, a student should not be pressured to enter a field in which he has high aptitude when his interests lie elsewhere. As has been indicated, aptitude exams have no way of successfully eliminating influential variables such as training and motivation. Further training may change an individual's "aptitude" quite dramatically. In addition, poor motivation may make high aptitude scores insignificant at best. Interest examinations may prove more useful in assessing learner motivation, and these, used in conjunction with other standardized measures, will help the counseling or placement officer to guide students in their career choices.

Achievement tests are used mainly by teachers for assigning grades to students, and it is normally the counselor's responsibility to draw the more far-reaching conclusions concerning a student's academic performance and looking at broad patterns exhibited by the student in terms of grades. Thus, while teachers may have different—or even poor—methods of determining "achievement scores" (i.e. grades) on an individual basis, the counselor has the responsibility of making more total judgments. Some grades may not appear to "fit" the pattern established by the student. It is up to the counselor to determine why. Variations of this sort are signposts often leading the counselor to significant discoveries. At times, a poor grade may simply mean that the student has had personal problems during that period of time, and the counselor should be interested in the nature of these problems as they relate to a potential job situation for the student. Similarly, a radical departure from an established pattern may indicate a personality conflict has existed between the student and a particular teacher or teachers. Again, this is good for the counselor to know. If he can discover what sorts of problems have affected the learner's achievement, it may help him to help the student make a more viable career choice.

REFERENCES

Airasion, P. W. and Madaus, G. F. "Criterion-referenced Testing in the Classroom." *Measurement in Education,* 1972, 3(4):1–8.

Bell, F. et al. "A Comparison of Three Approaches to Criterion Measurement." *Journal of Applied Psychology,* 1963, 47(6):416–418.

Block, J. H. "Criterion-referenced Measurement: Potential." *School Review,* 1971, 79:289–297.

Bloom, B. S. et al. *Taxonomy of Educational Objectives: The Classification of Educational Goals. Handbook I, Cognitive Domain.* New York: McKay, 1964.

Bloom, B. S.; Hastings, J. T.; and Madaus, G. F. *Handbook on Formative and Summative Evaluation of Student Learning.* New York: McGraw-Hill, 1971.

Borgen, J. and Davis, D. *Planning, Implementing, and Evaluating Career Preparation Programs.* Bloomington: McKnight Publishers, 1974.

Boyd, J. L., Jr. and Shimberg, B. *Handbook of Performance Testing.* Princeton, New Jersey: Educational Testing Service, 1971.

Edwards, A. L. *Techniques of Attitude Scale Construction.* New York: Appleton-Century-Crofts, 1957.

Fitzpatrick, R. and Morrison, E. "Performance and Product Evaluation." In R. L. Thorndike (ed.), *Educational Measurement* (2d ed.). Washington, D.C.: American Council on Education, 1971, pp. 237–270.

Flanagan, J. C. "The Critical Incident Technique." *Psychological Bulletin,* 1954, 51:327–358.

Flanagan, J. C. and Burns, R. R. "The Employee Performance Record: A New Appraisal and Development Tool." *Harvard Business Review,* 1955, 33(5): 95–102.

Glaser, R. and Nitko, A. J. "Measurement in Learning and Instruction." In Thorndike, R. L. (ed.), *Education Measurement* (2d ed.). Washington, D.C.: American Council on Education, 1971.

Graen, G. B. and Davis, F. V. "A Measure of Work Attitudes for High-School-Age Youth." *Journal of Vocational Behavior,* 1971, 1(4):343–353.

Gronlund, N. E. *Constructing Achievement Tests.* Englewood Cliffs, New Jersey: Prentice-Hall, Inc., 1968.

Harmon, P. "A Classification of Performance Objectives Behaviors in Job Training Programs." *Educational Technology,* 1968, 8(22):11–16.

Holland, J. L. *The Psychology of Vocational Choice: A Theory of Personality Types and Model Environments.* Waltham, Massachusetts: Blaisdell, 1966.

Krathwohl, David et al. *Taxonomy of Educational Objectives, Vol. II, Affective Domain.* New York: McKay, 1956.

Kuder, F. G. *Kuder Occupational Interest Survey, Research Handbook* (2d ed.). Chicago: Science Research Associations, 1962.

Kuder, F. G. *Kuder Preference Record—Occupational, Form D, Research Handbook* (2d ed.). Chicago: Science Research Associates, 1957.

Lawson, T. E. "Formative Instructional Product Evaluation." *Educational Technology,* 1973, 8(5):42–44.

Mager, R. F. *Developing Attitude Toward Learning.* Palo Alto, California: Fearon, 1968.

Mager, R. F. *Measuring Instructional Intent.* Belmont, California: Fearon, 1973.

Mager, R. F. *Preparing Instructional Objectives.* Palo Alto, California: Fearon, 1962.

Mager, R. F. and Beach, K. M., Jr. *Developing Vocational Instruction.* Palo Alto, California: Fearon, 1967.

Moore, M. R. *A Proposed Taxonomy of the Perceptual Domain and Some Suggested Applications.* (Technical Report No. TDR-67-3), Princeton, New Jersey: Educational Testing Service, 1967.

Nitko, A. J. *Criterion-referenced Testing in the Context of Instruction.* Learning Research and Development Center, University of Pittsburgh, 1972.

Popham, W. J. (ed.) *Criterion-referenced Measurement.* Englewood Cliffs, New Jersey: Educational Technology Publications, 1971.

Popham, W. J. and Husek, T. R. "Implications of Criterion-referenced Measurement." In Popham, W. J. (ed.), *Criterion-referenced Measurement.* Englewood Cliffs, New Jersey: Educational Technology Publishers, 1971, pp. 17–37.

Salomone, P. and Muthard, J. E. "Canonical Correlation of Vocational Needs and Vocational Style." *Journal of Vocational Behavior,* 1972, 2(2):163–171.

SRA Catalog for Business—Tests and Training Programs. Chicago: Science Research Associates, 1973.

Scott, W. A. and Wertheimer, M. *Introduction to Psychological Research.* New York: Wiley, 1966.

Shaw, M. E. and Wright, J. M. *Scales for the Measurement of Attitude.* New York: McGraw-Hill, Inc., 1967.

Simpson, B. J. "The Classification of Educational Objectives, Psychomotor Domain." *Illinois Teacher of Home Economics,* 1966, 10:110–144.

Stephenson, W. *Study of Behavior: Q Technique and its Methodology.* Chicago: University of Chicago Press, 1953.

Strong, E. K., Jr. *Vocational Interests of Men and Women*. Palo Alto, California: Stanford University Press, 1943.

Super, D. E. "A Theory of Career Development." *American Psychologist*, 1953, 8:185–90.

Super, D. E. "Vocational Development Theory in 1988: How Will it Come About?" *Counseling Psychologist*, 1969, 1:9–19.

Thurstone, L. L. "Comment." *American Journal of Sociology*, 1946, 52:30–50.

Walsh, W. B. and Barrow, C. "Consistent and Inconsistent Career Preferences and Personality." *Journal of Vocational Behavior*, 1971, 1(3):271–278.

Walsh, W. B. and Lewis, R. "Consistent, Inconsistent and Undecided Career Preferences and Personality." *Journal of Vocational Behavior*, 1972, 2(3): 309–316.

Wentling, T. L. "Measuring the Achievement of Competencies." *Educational Technology*, 1973, 8(5):48–50.

Wilson, C. L. "On-the-Job and Operational Criteria." In Glaser, R. (ed.), *Training Research and Education*. Pittsburgh: University of Pittsburgh Press, 1962, pp. 347–377.

Wittirock, M. C. and Wilfy, D. E. *The Evaluation of Instruction: Issues and Problems*. New York: Holt, Rinehart and Winston, 1970.

4

The Follow-up as an Evaluative Tool: The Student Follow-up

WHY CONDUCT A FOLLOW-UP STUDY?

A real follow-up study is much broader than a statistical placement report and fundamentally involves contacting graduates and dropouts from an educational or training program to gain input for program planning and assessment. Perceptions of past training, success in subsequent employment, and further education are examples of information pertinent to the maintenance and improvement of the programs.

Follow-up studies are designed to evaluate the product of career programs—the graduate. The primary goal of such education, the preparation of individuals for employment, can best be assessed by examining the placement records of graduates and gathering job performance data from employers. In addition, very important information regarding the strengths and weaknesses of a program may be gathered from the former students, who are in the best position to judge such characteristics.

Follow-up techniques include the mail survey, personal interview, and telephone interview—the scope and magnitude of the study will determine the most appropriate technique. A study of the graduates of even a very small school or program can be quite cumbersome, and so the mail survey is usually the most viable method for contacting former learners.

There are many reasons for conducting a follow-up study, and the results of a follow-up may range from a simple survey of the number of former learners receiving employment to a very intensive study which provides feedback from former learners regarding the appropriateness of their preparation to their career choices and plans, and the exemplary qualities or deficiencies of their educational program. The design of a follow-up study, like the design of any educational endeavor, should be based on a well-formulated plan. Such a plan should consist of an overall objective for the study and additional subordinate objectives which further define the focus of the investigation. The objectives for follow-up studies below are by no means exhaustive; they are but examples.

To Determine the Career Patterns of Former Participants of Various Programs

A follow-up, especially one carried out on a one-, three-, and five-year interval, may provide useful information regarding the career patterns of former learners. Determining both the path of advancement and the pattern of salary and wage increase is an important aspect of the follow-up study. To instructional and guidance personnel this type of information is important in that it affords them the opportunity to assist students in choosing occupational fields and training programs commensurate with their career and life goals. Equipped with the understanding of the career patterns of former students, educators may tailor their programs more appropriately to help students make job transitions.

To Determine the Immediate Demand for Positions within the Community

A placement survey can provide an indication of the types of jobs which students are entering upon completion of their educational or training program. From this information, an evaluator can make an estimate of the jobs which are available. Further, follow-up information can provide reasons to explain why former students are not entering specific jobs for which they have been prepared. Perhaps there are no available positions in that field. Although somewhat indirectly, a follow-up study may also provide general job-demand information.

To Determine the Mobility of Program Graduates

Movement within a firm or corporation, from job to job, or from one locality to another may be assessed via a follow-up study. Geographic mobility (place to place) data should be considered in the planning of new programs or the deletion of current ones. If a certain program is designed to prepare individuals for a particular occupation within a community, yet follow-up information indicates that the graduates of the program are moving from the community and accepting jobs in other geographic and occupational areas, then the program should probably be deleted or reassessed.

To Determine the Adequacy of the Educational or Training Program in Preparing Individuals for Job Entry

Usually former learners are interested in expressing their feelings about how well their educational experience has helped them in their subsequent employment. Learners often indicate certain job tasks which they have found to be most difficult in their employment situations. This information can help the educator or training director to revise or expand instruction in specific areas. By supplying data on learner performance or on the availability of employment positions, the follow-up can confirm the necessity for maintaining a particular course or program. Likewise, direct feedback regarding the worth or worthlessness of certain programs or courses can support their retention, revision, or removal.

To Determine the Adequacy of Preparation for Entry into Advanced Training Such As Community College, Industrial Training Program, University, or Adult Education Program

Former students or trainees are willing to point out the strengths and weaknesses of their past education in terms of preparing them for subsequent educational programs. Once these students have moved into advanced training programs they are perhaps the best judges of the pressures and expectations of higher education and can provide more objective assessments of the training programs they have experienced previously. Among other things, information may point up the need to coordinate the district or firm's occupational program offerings (vertical articulation) with those at other educational and training levels.

To Determine the Adequacy of Ancillary Services Such As Guidance, Counseling, and Placement

The contribution made by guidance, counseling, and placement services to the short- and long-range placement of learners in jobs is difficult to isolate from that of the instructional program. However, learners may provide information regarding specific strengths and weaknesses of the ancillary services, giving specific suggestions for improvement. Once again, these students are often better equipped to assess such services after they have gained experience on the job or in other more advanced programs and have actually experienced the results of guidance and placement services.

To Determine Realistic Job Descriptions for Positions Obtained by Former Students or Trainees

Former students and trainees can provide job descriptions for their present job. Job descriptions obtained in this way will serve as an axis around which job analysis will revolve. Once descriptions and requirements are obtained, instruction can be assessed in light of these descriptions by the educational or training program staff.

To Emphasize the Primary Objective of Career Education to Staff and Students

Inherent in all follow-up objectives is an emphasis on the primary objective of occupational education—the preparation of individuals for a productive career. But more than this, a follow-up study can help staff members to evaluate their own efforts. The follow-up can illuminate the real goal of the instructional program and alert the educator or trainer to his responsibility for maintaining contact with employers, staying abreast of their needs as well as those of students. To learners, both currently enrolled and graduated, the follow-up accentuates the relationship of career education to the world of work and, in addition, provides an opportunity for former students to supply input into the future role and function of educational institutions and programs.

To Provide Information for Required Reports

A somewhat auxiliary purpose of the follow-up study is to provide information for reports which are required by federal, state, local agencies, or corporate management personnel. For the past several years, each state has been required to report the number of placements and area of placement of all occupational students who have been enrolled in a program reimbursed by federal funds. This state requirement has led, in many instances, to states' requiring local education agencies to supply this placement information.

Each of the preceding purposes for conducting a follow-up study can be closely related to one or all of the others. While an agency's purpose for conducting a follow-up may be narrowly defined, follow-up questions will probably gather a wide range of material, some of which will also contribute to the achievement of other purposes. This is fine, and even desirable, and since it is not wise to bombard any student with redundant and annoying follow-up questionnaires, it is an excellent idea to coordinate follow-up activities with those of other departments or courses. The cost will not be appreciably greater for a more comprehensive survey, and additional data collected for other purposes will often alter or improve the basis for interpretation.

WHO SHOULD CONDUCT THE FOLLOW-UP?

Each of the groups mentioned below will have its own ideas about what information should be collected. Their input at an early stage will increase the efficiency of the follow-up survey by eliminating duplication of efforts, by insuring that all important areas are covered, and by guaranteeing utilization of results. Individuals who are involved identify with the investigation and are more likely to assume the personal responsibility to *do* something with the results. The involvement and support of many groups is necessary in the planning and conduct of a meaningful follow-up study.

School or Agency Administration

The commitment of the local administration is necessary for many types of internal evaluation. In some cases, administrative support will release the support of other staff members for the follow-up activities; and in other cases the administration must be sufficiently committed to the study to provide necessary staff time and printing and mailing costs. Finally, if any use is to be made of evaluation results in terms of change or realignment of instructional and supportive programs, the administration must be involved.

Governing Board and Citizens' Advisory Council

The Board of Education or the Board of Directors can provide support in the community, advising local business and industrial representatives of the need for and usefulness of the follow-up study. Also, board members are many times employers and may be asked to react to follow-up questionnaires in the formative or developmental stages. Like the governing board, the local advisory council is usually composed of community members who employ present or former students or who work with them in some way. Advisory council members can also provide consultant help in the development of evaluation instruments and procedures.

Guidance Personnel

In many cases within the public schools, guidance personnel assume the primary responsibility for conducting a follow-up study. The desirability of this arrangement, however, depends upon the scope of the study. The follow-up of only one specific program may require that the director of that program conduct the study with the help of the guidance staff and other personnel.

Not only do guidance personnel provide the instructional staff with support in the follow-up, but they have a vested interest in the outcome of the study. Follow-up data can determine both the effectiveness and perceived effectiveness of the guidance staff and their related functions.

In most educational settings the guidance staff maintains cumulative records which many times represent the primary source for obtaining student addresses and determining each former student's program of study. In the case of an internal training program of a particular industrial firm, the training director may assume the primary responsibility for conducting the follow-up.

Instructional Staff

The instructional staff, the group most capable of making changes in specific educational programs, *must* be involved in the follow-up study. Essential to the implementation of change as a result of the follow-up, the instructional staff can also contribute immensely to the procedural aspects of the study. Instructional or guidance staff should be involved in orienting students to the purpose and procedures of the study prior to their exit from the educational institution. Also, instructional staff members can help to locate former students once they have left school. In many instances, the name and signature of a familiar instructor or department chairman on the letter accompanying the instrument can help to personalize the follow-up and significantly increase the response to the survey.

Student Body

A recent trend in educational decision making regardless of the level has been toward the involvement of students in the determination of educational procedures and content. In a follow-up, the involvement of students in planning is vital to the success of study. Student involvement will promote ego identification and should aid in obtaining a good instrument return rate in future years. Also, student representatives can provide useful input regarding the clarity of the instrument. A simple slip in the choice of words can be disastrous to the success of a follow-up study. If the meaning of a question is interpreted differently by staff members and former students, the information gained is not reliable.

DEVELOPMENT OF THE FOLLOW-UP INSTRUMENT

Before anything else is done, the purpose and objectives for the follow-up must be established. First, an overall or primary objective for the study should be formulated. Once the primary study objective or purpose has been established, subordinate objectives of the study can be determined. Following is an example of a primary objective and several accompanying subordinate objectives:

Primary Objective: To determine the adequacy of the educational program in preparing individuals for job entry.

Subordinate Objectives: To determine if program content is consonant with job requirements.
To determine how many students entered jobs for which they were trained.
To determine, for those who did enter, job retention rates.
To identify strengths of the program.
To identify weaknesses of the program.

Once the objectives for the study have been established, an instrument that will best serve these stated objectives must be identified or constructed.

Appearance of the Instrument

To attract and hold attention, follow-up instruments must be visually appealing. Instruments should be prepared and duplicated on good quality paper, preferably colored paper. Research has shown that colored paper elicits a better response rate than white paper. This difference in response rate, in one instance, was over 15 percent.

Regardless of paper color, the instrument should appear neat and organized. Take care to check for the logical placement of items. That is, items to be answered by all respondents should be included at the beginning. Also, similar items should be grouped to facilitate and thus encourage response.

The instrument should also provide sufficient space for all responses. Instruments with too little space for response have a poorer rate of return, and the amount of space per item will have an effect on whether respondents will answer those items.

Finally, the instruments must be easy to read. The style of type must be appealing and sharp. Also, reproduction of the instrument must yield clean and legible copy. If possible, printing should be chosen over mimeographing or spirit duplicating as a method of reproduction. It has been found that the type of copy, just as the color of paper, plays an important part in a good return rate for follow-up instruments.

Items of the Instrument

Items should be related to the previously defined objectives for the follow-up. Just as highways are chosen once a destination has been defined, items must be written which will elicit information useful in achieving the study objectives. If you already know what program the former student or trainee was involved in, there is no need to ask him for this information. Do not require the follow-up respondent to provide information that is already available.

Brevity is also an important factor in the construction of individual items. The recommended maximum word length for an item is twenty words. Most items can be written in much less. Wording of items should be simple; if an item is long and complicated it may be misinterpreted or omitted. Frequently, two simple questions are better than one complicated one.

Probably the most important factor in the formulation of items for a follow-up instrument is the choice of wording. It is important that both the designer of the follow-up instrument and the respondent have the same issue in mind for each item. Payne (1968) gives additional suggestions regarding item preparation:

1. Never use double negatives.
2. If the antecedent is not very clear, restate it.
3. Check all meanings of words.
4. Avoid use of "concept words."
5. Stick to familiar words—if they do not have too many meanings.
6. To make questions readable, do not abbreviate words.
7. Avoid misplaced emphasis by underscoring words which should be emphasized.
8. Use a minimum of punctuation.

It is also wise to define any terms which may be unclear or questionable to the former student.

Most follow-up studies are directed toward obtaining information regarding the educational program and ancillary activities. The diversity of this type of information necessitates the use of several types of instrument items to elicit the information most efficiently. Item variation also changes the response mode for the former student. This is especially important when a lengthy instrument is utilized; variation helps to prevent the respondent from becoming bored with the instrument or establishing a constant pattern of response.

Follow-up instrument items can be classified into five categories: dichotomous response, multiple choice, rating, ranking, and open-ended items.

Dichotomous Response Items

These items offer the former student or trainee two alternative responses. They may have response choices such as yes-no, true-false, employed-unemployed, and the like. Below are several examples of dichotomous response items.

EXAMPLE ITEM 1

Are you in full time military service?

☐ Yes

☐ No

EXAMPLE ITEM 2

If you are in school now, check one box below.

☐ In school full time

☐ In school part time

EXAMPLE ITEM 3

If you work part time (less than 30 hours per week) check the reason why.

☐ That is all I care to work

☐ That is all I can get

As can be observed, the dichotomous item is easily understood and responses come readily. Only very simple instructions are needed. Results of the follow-up responses for this type of item are very easily reported with a frequency count (e. g., 231 responded *yes* and 442 responded *no*) or recorded percentages (e. g., 34 percent *yes* and 66 percent *no*).

Multiple choice Items

Although the dichotomous item has several strengths and can be used efficiently for gathering some types of information, there are other, more efficient ways that may be appropriate if space is a problem. For example, Items 1 and 2 above, and other dichotomous items of a similar nature, can be combined to form a multiple choice item. By combining Items 1 and 2 the following may be formulated:

EXAMPLE ITEM 4

What is your current employment or schooling status?

☐ In school full time

☐ In school part time

☐ In military service

☐ Housewife

☐ Unemployed

☐ Employed part time

☐ Employed full time

Example Item 4 provides information identical to that provided by Items 1 and 2, and four other alternatives have been added which could logically have made up two other dichotomous items. When appropriate, the multiple choice item is much more economical than the dichotomous item in terms of both time and space. The respondent can read the multiple choice item more quickly than two dichotomous items, and tabulation of results is simplified.

Alternatives offered in the multiple choice follow-up item should represent all possible responses. The respondent should not be placed in the situation where he is unable to place his response into one of the given alternatives. The instrument developer may find that it is difficult to perceive all possible choices to items. It is often helpful to have other individuals review the items and comment on them. Another approach, although more time consuming, is to list only the item stems (e. g., what is your employment status?) on a sample instrument and mail it to a number of former students. After receiving the returns, the instrument developers should categorize all open responses which were given to the item stems. Once responses have been categorized, item alternatives can be written to encompass all responses given.

If listing all item alternatives would be too lengthy, as in the listing of monthly or weekly salary, or if possible responses are continuous, it may be appropriate to construct the item incorporating ranges of responses for alternatives such as in Example Item 5.

EXAMPLE ITEM 5

If you are presently employed, please check one box below to indicate your approximate hourly wage.

☐ $2.01 to $2.50 per hour
☐ $2.51 to $3.00 per hour
☐ $3.01 to $3.50 per hour
☐ $3.51 to $4.00 per hour
☐ $4.01 to $4.50 per hour
☐ $4.51 to $5.00 per hour
☐ $5.01 to $5.50 per hour
☐ $5.51 to $6.00 per hour
☐ $6.01 or more per hour

Rating Items

A third type of item which is appropriate to a follow-up instrument is the rating item, a specific type of multiple choice item in which the alternatives are descriptors or ratings related to the subject presented in the item stem. The rating item is of great importance in gathering information relative to the educational program completed by the respondent. Example Item 6 is such a rating item.

EXAMPLE ITEM 6

How would you rate the value of the help which you received from the counselor(s) in choosing a career?

☐ High
☐ Average
☐ Low

To give respondents a more objective base for making such a rating, and to increase the consistency of interpretation of the item (reliability), qualifiers or guidelines may be attached to the alternatives. By adding qualifiers to Example Item 6, it becomes the following:

EXAMPLE ITEM 7

How would you rate the value of the help which you received from the counselor(s) in choosing a career?

☐ High. They helped me as much as I needed.
☐ Average. They helped me some.
☐ Low. They didn't help me at all.

The rating item can also be constructed to incorporate something similar to a Likert* scale, which can be applied to a series of items. This type of rating is not limited to one set of alternatives but may incorporate many, one of which could be an agreement scale. Example items 8 and 9 show the Likert type of rating item.

EXAMPLE ITEM 8

My counselor was very knowledgeable concerning occupations.

Strongly Agree	Agree	Neutral	Disagree	Strongly Disagree
☐	☐	☐	☐	☐

EXAMPLE ITEM 9

In general, how much help was your high school occupational training in the following areas:

	None	Little	Some	Much
a) Knowing how to use tools and equipment	☐	☐	☐	☐
b) Knowing what one does in this kind of job	☐	☐	☐	☐
c) Using time and energy productively	☐	☐	☐	☐
d) Finding needed job related information	☐	☐	☐	☐

*A scale incorporating a linear response mode. See Chapter 3 for a detailed description.

	None	Little	Some	Much
e) Being able to talk to the boss about job problems	☐	☐	☐	☐
f) Getting along with the customer, being patient, and so on.	☐	☐	☐	☐
g) Getting along with other workers	☐	☐	☐	☐
h) Understanding union membership	☐	☐	☐	☐
i) Handling new or unpleasant situations	☐	☐	☐	☐
j) Applying for a job	☐	☐	☐	☐
k) Interviewing for a job	☐	☐	☐	☐

As Example Item 9 demonstrates, ratings can be made on a number of statements within a short period of time and require only a minimal amount of space on the instrument.

Ranking Items

A fourth type of item is the ranking item. Although it is useful in many cases, this type has several limitations. One is the number of items which the respondent may be asked to rank. It is a very difficult task to rank a long list of items. An additional limitation is that the item might present alternatives which are so close to one another that the respondent has trouble discriminating between them. However, a logical, well-conceived ranking item can be useful in gathering follow-up information as in the one below.

EXAMPLE ITEM 10

Please rank the following instructional activities in terms of how you learned the best.

☐ Lecture
☐ Demonstration

☐ Workbook assignments
☐ Project activity
☐ Reading
☐ Homework
☐ Term papers

When a longer list is necessary, the length limitation can be overcome by asking the respondent to pick the one or two most desirable and least desirable options rather than ranking all of the alternatives.

Open-ended Items

The natural limitations imposed by a structured item are alleviated by the open-ended item, one which requires the respondent to formulate his own answer to a question. The open-ended item can elicit information that the instrument developer has overlooked, and can evoke suggestions from former students for improving instruction, ancillary services, or any other program component. Example items 11 and 12 are open ended.

EXAMPLE ITEM 11

What are your job duties? (Job duties are tasks you are required to do in your job, such as making beds, ordering supplies, preparing food, reading blueprints, laying out machine parts, repairing equipment, and the like.)

_____

_____

EXAMPLE ITEM 12

What learning experiences do you feel should be added to the occupational program in which you were enrolled?

_____

_____

The disadvantage of the open-ended item is the difficulty encountered by the evaluator in summarizing the results. Such summarization is not a great concern for small scale follow-ups, but in a large scale (school or training program) survey it can present a problem. Most open-ended responses can be classified into categories which can be summarized. Much time will be required to tabulate the open-ended responses which would not be needed for other types of items. However, this type can provide information that no other can. The additional time to record and summarize results may be greatly overshadowed by the wealth of information gained.

Directions

Directions to the former student will affect the overall validity of the follow-up study. The respondent must mark the instrument items in a consistent manner. Directions should be concise and complete and should be placed close to the items so that the respondent will not have to flip back and forth through the questionnaire. Every effort should be made to allow the respondent to concentrate on the question itself. Following are suggestions for giving clear, written directions on the questionnaire:

1. Make them brief.
2. Group questions according to different types of response or marking.
3. Set off directions with heavy, large, distinctive lettering.

In addition to directions for specific types of items, overall directions should be supplied emphasizing the purpose of the follow-up. The respondent must be convinced that the questionnaire is worth his time. Directions should include a deadline or desired return date. Inclusion of a return date has been shown to be a factor contributing to an increased return rate for mailed questionnaires.

Instrument Format

The format of the follow-up instrument should be carefully considered, both intrinsically and as a factor contributing to the rate of return. The mail follow-up must "stand alone," establishing rapport with the respondent which would otherwise be accomplished by the interviewer in a telephone or personal interview. Once this "rapport" has been established, the sequencing of items is important to maintain contact with the former student. The instrument should have a smooth-flowing sequence which is easy for the respondent to follow.

The preliminary items of the instrument should be easily answerable and should relate directly to the avowed purpose of the follow-up. The first items encountered by the respondent may determine whether the instrument is completed at all. When possible, items should be grouped according to their underlying objective. For example, all items related to an individual's current status should be grouped. Major divisions of items in a follow-up instrument could include personal information, employment information, educational program information, ancillary services information, and further recommendations, to name but a few. Within these major categories, items should be ordered according to their response mode. Items possessing a rating format should be grouped together to require fewer mode changes on the part of the respondent and to minimize the directions required throughout the instrument.

Another format to be considered is the branched-item format. Branching is the transfer of the reading and responding path of the respondent based upon his current response to an item as shown below.

EXAMPLE ITEM 13

What is your employment status?
　　Employed　　□
　　Unemployed □ If you checked unemployed, skip to
　　　　　　　　　　Item 19.

The utilization of the branching item can save respondents the trouble of reading items which do not apply to them.

A final consideration for the format of the follow-up instrument is the overall instrument length, and for this there is no standard length. The interest of the group being followed up, the orientation given to the respondents, and the overall purpose of the follow-up all have an effect on how former learners will be motivated to respond. A disadvantage of a lengthy instrument is that the respondent may be motivated to dispose of the instrument and never respond. Several researchers have stated that a one-page or postcard questionnaire is more likely to be returned than a two- or three-page questionnaire. Again, other factors will determine the ultimate or most desirable length.

In addition to organizational considerations, there are several factors to be considered relative to the layout of the follow-up instrument. The title should appear on the first page of the instrument. The terms "questionnaire" and "checklist" should be avoided, however, as these terms have been found to be irritating to some individuals. "Form" or "instrument" are terms more acceptable.

The name of the individual or agency sponsoring the follow-up should also appear on the instrument. General directions should be given for the entire instrument which should include a brief presentation of its purpose and the deadline for return or desired return date. The address to which the completed instrument should be mailed should also appear in plain sight.

The layout of the instrument should provide suitable space for the response to all items. Do not expect the former student to crowd or squeeze his answers. Any inconvenience to the respondent may have an effect on the completion and return rate for the instrument. All items should parallel the bottom of the page, including all rating categories. That is, all column headings should be printed horizontally rather than vertically. Example Item 14 below shows the desirable presentation while Example Item 15 illustrates the undesirable.

EXAMPLE ITEM 14

THIS

Strongly Disagree	Disagree	Neutral	Agree	Strongly Agree
☐	☐	☐	☐	☐

EXAMPLE ITEM 15

NOT THIS

Strongly disagree	Disagree	Neutral	Agree	Strongly agree
☐	☐	☐	☐	☐

Major categories of the instrument such as "personal informa-tion" should be emphasized in bold or a larger type face. Also, all pages should be numbered. Pages printed on both sides should have "(over)" printed at the bottom of the first side.

Validation of the Instrument

Once the instrument has been prepared, it should be reviewed for clarity, meaning, and appearance. A copy of the instrument should then be submitted to a few selected individuals. The school adminis-tration, selected members of the citizens' advisory council, guidance staff, selected instructional staff members, and—most importantly—the student group should be represented. Since the success of the entire follow-up depends upon the support of these groups, any opportunity to involve them should be capitalized upon. The groups should review the overall content of the instrument and criticize wording, format, and other aspects of the instrument.

Of all groups, the student body or trainee group should be utilized the most extensively. The instrument should be administered to a group of current students and to a group of former students as a pilot test for the instrument. The pilot test will provide information which will be expanded during the actual follow-up study, but, more important, it will point up inconsistencies and problems of interpretation. When the instrument is administered to the group of in-school students, a request should be made asking the respondents to comment on specific items, to indicate problem areas of the instrument, and to make suggestions for its improvement.

The pilot test will also provide the opportunity to test the procedure for administration and to put the wheels in motion relative to processing the returns. These aspects will be considered in greater detail in sections to follow.

ADMINISTRATION OF THE FOLLOW-UP STUDY

Follow-up studies, like any other educational endeavor, should be well planned from start to finish. Both overall objectives of the follow-up and subordinate objectives should be firmly established and held in mind throughout the study. Once objectives are established, the primary responsibility for coordinating the entire effort should be assigned to one individual. This individual will require support in proportion to the magnitude of the study but should assume a leadership role throughout.

Determining Groups to Follow Up

Inherent in the determination of the need and objectives for the follow-up is the selection of individuals to be included in the follow-up survey. Resources available will play an important part in determining the scope of the study. However, the evaluative focus will be the primary determinant in the selection of the students or trainees to be surveyed. If evaluation focuses on a specific course, the former learners of that specific course should be followed up. Likewise, if the focus is on the evaluation of a certain program or of a total institutional program, then the group surveyed will be larger in number.

A program is a series of courses organized in a sequence to provide a student with a saleable skill. For example, a secretarial training program might comprise courses in typing, shorthand, office procedures, and so on. A total institutional program includes all career programs offered by a specific educational agency. A follow-up, when economically feasible, should not be limited to occupational graduates of an institution. It is important to have a picture of the entire former student body. Even college-bound students or those enrolled in advanced educational programs may provide useful information regarding the completed program and its related components.

Regardless of the scope of the follow-up, a group or subgroup including individuals who have "dropped out" of the program should not be overlooked. Dropouts may be able to provide information that no other group can provide regarding the weaknesses of an educational or training program. Without the dropout response, the follow-up study will give a distorted picture of the former learners.

It is highly probable that dropouts will prove to be a difficult group from which to elicit information. Dropouts are consistently less responsive to follow-ups than are program completors. This fact may necessitate special consideration in terms of locating and properly motivating the dropout.

When feasible, all students who have participated in an educational or training program should be included in the follow-up. But when the number is very large, and economic and personnel constraints prevent follow-up of each former student, it is advisable to draw a sample from the total group.

The term "sample" used in this sense refers to a subgroup chosen from a larger group and treated as representative of that group. If sampling is to be reliable, care must be taken to select a subgroup which is truly representative of the larger group. One method of sampling is to randomly select names of former learners from a list including all names. A further step can be taken to ensure accurate representation of individual programs by using stratification. *Stratification* is simply the breaking of a large group into subgroups, followed by random sampling from these subgroups. For example, the list of all former students for the past year may be divided into those who were enrolled in the general curriculum, college level curriculum, or occupational curriculum. Next, a random sample of 40 percent of each of these three groups could be drawn and included in the follow-up study.

Choosing the Method for Follow-up

Methods for follow-up have generally been limited to the personal interview, telephone interview, or mail survey. Each technique has advantages and disadvantages which must be weighed by the director of the follow-up against the purposes, scope, and resources available for the study at hand.

Most sociological research studies which involve the gathering of data from the public rely heavily on the personal interview. The personal interview allows the interviewer the opportunity to establish rapport with the respondent and to convince him of the importance of the study. In this way, a greater percentage of response is attained. Moreover, the interviewer can probe into the underlying reasons for specific responses to questions. Many times this is as important as recording the actual responses. These attributes make the personal interview one of the most accurate methods for gathering information regarding a former student and his feelings about his training program. However, for a local school-directed follow-up study of former graduates, the disadvantages of the personal interview may by far outweigh its advantages.

A distinct disadvantage of the personal interview is the cost in terms of required personnel. Interviewers must be hired or available staff must be reassigned to the task of contacting former students. Also, the interviewers must be trained in interviewing, if trained interview personnel are not utilized. And regardless of training, all must be instructed in the use of the interview questionnaire or instrument.

Another cost involved, aside from paying and training interviewers, is the travel of the interviewer. Considering the mobility of former students of an average educational program, the cost of locating and traveling to the former student's residence may be prohibitive. Moreover, if graduates have moved too far from their place of schooling, it may not be at all feasible to contact them in person.

A method for follow-up which can overcome some of the disadvantages of the personal interview, while maintaining some of the same advantages, is the telephone interview. The telephone interview allows the interviewer to explain the purpose and importance of the study and to ask the set of questions which has been prepared. Although the cost of interview personnel is still a sizeable one, travel costs are avoided with the telephone interview.

Personal and telephone interviews have proved standard techniques in sociological research and public opinion polls. However, the task of learner follow-up is somewhat different than most research and opinion surveys. Traditional research surveys involve the sampling of individuals on a random basis from states, counties, cities, city blocks, or telephone directories. A follow-up study differs in that a specific group of individuals is the focus of the study. Thus, mobility may be an inhibitory factor. It should not be assumed, however, that sampling is not applicable to follow-up studies. Samples may be drawn from a specific group of former students.

The focus of the follow-up on a specific group points up the advantages of a mail questionnaire. This questionnaire can reach most former students regardless of their geographic location. Respondents are equally accessible whether in Hartford or Honolulu. Another advantage of this method is the low cost involved. A mail survey can cost as much as twenty times less than a personal interview survey, even considering multiple mailings to those who do not respond immediately. The mail instrument may also be capable of gaining follow-up information which an interview would fail to gain. For example, more people are willing to give income information by mail than by interview. These advantages will most likely place the mail method at the top of the methods list for follow-up studies, although care must be taken to minimize the greatest disadvantage of the mail questionnaire—its rate of return. Several precautionary measures, to be discussed in a later section, will help to ensure that the former student or trainee is properly motivated to complete the instrument. One means of gaining the cooperation of former participants in responding to the follow-up is to orient them prior to the study.

Orientation of Respondents

Past experience has shown that orientation of the student or trainee, before he receives the follow-up instrument, will increase the return rate of the instrument. An extensive study conducted by Norman (1948) has uncovered the following reasons why individuals do not answer a mailed questionnaire:

1. Indifference
2. Negligence
3. Suspicion
4. Lack of understanding
5. Fear of affecting status
6. Minimizing the importance of personal data

These factors can be more broadly classified into three categories: comprehension, knowledge, and motivation. These three factors will determine whether the respondent answers the questions of the follow-up instrument or, of equal importance, whether the instrument is returned.

Comprehension refers to the respondent's understanding of the purpose of the study and, more precisely, to his understanding of the meaning of the items. In the context of the questionnaire, knowledge is the respondent's ability to complete the items of the instrument. To be able to respond, the former student must, in addition to understanding the question, possess the knowledge to answer it. To be motivated to complete and return the instrument, the respondent must be convinced that the study is important enough to warrant his time and effort.

An orientation of respondents in addition to other steps will increase the rate of completion and return of the follow-up instrument. An orientation session for learners prior to their graduation or program completion is ideal. At this session, the purpose of the follow-up and the plans for utilizing the results should be discussed with the learners. Learners should be informed that each of them will be receiving an instrument through the mail at certain time intervals (to be determined by the educational agency). If feasible, a copy of the instrument should be presented to the students for their review and reaction.

If an orientation of students is impossible (if, for example, the student body to be surveyed has already left the educational agency), several actions can be taken to maximize the motivation of the respondent with regard to the follow-up study. A postcard mailed to former students prior to the distribution of the follow-up instrument, containing a brief description of the study and an indication that a second letter and instrument are on the way, has proved to be a valuable means of orienting the respondent. The same can be accomplished by making a short telephone call to the respondent. Of course, the scope of the study and resources available may prevent telephoning. If the agency does not publish an alumni newsletter, an ad with the local newspaper, radio, or television station can also make the former students aware that a study is being conducted and for what reason. A task necessary to the effective follow-up is the location of all former students.

Locating Former Students

The evaluator's success in locating respondents has an obvious relationship to the success of the entire study. If the results of a follow-up study are to be useful and important to the evaluation and, subsequently, to decision making, a large percentage of former students must be included in the study. At the time of the orientation, measures may be taken to facilitate location of former students.

One method of keeping in touch with former students involves the distribution of a perforated card to each student (see Figure 4–1). This two-part card has the student's name on both parts. The small part is to be completed at the time of the orientation, to record both his present address and his parents' name and address. This portion should be collected and filed by the director of the follow-up. The larger portion of the card is a postcard designed to fold easily for storage in the learner's wallet or purse. In the event of any move subsequent to their exit from the educational program, students can fill in the change-of-address information on this card and drop the card in the mail. With the cooperation of former students, these cards will allow the educational or training agency to maintain correspondence with its alumni.

Alternative to the student card is a folded, two-part card mailed to the parents of former students several weeks prior to the mailing of questionnaires. The "parent card" informs parents of the study's purpose and the importance of gaining the cooperation of their son or daughter in completing the forthcoming instrument. The card also

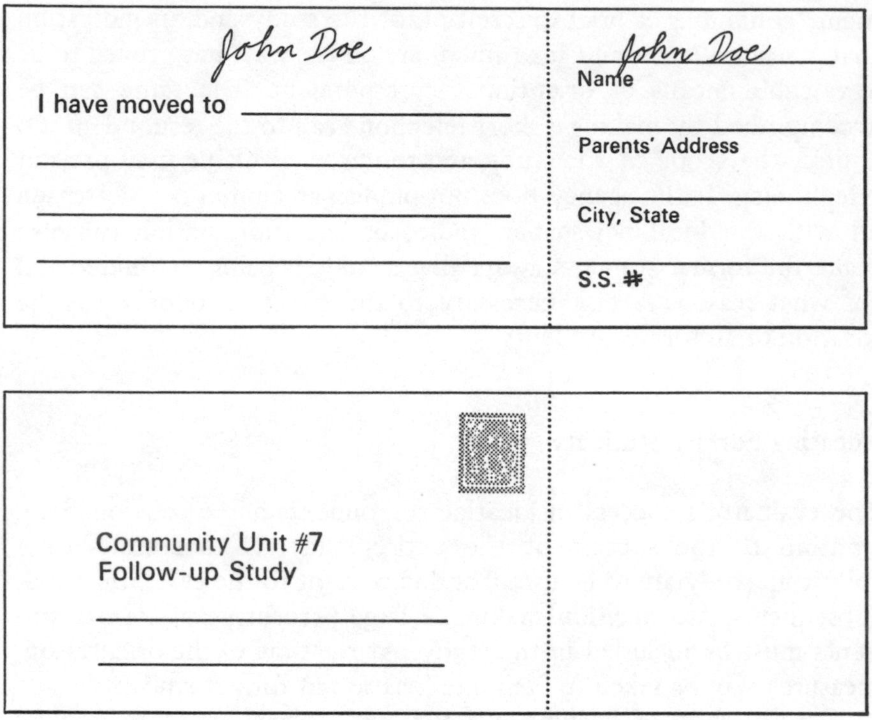

I have moved to _____

John Doe

Name   _____*John Doe*_____

Parents' Address _____

City, State _____

S.S. # _____

Community Unit #7
Follow-up Study

_____

_____

FIGURE 4–1   *Example of Student Change-of-Address Postcard*

provides a second section to be torn off and returned to the school either confirming or correcting the former student's registered address (see Figure 4–2).

Several less involved and less costly steps can be taken to help ensure the transmittal of the follow-up instrument to the former student. Simple placement of "please forward" on the envelope containing the instrument will command the attention of many parents. Another way of locating former students who may have changed their place of residence is to advertise the follow-up study via local newspaper, radio, or television. In addition to giving an explanation of the study, a request can be made that former students who have moved inform the school of their new address.

Of course, there are many more approaches to locating respondents; telephone directories, city directories, and credit bureaus are but a few. The scope of the study, size and type of community, and many other variables will dictate the most efficient method or methods for locating respondents.

Distribution of Instruments

Once the follow-up instrument has been developed and the groups of former students identified, the instrument is ready to be mailed. A letter should accompany the questionnaire in all surveys, to explain the study and to motivate the recipient to respond. Address the letter personally to individual former students, and design it to arouse their interest in the study. Keep the letter short. This letter should indicate the purpose of the study, uses to be made of the findings, and a date by which the questionnaire should be returned. Emphasize the importance of obtaining a response from everyone, and assure the former student that his information will be held in confidence.

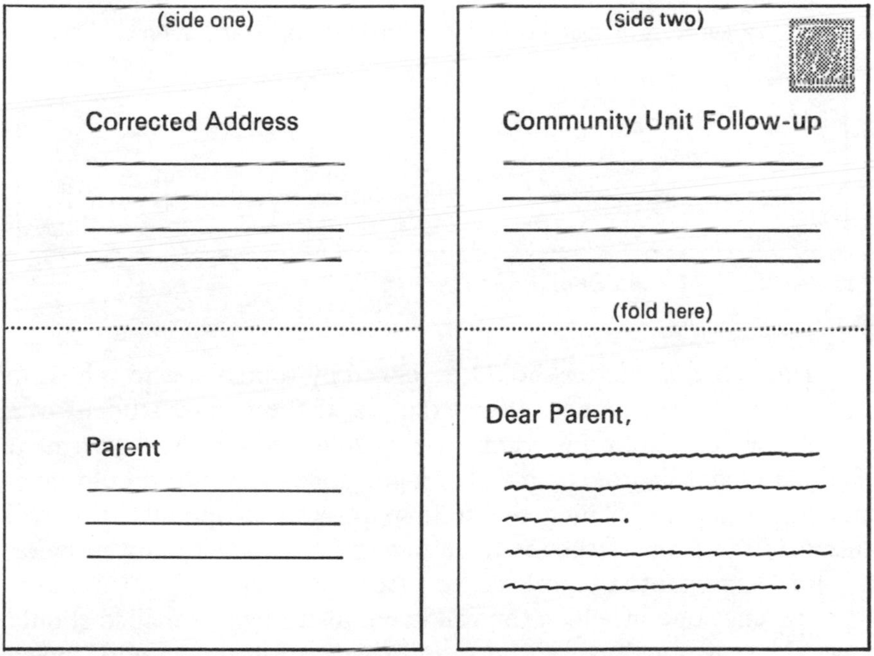

FIGURE 4—2   *Example of Parent Change-of-Address Postcard*

```
┌─────────────────────────────────────────────────────────────┐
│                [YOUR INSTITUTION'S LETTERHEAD]                │
│                                                               │
│                                                               │
│                                                               │
│  Dear Stu,                                                    │
│                                                               │
│      You as a graduate of the class of 1973 from (your        │
│  institution) are one of our most valuable sources for        │
│  suggestions on how to improve our instructional offerings.   │
│  We believe that you can help us improve our offerings so      │
│  that we can better serve the students and community of        │
│  (your town).                                                 │
│                                                               │
│      Would you please help us in our efforts by taking a few  │
│  minutes to complete and return the enclosed form? We have    │
│  enclosed a stamped envelope and we hope to receive your      │
│  reply by November 15.                                        │
│                                                               │
│      Please be assured that all information you supply will be │
│  held in confidence and that your name will never be          │
│  associated with any response.                                │
│                                                               │
│      We appreciate your cooperation in this important effort.  │
│                                                               │
│                                  Sincerely,                   │
│                                                               │
│                                                               │
│                                  (Signature and title of      │
│                                  administrator, teacher,      │
│                                  or counselor)                │
└─────────────────────────────────────────────────────────────┘
```

FIGURE 4–3   *Example Follow-up Letter*

If possible, the letter should be signed by someone who is held in high regard by the student. For example, if the former student of a distributive education program is being followed up, the department chairman, coordinator, or possibly a guidance counselor should sanction the study by signing the follow-up letter. Hopefully, this will motivate the former student to return the completed questionnaire. Figure 4–3 presents a sample cover letter.

The envelope in which the follow-up instrument is mailed should have the return address of the sponsoring institution. In addition to the questionnaire, enclose a stamped, self-addressed envelope.

A considerable amount of research has been conducted in an

attempt to determine the effectiveness of alternative incentives. Rewards such as pencils, packages of instant coffee, and money do have an effect on the return rate of questionnaires. But additional costs must be considered, and the characteristics of the group being surveyed should dictate the chosen incentives.

The distribution of instruments should be carefully timed. Early in the school term and early in the week seem to be the best mailing times for a good return rate. As a rule, the instrument should arrive in the former student's mail on Monday or Tuesday. Periods of stress such as holidays, vacation time, election time, and income tax time should be avoided.

Finally, before instruments are placed in envelopes and mailed, questionnaires must be coded. Even if respondents are requested to sign their names to the instrument, many will not. It is important to the administrator of the follow-up study to know who has failed to respond so additional action can be taken to obtain their responses.

The simplest method of coding instruments is to assign a number to each person on the list of former students. The same number should be placed on the back of each individual's questionnaire. If such a code is used, each individual should be informed of the reason for numbering and should be assured that the results of his questionnaire will remain confidential.

Follow-up of Nonrespondents

The goal of the administrators of follow-up studies is, of course, 100 percent return of the completed instruments. However, as indicated previously, return rate is the greatest disadvantage of a mail survey. Research has shown that in many mail surveys the people who do not respond to the study are of a different sort than those who do. If this is true, and a return rate of only 50 percent is achieved, the results are not likely to be realistic. Several measures may be taken to ensure realistic data which lack bias.

The most effective means of reducing nonrespondent bias is to obtain a high percentage of return by repeat contact with the nonrespondents. Essentially, this involves the mailing of additional reminder cards, letters, additional instruments, or a combination of these. A 60 percent return is considered good, but it is not sufficient

```
┌─────────────────────────────────────────────────────────────┐
│              [YOUR INSTITUTION'S LETTERHEAD]                  │
│                                                               │
│                                                               │
│                                                               │
│   Dear Stu,                                                   │
│                                                               │
│       In case you did not receive our earlier letter, this second │
│   copy of our form is designed to obtain suggestions from you for │
│   improving the offerings of our school.                      │
│                                                               │
│       Many of your 1973 classmates have already returned their │
│   forms.  Won't you please help us improve the opportunities avail- │
│   able to future students?  We have enclosed, for your convenience, │
│   a stamped envelope.  We would appreciate it very much if you │
│   would complete this form and return it to us immediately.   │
│                                                               │
│                           Sincerely,                          │
│                                                               │
│                                                               │
│                                                               │
│                           (Signature and title of             │
│                           administrator, teacher,             │
│                           or counselor)                       │
└─────────────────────────────────────────────────────────────┘
```

FIGURE 4–4   *Example Reminder Letter*

to eliminate the effect of bias. An 80 percent return is considered necessary to sufficiently alleviate such bias in a small, heterogeneous group such as former learners.

In a national study of secondary school students—Project TALENT—it was determined that an additional questionnaire was more effective than a reminder card or letter alone in eliciting responses. Therefore, since additional costs would be minimal, another instrument should be mailed with the reminder. Figure 4–4 presents an example of a reminder letter. Follow-up letters to nonrespondents should be mailed two weeks following the initial mailing. Subsequent mailings should be sent at two- or three-week intervals. Depending on the age of the former students, a letter sent to the parents, which indicates the purpose of the study and the need for a good return, might improve the return from nonrespondents.

Personal contact of a sample of nonrespondents is another strategy for ensuring that the results of the study are not biased. Telephone a small percentage of the nonrespondents, asking them to complete the instrument verbally over the phone or encouraging them to complete it and mail it. The information gained from this small group can be compared to that obtained from the regular respondents. If there is little or no difference between groups, then a lack of bias can be assumed and analysis of the results can begin. If a bias does appear, then further steps should be taken to increase the return.

PROCESSING FOLLOW-UP RESULTS

To be effective in evaluating programs and courses, a follow-up study must be carefully planned and executed. Careful development of the instrument and efficient administration of the study will facilitate the utilization of the follow-up findings.

Tabulating Responses

The first step which should be taken, once an adequate return has been received, is the tabulation of responses. The magnitude of the study as well as the financial and physical resources of the educational agency will determine the means by which the results are to be tabulated. For very small studies (under 100) results are best tabulated by hand. This involves the use of an uncompleted instrument to tally the responses. If a study involves over 100 former students, it may be advisable to use data processing equipment for tabulating and summarizing questionnaire responses.

In a larger study, the handling of responses may be very cumbersome and it is often difficult to maintain accuracy without the use of data processing facilities. Such processing requires that the responses on the questionnaire be transferred to a punched data processing card. The transfer of responses from the questionnaire to the punched card is done by coding—the assignment of a number to each response. Once responses are coded, they are punched into specific columns of the punch card. An accounting machine or computer is capable of reading the cards and making tabulations, calculating

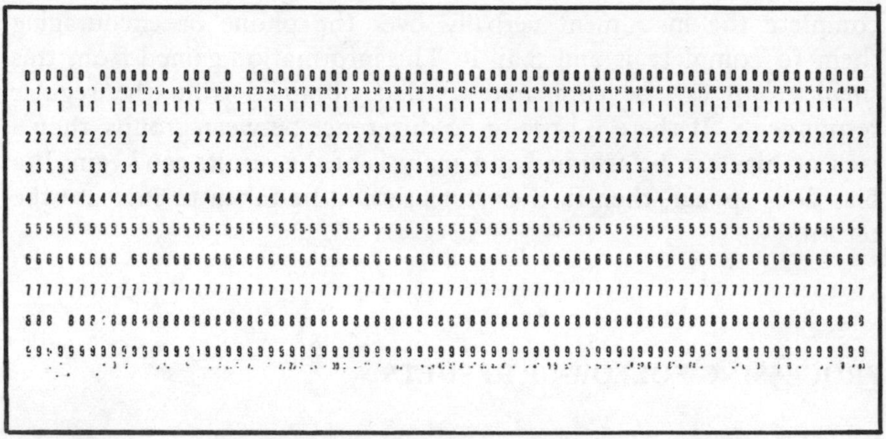

FIGURE 4–5   *Example Punched Item as Recorded on Data Card*

averages, and printing summaries of the results. Figure 4–5 shows an item which has been coded and punched.

Summarizing Responses

Once responses have been coded and transferred to punch cards, summaries can be generated. The director of the follow-up study will be required to identify the type of summary desired and to communicate his needs to data processing personnel. One possible summary format would be the presentation of percentages of the group who have responded to the alternatives for each item. For example, Item 4) in Figure 4–6 represents a computer output summary of tabulated responses to the following item:

4) What is your current employment or schooling status?
    ☐ In school full time
    ☐ In school part time
    ☒ In military service
    ☐ Housewife
    ☐ Unemployed
    ☐ Employed part time
    ☐ Employed full time

SCHOOL CODE= 419   FOLLOW-UP RESULTS FOR 1973-74 SCHOOL YEAR

4)   WHAT IS YOUR CURRENT EMPLOYMENT OR SCHOOLING STATUS?

25% - IN SCHOOL FULL TIME

10% - IN SCHOOL PART TIME

05% - IN MILITARY SERVICE

10% - HOUSEWIFE

15% - UNEMPLOYED

05% - EMPLOYED PART TIME

30% - EMPLOYED FULL TIME

FIGURE 4–6   *Example Report Summary for One Item*

4)   WHAT IS YOUR CURRENT EMPLOYMENT OR SCHOOL STATUS?

MALE	FEMALE	
10%	30%	IN SCHOOL FULL TIME
10%	10%	IN SCHOOL PART TIME
10%	00%	IN MILITARY SERVICE
00%	20%	HOUSEWIFE
15%	15%	UNEMPLOYED
05%	10%	EMPLOYED PART TIME
50%	15%	EMPLOYED FULL TIME

FIGURE 4–7   *Example Report Summary for Cross-Tabulation Item*

Responses can be analyzed and presented in more detail by cross-tabulations with some other factor such as sex or occupational area. The results of Item 4), represented in Figure 4–7 above, have been cross-tabulated by the sex of the respondents to identify differences between males and females in employment and schooling status. In addition to percentages, other formats can be utilized to present survey findings. These include averages, tallies, and histograms. Examples of these three formats are presented in the next chapter.

UTILIZING RESULTS

Altering Objectives and Content

The follow-up study may be conducted for very specific purposes—to determine the mobility of former students, or to determine the number of students who apply for entry into community colleges, industrial training programs, universities, or adult education programs. Information on the mobility of program graduates may ultimately affect the content of program objectives. Ultimately, a change in objectives and content will probably affect teaching methods, scheduling, and other factors, but generally these sorts of changes will need to be confirmed by other types of evaluation—consultative team evaluations, employer surveys, and cost-benefit evaluations.

Naturally, the most informative follow-up will combine information on a number of factors, and it is recommended that the evaluator collect as much information in one mailing as he possibly can. Often, defining the purpose of a follow-up too narrowly will lead to misconception about what is needed. Let's look at how one school district might be misled by follow-up information which covers only one factor. Example item 16 is a sample item which represents the compiled results from a follow-up of occupational students.

EXAMPLE ITEM 16

What is your current employment status?

☐ In-school   (45%)
☐ In school part time   (5%)
☐ Military service   (5%)
☐ Housewife   (20%)
☐ Unemployed   (3%)
☐ Employed part time   (5%)
☐ Employed full time   (20%)

From this example, we can see that a good proportion of students are in school after graduation from the program. In this particular example, the evaluator should look carefully at the objectives and content of his program. From this example, he might easily conc.ude that heavy emphasis should be placed on articulation with continuing education institutions. However, the results from only one question may be misleading. Suppose that the same survey turned up responses to the question presented in Example Item 17.

EXAMPLE ITEM 17

What were your reasons for continuing your education?

☐ I did not find a job in my field.   (35%)
☐ I did not feel adequately prepared for a job. (18%)
☐ I did work, but I did not feel challenged.   (8%)
☐ I always intended to go to school.   (45%)

Responses to a question of this sort can considerably alter the evaluator's conclusions regarding Example Item 16. Here, for example, a large proportion of students answered that they had gone to school because of an inability to find employment. Emphasis of the school might well be shifted to better prepare students for careers out of school than toward articulation of programs. Again, however, caution should guide the evaluator in this area. Certainly, if it is found that the articulation of programs is poor, the evaluator will not want to ignore this problem. Objectives for programs should accommodate this problem as well; only priority should be affected by the knowledge that most students would prefer to find employment after graduation.

The open-ended response item can provide a valuable source of information for making changes in objectives and content. Example Item 18 is such an item.

EXAMPLE ITEM 18

What skills should have been given more emphasis in your training program?

_____

_____

_____

The results of this type of item are, due to the nature of the item, more difficult to tabulate or average than other item types. However, responses to this item can be categorized with similar responses, and general tabulations can be presented such as the following:

> Skills former students feel should be emphasized:
> 21/130 Transcription
> 15/130 Telephone skills
> 14/130 Personal relations with co-workers

Interpretations are easily made from open-ended results.

Dissemination of results is particularly critical in evaluation that will alter or revise objectives and content. Undoubtedly there are persons on any staff who have strong feelings about the emphasis of a particular program. Dissemination of results to the entire staff will allow these people to understand the need for alteration of their objectives, or will stimulate them to make a case in support of their own interests. This may turn up new information which may indeed change the implications of previous follow-up data. By disseminating results for discussion, the evaluator is not only helping to insure utilization of results but is conducting a more thorough evaluation and checking the validity of his own interpretation.

In the case of evaluation results that indicate a change in objectives and content, the evaluator will again save time and effort by requesting the aid of the whole staff. Staff members should be asked to suggest amendments to objectives and, ideally, a meeting should be held at which staff members can present, promote, and defend their suggested changes.

Altering Job Descriptions

If revising job descriptions has been the purpose of your follow-up from the beginning, utilization of results may prove gratifyingly simple. If you have identified the general employment trends of graduates and have requested descriptive information concerning their current jobs, most of your work is complete. Again, it is best to request the aid of staff members—and perhaps employers—in interpreting and verifying this information. But a well-constructed item can ensure that this task is nearly complete. See the following example for graduates of a secretarial program.

EXAMPLE ITEM 19

Estimate the percentage of time you spend in the following tasks on an average day:

___ Typing
___ Transcription
___ Stenography
___ Duplicating
___ Operating calculators

Although different types of jobs may differ in the amount of time required for typing, transcribing, and so on, a calculation of the average percentage of time spent on each task by most graduates will be of greatest use to the evaluator. In most instances, it is not possible to identify specific categories or levels of secretarial positions; titles vary, and even secretaries holding identical titles in the same organization will have varied responsibilities. What this sort of item will yield is a generalized job description applicable to graduates of a particular program.

Naturally, results which provide the evaluator with revised job descriptions also contribute to the revision of program objectives. Should it be found that a large percentage of time is spent on any task by program graduates, this emphasis should be adequately reflected within that program. However, a strict percentage of time correlation cannot and should not be made. It is possible, for example, that a graduate will spend 35 percent time on a task which he can master in a two-week period. The important thing, really, is that the graduate has mastered that task.

Altering Placement Services

Follow-up of students, which indicates that students have been placed in jobs for which they were not prepared, has implications for placement services as well as for revision of objectives. If jobs are available at different levels and if placement staff can identify areas in which their graduates are over- or under-prepared, it will be their job to make reasonable judgments about placement of students in the future. These sorts of decisions are highly situational, and the necessity of personal judgment on the part of placement staff cannot be diminished by any systematized approach.

REFERENCES

Baird, L. L. and Holland, J. L. *The Flow of High School Students to Schools, Colleges, and Jobs.* Iowa City, Iowa: American College Testing Program, Report No. 26, 1968, vol. 30.

Byram, H. M. *Evaluation of Local Vocational Education Programs: A Manual for Administrators, Teachers, and Citizens.* Columbus: Center for Vocational and Technical Education, The Ohio State University, 1965.

Cox, J. A. *Utah Project "Follow-up": Interim Report.* Salt Lake City: Utah Research Coordinating Unit for Vocational and Technical Education, 1969.

Craig, J. S. (ed.) *Conference on Follow-up Studies in Educational Research, November, 1965.* Madison: Center for Studies in Vocational and Technical Education, Industrial Relations Institute, University of Wisconsin, 1965.

Droege, R. C. and Crambert, A. C. "Follow-up Techniques in a Large Scale Test Validation Study." *Journal of Applied Psychology,* 1965, vol. 49, no. 4.

Eninger, M. U. *The Process and Product of T and I High School Level Vocational Education in the United States: The Process Variables.* Pittsburgh: Educational Systems Research Institute, 1968.

Evans, R. N. (Chairman, Committee on Vocational, Technical, and Practical Arts Education). *Review of Educational Research,* Washington, D.C.: American Educational Research Association, vol. 32, no. 4.

Follow-up Study of Career-oriented Curriculums 1968—Phase I. Selden, New York: Suffolk County Community College, 1968.

Glaser, E. M. and Houston, C. G. *An Evaluation Follow-up Study of the JOC Experimental Demonstration Project for the Communities of Denver and Pueblo, Colorado.* Los Angeles: Human Interaction Institute, 1967, 116:28.

Goff, M. L. "Follow-up Procedure for Post-Secondary, Vocational-Technical Graduates." Cheyenne, Wyoming: State Department of Education, 1967, 11:34.

Harris, W. M. *A Proposed Model for an Information Storage and Retrieval System for Reporting Job Placement Follow-through Data of Persons Trained in Industrial Education Programs in California Public Schools* (Tentative Draft). Sacramento: California State Department of Education, 1967.

Howell, K. M. and Felstehausen, J. L. *A Follow-up Study of Illinois Home Economics Job Training Programs, Final Report.* Springfield: State of Illinois, Board of Vocational Education and Rehabilitation, Division of Vocational and Technical Education, 1971.

Little, J. K. *Review and Synthesis of Research on the Placement and Follow-up of Vocational Education Students.* Columbus: The Center for Vocational and Technical Education, The Ohio State University, 1970, pp. 24—25.

Mailey, P. J. *A Vocational-Technical Student Follow-up System.* Olympia: Washington State Board for Vocational Education, 1966.

Management Surveys for Schools, Their Uses and Abuses. Washington, D.C.: American Association of School Administrators, 1964.

McKinney, F. L. and Oglesby, C. *Developing and Conducting Follow-up Studies of Former Students.* Lexington: Kentucky Research Coordinating Unit, 1971.

Michigan Department of Education. *Guidelines for Conducting Follow-up Studies of Vocational and Technical Education Students.* Lansing: Division of Vocational Education, 1965, 8:33.

Moore, "Increasing the Returns from Questionnaires." *Journal of Educational Research,* 1941, 35:138—141.

Norman, R. D. "A Review of Some Problems Related to the Mail Questionnaire Technique." *Educational and Psychological Measurement,* 1948, 8:235—245.

Norton, R. "Planning and Conducting Follow-up Studies." Paper read at the Multistate Evaluation Workshop, East Lansing, Michigan, 1970.

O'Conner, T. J. *Follow-up Studies in Junior Colleges: A Tool for Institutional Improvement.* Washington, D.C., American Association of Junior Colleges, 1965.

Oppenheim, A. N. *Questionnaire Design and Attitude Measurement.* New York: Basic Books, Inc., 1966, pp. 83—92.

Orr, D. B. and Neyman, C. A., Jr. "Considerations, Costs, and Returns in a Large Scale Follow-up Study." *Journal of Educational Research,* 1965, p. 58.

Payne, D. A. *The Specification and Measurement of Learning Outcomes.* Waltham, Massachusetts: Blaisdell Publishing Co., 1968.

Pucel, D. J.; Nelson, H. F.; and Wheeler, D. N. *Questionnaire Follow-up Returns as a Function of Incentives and Responder Characteristics.* Minneapolis: Department of Industrial Education, University of Minnesota, 1969, p. 34.

Santa Cruz County Schools Student Follow-up Survey, A Manual for Use by Administrators, Counselors, Teachers, and Data Processing Personnel. Santa Cruz, California: Board of Education, 1968.

Schwarzweller, H. K. *Research Design, Field Work Procedure, and Data Collection Problems in a Follow-up Study of Young Men from Eastern Kentucky.* (Rural Sociology Department, R. S. 21), Lexington: University of Kentucky, 1963.

Scott, C. "Research on Mail Surveys." *Journal of the Royal Statistical Society.* 1961, Ser. A, 124:143.

Sharp, L. M. and Krashegor, R. *The Use of Follow-up Studies in the Evaluation of Vocational Education.* Washington, D.C.: Bureau of Social Science Research, Inc., 1968.

Snelling, W. R. "Impact of a Personalized Mail Questionnaire." *Journal of Educational Research.* 1969, 63:126–129.

Squires, C. E. *An Instrument to Evaluate MDTA Institutional Training Projects in Arizona.* Phoenix: Arizona State Department of Vocational Education, 1968, 39:34.

5

The Follow-up as an Evaluative Tool: The Employer Survey

WHY AN EMPLOYER SURVEY?

An employer survey can provide valuable evaluative information to the managers of occupational programs. This type of survey can be executed in a number of ways; the scope of the survey, the number of employers to be surveyed, and the resources available to the local educational agency will determine the method to be utilized. For most occupational programs the mail survey is superior in terms of resource allocation. However, it is possible that in some instances the telephone interview will prove to be the most efficient method for conducting follow-up of learners through their employers.

An employer survey may vary from a simple survey of the number of available jobs in specific occupations to an estimation or rating of the competencies held by former students. Several objectives or goals for an employer survey are discussed below. Local program managers may combine many of these objectives or may formulate entirely different and additional ones.

To Assess the Performance of Former Students

If the viability of competency lists has been assessed by means of a survey, or through the use of advisory committees, the employer survey may focus on the competencies actually *possessed* by employees who are former occupational students. This can be accomplished by asking the employer to rate former students on each of a given list of skills. Another approach is to present a list of competencies, instructing the employer to identify those that the former student is lacking. This assessment may also be applied to "general competencies," such as "ability to get along with individuals," and such general assessments may be conducted regardless of the type of program being evaluated. A more detailed survey might focus on

166

specific job competencies such as "ability to adjust automobile brakes properly." At any rate, the focus of the employer survey should be determined by the unit being evaluated.

To Determine How Specific Program Graduates Compare with Graduates of Other Training Programs

It is often useful to know where individuals working in specific jobs have obtained their training or preparation for the job. This information can be valuable in discovering duplication of training efforts within a community. Whether duplications are or are not in existence, it may prove valuable to know how the graduates of your program compare to the graduates of others based upon employer rating. Some individuals may have entered specific occupations without any training. In this case, it may be useful to determine how they differ from those who have had training. Comparisons of this sort may be general in nature or may relate to specific competencies.

To Elicit Employer Recommendations for Improving the Occupational Program

This objective integrates many possible objectives for the employer survey. In addition to assessing competency lists and rating the performance of their employees, employers can make suggestions for improving the current offerings and better preparing learners for productive careers.

To Determine the Recruitment Practices of Employing Agencies

An important contribution of the employer survey is the better understanding of recruitment practices used by employing agencies. Employers may be asked questions regarding the sources used to locate new employees, or more specific questions may be asked dealing with the expectations of prospective employers. Both of these types of questions can help the local educational agency do a better job of selecting, training, and placing students in an appropriate way. Employers may be asked such questions as: *What competencies do you require that a clerical employee possess?* Or, *what characteristics do you desire in a prospective employee?* Even recruitment practices may throw some light on the relative merits of a program. Other questions might be: *How do you select among graduates of the same program?* Or, *How do you select graduates from different programs?* Answers to these questions may be useful in many ways; many times such answers will aid in the development of new programs or in the organization of job orientation courses.

To Assess the Competency List of a Specific Course or Program

The reaction of employers to competency lists is often invaluable in the evaluation of specific programs or courses (e. g., dental technician or legal secretary). A survey directed toward the assessment of competency lists will help the evaluator determine whether competencies identified by many instructors or program managers are realistically reflecting former students' actual job requirements.

To Estimate Supply and Demand for Individuals in Particular Occupations

A secondary benefit supplied by an employer survey is an estimation of supply and demand. Employers of graduates can be asked questions such as: How many employees did you hire last year? Five years ago? How many do you expect to hire within the next two years, and so on. Questions of this sort enable you as program personnel to gain a general feeling for employment trends. However, if an in-depth supply and demand study is your primary goal, then it should be undertaken in addition to the employer survey.

To Aid the Public Relations of the Educational or Training Agency or Institution

Another side benefit of the employer survey is improved public relations between the school and the employing community. Most employers are very willing to become involved in the instructional programs of the community, and any opportunity to involve them should be capitalized upon. The employer survey is an excellent way to involve employers in the development of the educational program.

These are all possible purposes or reasons for conducting the employer survey. You may have additional concerns to add to these, or several of these may meet your intended purposes for the follow-up survey.

WHO SHOULD BE INVOLVED IN THE EMPLOYER SURVEY?

One of the first things to do is determine who should work on the survey. Experience has shown that the team approach to the employer survey is the most efficient and useful approach. It is important to involve individuals who will not only contribute to the conduct of the survey but who will be responsible for carrying through and utilizing the results.

School or Agency Administration

In most cases, the program manager or the chief administrator of a particular program should assume the leadership role in conducting the employer survey. In some instances, this individual may wish to delegate responsibility for some of the individual activities to his staff. As is true with the student follow-up, the involvement of school or agency administration is essential if any use is to be made of evaluation results in terms of changes in instructional and supportive programs.

Instructional Staff

Moreover, the instructional personnel of the program under consideration should be involved in the development and implementation of the employer survey. Most likely it will be these individuals, the instructional personnel, who will actually make any program changes based upon the results of the employer survey, and their involvement will ensure their understanding of the necessity or importance of making changes. The involvement of instructional personnel may have additional benefits. Even if major program changes are not warranted by the evaluation, instructional personnel may be moved to change the orientation of their teaching as a result of their involvement in the employer survey.

Guidance Personnel

Counseling or placement staff members should also be involved in the employer survey. In many instances, these individuals are also involved in the conduct of a student follow-up survey, since they maintain student records and are many times responsible for reporting on the placement of students. Many times the placement staff members maintain a file of student names and employers which can become a very important source for identifying the employers of graduates and the focal points for the employer survey.

Citizens' Advisory Council

Another important group of individuals who can contribute significantly to the employer survey is the advisory committee. In some cases, the committee can play a primary role in the survey, participating in the development and tryout of instruments and the subsequent implementation of suggestions for utilizing the results. Because of their unique perspective, the advisory committee members will offer valuable reactions to collected information. Even if they do not participate directly, it may be beneficial to have members "sanction" the survey by supplying the letterhead of the committee chairman for the mailings. Because committee members are often well known in their community, this approach can elicit a much better response from employers. It is also possible to involve members in the telephoning of employers. The advisory committee should be involved from the beginning of the survey, beginning with the selection and establishment of purposes for the survey.

THE DESIGN OF THE EMPLOYER SURVEY

Like any other evaluation or other type of educational activity, the employer survey must be well planned. Planning must be based upon a well-conceived objective or desired outcome and must involve both those individuals who will conduct the survey and those who will utilize the results. Also, decisions will need to be made regarding the method to be used in the survey and in the selection and identification of those employers who will be questioned.

Determining the Desired Outcome

The desired "outcome" of the employer survey may be indicated by any of the objectives suggested at the beginning of this chapter, or it may reflect the combination of a number of these purposes or the addition of some that did not exist in the initial listing. Determining desired outcomes should help to delimit the scope of the employer survey. Although determining the post-program performance of former students might be the *desired purpose,* it is yet necessary to define the scope in terms of what class or what program is to be assessed for what time frame. For example, the more specific purpose might be the assessment of post-program performance of the former students of the electronics technician program for last year. Of course, the scope could be much broader than this; it could be assessment of the graduates of all industrially oriented programs, of all business education programs, or of all sales training programs. The desire of the institution and its staff along with the consideration of financial and personnel resources for conducting the survey will be factors which will contribute to the decision regarding scope. To delineate the purposes and scope of the survey, and to aid later development of the instrument, it is suggested that one or more broad key questions be stated. One possible key question was presented earlier: *How do the graduates of our electronics technician program perform in a work setting?* Another key question might be: *How do the graduates of our electronics technician program compare to those employees who have been trained on the job?* For some surveys, just one of these questions may be sufficient; however, if a broader survey is being conducted with emphasis on more than post-program performance of graduates, then a number of these key questions should be formulated.

Determine the Method to be Utilized in the Survey

Basically, there are three methods that can be utilized in the conduct of the employer survey—the personal interview, telephone interview, and mail survey. The specific advantages and disadvantages of each one of these methods was discussed in detail in Chapter 4, and only a summary will be presented in this chapter.

The personal interview is probably the most costly technique for collecting employer follow-up information. However, this method does allow the interviewer the opportunity to establish rapport with each employer and to convince him of the importance of the study. Also, the personal interview allows the interviewer to probe into the underlying reasons for specific responses to questions. If improvement of public relations is one function of the employer survey, then the personal interview technique is probably the most efficient means of achieving this goal. These attributes make the personal interview one of the most potentially accurate methods of gathering information. The primary disadvantage of the personal interview is its cost in terms of required personnel time and travel to the employment site. This in itself could limit the gathering of information from employers who are not in the immediate community.

The telephone interview can overcome some of the disadvantages of the personal interview while maintaining some of its advantages. The telephone interview allows the interviewer to explain the purpose and the importance of the study and to ask a set of prepared questions. Although the cost of interview personnel is still a sizeable one, travel costs are avoided with the telephone interview.

The mail questionnaire is probably the most efficient way of gathering employer survey information. Costs for this method are very low and the mail questionnaire can reach any employer regardless of his location. Probably the greatest disadvantage of the mail questionnaire is its rate of return, and precautionary measures should be employed to ensure that the employer is motivated to complete and return the survey instrument. Weighing these advantages and disadvantages against personnel and financial resources available to the local agency, the local education personnel should select one of these methods to be utilized for the survey. Special considerations for the development of the particular type of instrument will then be needed.

DEVELOPMENT OF THE EMPLOYER SURVEY INSTRUMENT

Once the survey method has been chosen, attention should be given to the development of an instrument to be used for structuring the interviews, instruments, and method for recording results from the survey. An instrument, whether used with a personal, telephone, or mail questionnaire survey, usually contains a series of questions to be asked of the employer with categories for his response. The entire instrument, including each of its items, must relate to the key questions and the overall purposes of the employer survey (discussed previously).

Key questions such as: *How do the graduates of our electronics technician program perform in a work setting?* delineate the focus of the survey. The evaluator may develop a series of these or may focus on one or two questions. Given just this one example key question, it can be seen that there are many facets to the performance of graduates in a work setting. Therefore it is necessary to define even more precisely the focus of the survey. Taking this key question, the evaluator would want to specify another series of questions, which we will consider here to be criterion questions, to make more specific our general concern about the electronics technician program. Some example criterion questions are: *How are general job traits of our graduates perceived by employers? How are specific job competencies of our graduates perceived by employers?*

Many similar questions can be derived from our general key question. Once criterion questions have been developed, then specific instrument items can be formulated. A number of items can be written to correspond to the first criterion question: *How are general job traits of our graduates perceived by employers?* Items may make direct reference to any of several job traits, including dependability, responsibility, initiative, and so on. The instrument item simply asks the respondent to rate an employee on a specific job trait. Example Items 1, 2, and 3 present these traits with a rating scale ranging from a low of 1 to a high of 9.

EXAMPLE ITEM 1

	Low	Average	High
Dependability: promptness, reliability in attendance	1 2 3	4 5 6	7 8 9

EXAMPLE ITEM 2

	Low	Average	High
Responsibility: willingness with which work is accepted and performed	1 2 3	4 5 6	7 8 9

EXAMPLE ITEM 3

	Low	Average	High
Initiative: ability to plan and direct own work	1 2 3	4 5 6	7 8 9

Another example involving the second criterion question, *How are specific job competencies of our graduates perceived by employers?* can also be utilized to specify and formulate instrument items. Here, specific job competencies are defined and expanded into instrument items. For evaluating an auto mechanics program, Example Items 4, 5, 6, and 7 have been developed from this initial key question.

EXAMPLE ITEM 4

	Very Adequate	Adequate	Inadequate	Cannot Determine
Use of micrometers	☐	☐	☐	☐

EXAMPLE ITEM 5

	Very Adequate	Adequate	Inadequate	Cannot Determine
Use of compression gauge	☐	☐	☐	☐

EXAMPLE ITEM 6

	Very Adequate	Adequate	Inadequate	Cannot Determine
Use of vacuum gauge	☐	☐	☐	☐

EXAMPLE ITEM 7

	Very Adequate	Adequate	Inadequate	Cannot Determine
Use of ammeter	☐	☐	☐	☐

You will note that a different scale has been used for rating these specific job competencies than was used for the general job traits. The scale possesses four rating categories ranging from *very adequate* to *inadequate*, with an additional category for *cannot determine*. These are but two of the possible types of rating scales which can be employed. There are many more types of questionnaire items, however, that can be included in the employer survey instrument, such as the multiple choice item, which has proved to be very useful. The example shown here is directed toward determining the sources of recruitment practices by employers.

EXAMPLE ITEM 8

What is your primary source for recruitment of employees?

    a) State employment agency
    b) Secondary school counseling offices
    c) Community college placement offices
    d) Walk-in applicants
    e) Newspaper ads

Rating items can also be used to obtain some type of measure of an employee's performance. Example Item 9 is directed toward rating the suitability of the employee for the kind of job held and has categories ranging from exceptionally able to not at all suited.

EXAMPLE ITEM 9

How would you rate the suitability of the employee previously named for the kind of job he holds?
    ☐ Exceptionally able
    ☐ Well
    ☐ Acceptable
    ☐ Poorly
    ☐ Not at all suited

Survey items can also be of the ranking type. The ranking item asks the employer to rank order either a list of items or to select out in rank order a small number of items within the list. Example Item 10 asks that the employer rank only three of the most important items. This rule should be followed when more than four items are presented since it becomes difficult to rank a very long list.

EXAMPLE ITEM 10

Below is a list of personal qualities and job skills. Check the box before the *three you consider most important for a person entering the job previously identified.*

☐ Ability to get along with others
☐ Initiative
☐ Positive attitude toward work
☐ Appearance and grooming
☐ Judgment
☐ Dependability
☐ Accuracy, quality
☐ Attendance and punctuality

The last type of item that can be included in the survey instrument is the open-ended item, and it can provide information that no other type of item can. Open-ended items are often of special value because, by giving an employer a free hand, the evaluation team may learn of problems they were previously unaware of and consequently did not ask questions about.

EXAMPLE ITEM 11

What would you recommend be added to our current electronics program?

_____

_____

_____

Specific suggestions for constructing the item types given here have been presented in Chapters 3, 4, and 7. The reader is referred to these chapters for more detailed information regarding the construction of questionnaire and survey items.

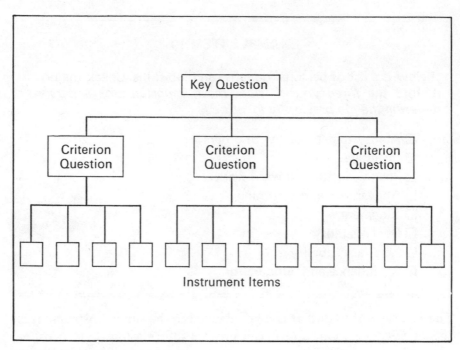

FIGURE 5–1   *Schematic of Instrument Item Development*

To summarize, the survey instrument begins in the form of a key question, becoming more specific with the delineation of criterion questions from which instrument items are lastly developed. Figure 5–1 presents schematically how this progression flows.

Once items have been prepared there are two other considerations or concerns. First, the items must be organized into an instrument in a consistent and meaningful format. Items should be grouped both according to similar format (i. e., items with similar rating categories should be combined) and according to criterion questions. Grouping facilitates response to the questionnaire and allows the employer to see the logic and significance of each individual item, which adds to the entire face validity of the instrument.

The final consideration for instrument development is the formulation of directions to go along with the instrument. They should be instructive to the employer, both in terms of the overall instrument and in terms of specific directions for each type of item included in the instrument. Overall directions should stress the importance of the survey being conducted as well as include an indication of who is conducting the survey.

Once the instrument items have been assembled and directions developed, the instrument should be perfected via a trial run and reviewed by several groups. The first step to the testing of the survey instrument is to have the staff of the program review each item contained in the instrument. This can be done either on an individual basis or in a group. If done individually, each staff member should be asked to read the instrument and to make comments on the form.

EVALUATION OF EMPLOYEE'S HIGH SCHOOL PREPARATION FOR EMPLOYMENT

To the Employer or Supervisor of:

Employee's Name

1. In what capacity are you related to the employee named above? (Check the box.)

   1 ☐ Employer   2 ☐ Supervisor   3 ☐ Other_____
                                                      (Write in)

2. What is the title of the job for which this employee is hired?_____
                                                      (Job title)

3. In the following aspects of employment, how well prepared was the employee previously named for the job for which hired? (Circle the number below the answer.)

-25

	Not at all	Poorly	Some-what	Well	Does not apply
1. Job know-how, application of technical knowledge and skill	1	2	3	4	5
2. Use of tools and equipment	1	2	3	4	5
3. Selection and care of space, materials, and supplies	1	2	3	4	5
4. Quality of work, ability to meet quality demands	1	2	3	4	5
5. Quantity of work, output of satisfactory amount	1	2	3	4	5
6. Cooperativeness, ability to work with others	1	2	3	4	5
7. Accepting advice and supervision	1	2	3	4	5
8. Dependability, thorough completion of a job without supervision	1	2	3	4	5
9. Initiative, doing jobs that need doing	1	2	3	4	5
10. Attendance, reporting for work regularly	1	2	3	4	5
11. Appearance, presenting a business image	1	2	3	4	5
12. Adaptable to new situations	1	2	3	4	5
13. Being able to talk to the boss about job related problems	1	2	3	4	5
14. Serving the public, patient, etc.	1	2	3	4	5
15. Safety habits, minimizing chance for accidents	1	2	3	4	5

4. How would you rate the suitability of the employee previously named for the kind of job held? (Check the box that applies.)

   1 ☐ Exceptionally able
   2 ☐ Well
   3 ☐ Acceptable
   4 ☐ Poorly
   5 ☐ Not at all

5. Below is a list of personal qualities and job skills. Check the box before the three you consider most important for a person entering the job held by the previously named employee.

   1 ☐ Ability to get along with others— other workers, customers, patients
   2 ☐ Initiative
   3 ☐ Positive attitude toward work
   4 ☐ Appearance and grooming
   5 ☐ Judgment—ability to make decisions, ability to plan and organize
   6 ☐ Competency in using job tools, machines, and materials
   7 ☐ Dependability
   8 ☐ Accuracy, quality, and thoroughness
   9 ☐ Attendance and punctuality
   10 ☐ Work quantity
   11 ☐ Other_____
                  (Write in)

Use the back of this sheet for other suggestions concerning high school occupational training.

FIGURE 5–2   *Example Employer Survey Instrument (reproduced from "Follow-up Report on Illinois" by Felstehausen et al., Charleston: Eastern Illinois University, 1973).*

The instrument should then be returned to the person in charge of instrument development for his synthesis of the comments and resultant revisions. In the case of a group review, the staff should discuss each item with the person in charge of the instrument development, who would make notations for subsequent changes. The second important task in testing the instrument is to have the advisory committee review it. Committee members, many of them employers, are in a very good position to judge the content and format of the employer survey instrument. This is also an excellent way to involve the advisory committee in the total effort of the employer survey. A third step to consider is mailing out the instrument to several employers, asking them to react to the content of the instrument, but usually this information can be gained from advisory committee members. Figure 5–2 is an example of a concise but complete employer survey instrument.

ADMINISTRATION OF THE EMPLOYER SURVEY

Once the instrument has been developed and reviewed by both staff and advisory committee members, there remain several steps to be taken in the actual administration of the survey. Employers must be selected, their addresses or telephone numbers identified, an introduction must be developed, coding and recording of responses must be planned, follow-up methods determined, and interviewers may need to be trained.

The Selection of Employers

The first step in the actual administration of the employer survey should be the identification of employers to be surveyed and their addresses or telephone numbers obtained. If a student or learner follow-up study has been conducted within the last several years, this study may be used as a source. Or, if a student or learner follow-up is being conducted in conjunction with or simultaneously with the employer survey, an item may be included in the student follow-up survey asking the name and address of the student's employer and immediate supervisor. For an employer survey, it is important to specify each individual's name rather than simply sending the survey to the employing agency. Because this personalizes the survey, it helps to ensure an adequate return or response to the instrument.

If a learner follow-up is not being conducted, it may be necessary to telephone the individual former student and ask him the name of his immediate supervisor or employer, or it may prove to be just as easy to conduct a learner follow-up. In many cases, this type of activity can be conducted by clerical or secretarial staff members. Also, it is often possible to telephone the student's parent, whose name can be obtained from student records, requesting that he indicate the student's place of employment and immediate supervisor.

Development of a Cover Letter or Interview Introduction

If a mail survey is being conducted, a cover letter must be prepared to accompany the instrument. This letter should attempt to establish rapport between the educational or training agency and the employer, indicating the purposes of the survey and giving some indication of how the results will be utilized. Since the mail survey instrument pretty much stands alone, it is important that the employer be convinced that his contribution will be of some use and will warrant the time spent on completing the instrument. Many times it is advantageous to involve the advisory committee in the development of this letter. Figure 5–3 presents an example cover letter designed to accompany a survey instrument. In addition to involving the committee in the development of the letter, it may prove fruitful to duplicate this letter on the letterhead of the advisory committee chairman, adding his signature. This indicates that the advisory committee has sanctioned the survey, and employers and supervisors within the community may be more likely to respond to such a survey instrument than to one mailed solely by the educational or training institution.

```
┌─────────────────────────────────────────────────────────────────┐
│                  [YOUR INSTITUTION'S LETTERHEAD]                  │
│                                                                   │
│                                                                   │
│                                                                   │
│  Dear Employer or Supervisor:                                     │
│                                                                   │
│      We are currently evaluating the effectiveness of the occupa- │
│  tional training we provide high school youth.  One of our occupa-│
│  tional training objectives is to equip students with job skills  │
│  required to enter the world of work.  As the employer or supervisor│
│  of one of our former students, you can help us determine if we are│
│  doing what we have set out to do.                                │
│                                                                   │
│      Will you take a few minutes to assess the preparation for    │
│  employment of the employee named on the enclosed evaluation form?│
│  This is designed to give us vital information for determining the │
│  effectiveness and identifying strengths and weaknesses of present│
│  occupational training programs.  No employee, employers, supervisor│
│  or business will be identified in the results of this study.  All│
│  responses to questions will be kept in strict confidence.        │
│                                                                   │
│      Would you complete the evaluation form as soon as possible   │
│  and mail it in the enclosed stamped envelope?  Thank you for your│
│  valuable contribution to the improvement of job training for future│
│  students.                                                        │
│                                                                   │
│                              Sincerely,                           │
│                                                                   │
│                                                                   │
│                                                                   │
│                              (Signature and title of a            │
│                              local school administrator)          │
└─────────────────────────────────────────────────────────────────┘
```

FIGURE 5–3   *Example Employer Survey Cover Letter—First Mailing (adapted from "Follow-up Report on Illinois" by Felstehausen et al., Charleston: Eastern Illinois University, 1973).*

If a telephone interview is used in the employer survey, an introduction to be delivered by the interviewer must be developed. This introduction must establish rapport, indicate the purposes of the survey and, in some way, convince the employer or survey respondent that the survey is of importance and worthy of the time that it will require. This introduction should not necessarily be *read* to the employer, but the interviewer should be given adequate guidelines for conducting this portion of the interview.

Coding and Recording of Responses

In a survey of this nature, it is important to receive as high a return or response rate as possible, and precautionary and remediary steps should be taken to increase the response rate. The follow-up of nonrespondents is one means of increasing the rate following the initial mailing of a survey instrument. Likewise, in the case of a telephone interview, the repeated telephoning of individuals who do not answer initially should be employed. To follow up nonrespondents, it is necessary to record who has responded and who has not responded, and this means that instruments must be coded. An identifying code should be located someplace on each mail questionnaire or someplace on the recording form for each telephone interview. On the mail questionnaire the respondent should be informed of the purpose of the code either in the directions to the instrument or in the cover letter. This will help to alleviate any fears that the respondent will be singled out in the reporting of results.

Training of Interview Personnel

When the telephone or personal interview technique is utilized in the employer survey, it will be necessary either to hire interviewers or use current staff as interviewers. If experienced interviewers are used, they will need to be oriented to the specific instrument and items to be included in the interview. Also, methods for recording responses and techniques for handling nonrespondents should be clarified.

If current secretarial or professional staff members are utilized in the interviewing role, then possibly more attention should be paid to this orientation. It is important that interviewers do more than simply read questions and mark responses to them. The personal and telephone interview are probably two of the most efficient and effective ways of facilitating public relations between the educational agency and the employing community. Consequently, it is important to make a good impression upon the employers during the conduct of the survey. The director of the employer survey will probably want to refer to an existing guide for input concerning interviewing techniques to pass on to his interview staff. Figure 5–4 contains several hints for inexperienced interviewers.

Principles of Interviewing

Interviewing is a basic method—a machine—of the Three Phase Evaluation System. An interview then, is not just a conversation; it is, rather, a carefully thought out technique for finding out from respondents (the people we interview) how things are and how people feel and think. The interview itself is not intended to change or influence the respondent. The interviewer, therefore, must be an understanding person, capable of accepting what the respondent says without judging or rejecting him.

We know that in order to understand a person we must know what some of his needs are. A respondent in an interview situation has needs which the interviewer must understand and try to meet:

___ the respondent needs to see the interviewer as someone who is not a threat to his immediate or future well-being, nor to his self-esteem;

| he needs to see the Evaluation itself as not posing a threat;

| he needs to understand, even in a limited way, the purpose of the evaluation, the reason he was selected and why his cooperation is required;

| he needs to see the interview situation as a pleasant way of spending some time;

| he needs to feel, after the interview is completed, that he has had a real opportunity to express himself freely on the subject.

To meet these needs of the respondent, the interviewer must be very conscious of what he is doing and how he is doing it. Certain techniques should be followed to help insure a good interviewing relationship, as well as to obtain an accurate, unbiased interview. Let us now turn to a discussion of some of those techniques and procedures.

Establishing and Maintaining Good Interviewing Relations

A good interviewing relationship requires that the respondent feel relaxed and at ease with the interviewer—to the point where he feels free to say what he really thinks or feels about a given subject, without fear of criticism or disapproval. To maintain an atmosphere of this kind, the interviewer must have a sympathetic interest in people and the ability to recognize and understand their feelings. He must respond in both an encouraging, reassuring or supportive way. But support should not influence or bias the content of what they say. Assuming you have the basic conviction and sincerity necessary to good interviewing, you will rapidly become sensitive to the moments in an interview where encouragement or reassurance is needed, but some standard professional procedure will help you both to minimize the need and to deal with it when it arises.

Generally, keep the following points in mind while conducting an interview:

a. Be friendly and informal but, at the same time, professional in your manner. Remember that you are a stranger, and everything you say or do should help to gain the respondent's confidence in you as well as in himself.

b. Be a sympathetic, interested and attentive listener. Encouraging nods, "uh-huh's," "I know how you feel," and similar gestures will convey to the respondent that he is understood and that his opinions are valued and appreciated. But don't overdo it! There's nothing quite so distracting to the average person as the listener who keeps up a running stream of "uh-huh," "is that so," when it's not needed. A nod of the head is usually a much more articulate way of showing your interest than a constant clucking in the background, which many respondents will feel is a camouflage for a lack of genuine interest in them and their problems.

c. Be neutral with respect to the subject matter. Do not express your own opinions either on the subjects being discussed by the respondent or on the respondent's ideas about those subjects. You must never betray feelings of shock, surprise, indignation or disapproval at what the respondent is saying either by word or involuntary gesture. Your job is to understand and accept what he is saying, not to approve or disapprove of it, nor to agree or disagree with it.

d. Be observant. Be alert to the way in which the respondent expresses himself and to the gestures he uses. These signs may serve as cues that the respondent is becoming uncomfortable and ill-at-ease or that he is not expressing what he really feels.

e. Last but not least, be at ease yourself, in the interview situation. If you feel hesitant, embarrassed, hurried, or awkward, the respondent will soon sense this feeling and behave accordingly.

Beyond these standard points applicable to all inverviews, there are some respondents or situations that require encouragement or reassurance either in getting the interview started or during its course. The cardinal principle in all of these cases is to put the respondent at his ease and to get him interested in the interview, so frequently you will know what to do simply by putting yourself in the respondent's position, and asking yourself how you would be feeling under those circumstances.

FIGURE 5–4 Interviewing Hints (reproduced from "Team Member Handbook," Springfield: State of Illinois, 1974).

Follow-up of Nonrespondents

A good response requires that the response rate be representative of all employers of students of a particular program. The size of the survey, of course, will determine the exact response rate required. However, in most instances 70 or 80 percent return of a mail questionnaire is thought to be adequately representative. As recommended in the discussion of the student follow-up survey (see Chapter 4), it is possible to resurvey a sample of those individuals who did not respond and to compare their responses with those of the initial responding groups. If no differences occur, then it can be assumed that the obtained sample is representative of the total group being surveyed. However, if the differences do occur, then it will be necessary to take further remedial action in obtaining a better response to the survey.

EMPLOYER/SUPERVISOR SURVEY REMINDER NOTICE
SECOND MAILING

Dear Employer or Sxpervisor:

HELP!!! We're looking for a MISSING EVALXATION FORM! If yox've retxrned yoxr "Evalxatin of Employee's High School Preparation for Employment" form yox've already helped and don't need to read the rest of this message.

This message may be a little hard to read becaxse the u is missing on oxr typewriter. The other 44 keys are fxnctioning properly, bxt one key makes a big difference. Oxr sxrvey is mxch like the typewriter. If we're to have a meaningfxl sxrvey, yox are important.

Yox are <u>only one person</u>, bxt one person can really make a difference jxst as <u>only one key</u> made a disaster oxt of this message! Yox can make yoxr contribxtion to the improvement of employment preparation of fxtxre high school stxdents simply by mailing yoxr completed evalxation form today.

THANK YOX

FIGURE 5–5   *Example Reminder Card for Nonresponding Employers (reproduced from "Follow-up Illinois" by Felstehausen et al., Charleston: Eastern Illinois University, 1973).*

[YOUR INSTITUTION'S LETTERHEAD]

Dear Employer or Supervisor:

In case you did not receive our earlier letter, this second copy of the evaluation form is being sent so you will have the opportunity to let us know how you feel about the high school occupational training provided youth.

The early responses to our request for information from the employer/supervisors of our former students have been rewarding. An analysis of returns seems to indicate that employer/supervisors welcome the opportunity to assist school personnel in providing realistic employment education for students.

Won't you help us improve the occupational training of future students by mailing your completed evaluation form today? We have enclosed, for your convenience, a stamped envelope addressed to the data processing agency at our institution. Again let me assure you that your answers will be kept in strict confidence.

Thank you for your assistance.

Sincerely,

(Signature and title of a
local school administrator)

FIGURE 5–6   *Example Cover Letter for Third Mailing to Nonresponding Employers (reproduced from "Follow-up Report on Illinois" by Felstehausen et al., Charleston: Eastern Illinois University, 1973).*

In order to follow up on those individuals who have not responded, it is necessary to have a record of the individuals whose responses you have received. Those who have not responded then become the focus of the follow-up of nonrespondents. For the mail survey, normal procedure involves the mailing of a follow-up letter or card to those individuals who have not responded, along with an additional copy of the survey instrument. Figure 5–5 presents an example follow-up card for the nonrespondents of a mail employer survey. Figure 5–6 represents a second follow-up letter which should be mailed if the particular respondent has not responded after the initial reminder.

Another means of following up nonrespondents to the mail survey is to contact those individuals by telephone, asking them to react or respond to the survey by mail—or by giving their verbal response on the phone. In the case where the telephone interview is utilized for the entire survey, then continual contact should be attempted with those individuals of the survey until an 85 or 90 percent return has been achieved. Of course, in most instances it will happen that not all employers will wish to spend the time in answering questions over the telephone. In these cases, the fact will simply need to be accepted. However, if a great number of employers express a negative attitude toward the survey, possibly the administrators of the survey should reassess their approach.

SUMMARIZING AND PRESENTING THE RESULTS

Once all responses to the survey have been obtained, or at least a good proportion of the responses, you will want to begin summarizing the information which has been gathered. There are two basic means of summarizing questionnaire or survey information. If a small survey involving less than 100 individuals is being conducted, a hand tally of the results is probably the most efficient means of summarization. Hand tallying can usually be done by a clerical staff member and does not require the professional abilities of an administrator or of an instructor. However, if a much larger survey is being conducted, for example the employers of the entire occupational student body for a particular year or number of years, you may wish to use the computer to summarize the results. Of course, the availability of the computer or other data processing facilities will influence this decision. Computer summarization has the advantage that it is much faster and much easier to manipulate numbers, but the time saved here must be weighed against the time necessary to keypunch responses onto computer cards. The means of reporting which is desired on the part of the survey staff will, of course, have an influence on the way the summarization is handled.

Once the results have been summarized, they should be presented in a simple and meaningful manner. The audiences of this report will probably be the instructional staff, advisory committee, administration of your institution, and possibly even students of the involved programs. Therefore, the report in which the results are presented should not be a technical research report but should be a report which everyone can understand. There are several different techniques or formats for presenting survey results.

First of all, simple tallies can be presented. Example Item 12 shows how the responses to a particular rating item—initiative—can be presented with categories of low, average, and high.

EXAMPLE ITEM 12

	LOW	AVERAGE	HIGH
Initiative	~~HHT~~ II	~~HHT~~ ~~HHT~~ ~~HHT~~	~~HHT~~ ~~HHT~~ ~~HHT~~

Each line represented in these categories indicates one individual's response.

Percentages can also be used for presenting responses to the same item with numbers within each category indicating the percentage of the total group who responded in a particular way. Example Item 13 shows this method.

EXAMPLE ITEM 13

	LOW	AVERAGE	HIGH
Initiative	20%	40%	40%

Also histograms or bar graphs can be used to show relationship of specific groups on individual items. For example, Example Item 14 compares the employer rating of males to those of females on the item "initiative."

EXAMPLE ITEM 14

		Low	Average	High
Initiative	Male			
	Female			

Averages may also be used to show responses to a particular item of the survey. In Example Item 15 a numerical value has been assigned to each of the rating categories—(1) for low, (2) for average, and (3) for a high rating. Simply, then, this involves calculation of an average for all responses. In the case of Item 15, the average was 2.3, located between average and high.

EXAMPLE ITEM 15

	(1)	(2)	(3)
Initiative	Low	Average	High
		$\bar{x} = 2.3$	
		(AV.)	

In addition to presenting item responses or item characteristics, the report or presentation of the results should contain an explanation of how the information was collected. This information can usually be presented in an introduction to the survey report. It will also be important to utilize the results in a meaningful way.

UTILIZING RESULTS

Results of the employer survey may be used to improve programs, revise objectives, delete programs, add courses, revise sequencing, or for any number of other purposes. To be utilized properly, results must be disseminated to all staff members who are involved with the program in question. The staff should be encouraged to take an active role in recommending changes they feel are indicated by the results of the survey. The best way of encouraging this is to hold a meeting at which appropriate staff members can discuss evaluative findings and explore means of addressing identified problems.

It is possible that an investigation conducted for one purpose will turn up evidence that has implications for another. For example, an employer survey conducted to enable instructors to revise objectives may collect information that indicates a new course should be added. For this reason, even the identified, prespecified purpose for conducting the evaluation may not give a complete picture as to who should be involved in the summary meeting.

If the employer follow-up survey has been conducted at a course level, the instructor may have no plans to hold a meeting of the entire staff. However, he may turn up information he feels will be useful to staff members and may want to bring it up at a departmental meeting. If the employer survey has been conducted by the program manager, and relates to the overall program, it is advisable to hold a meeting to be attended by all related staff members, at a minimum.

The program manager, whether or not responsible for conducting the employer follow-up survey, will be in a position to recommend a number of changes to his staff, but he should still encourage the participation of staff in the decision-making process. If staff members are to be involved in implementing the changes indicated by evaluation, it is essential that they be involved in the planning stages. It is further essential that changes suggested be viable and practical, and this will be more likely if staff members are involved in the decision-making process.

Some decisions cannot be made by staff members or the program managers alone. Some must be made by the administration or by the governing board. Consequently, the most efficient means for initiating the utilization of results may be to involve representatives from each possible decision-making level in the discussion of results. This may eliminate unnecessary requests, as an administrator can offer an informed opinion as to the feasibility of any given alternative and can help staff members formulate requests for changes.

Chapter 9 of this book will present more detailed information regarding the utilization of all evaluation results including those of the employer survey.

6

The Consultative Team Evaluation

WHY HAVE A CONSULTATIVE TEAM EVALUATION?

A consultative team evaluation involves the visitation, observation, and analysis of an instructional endeavor by a team of individuals for the purpose of providing suggestions for improvement. Members of a consultative team can be selected to meet the special needs of the education or training organization. With some external evaluation teams—such as an accreditation team, a state-sponsored team, or a supervisory team—the program personnel may rightfully feel uneasy if they are concerned about where they may fall on the overall rating. However, when the emphasis of the team is consultative, teams are often selected by the program manager or other involved personnel. Program personnel can elicit the team's judgments and suggestions for improvement, and the threat of evaluation is minimized.

The consultative team evaluation is much more than just a group of consultants making recommendations. Just as a medical team carefully examines an ailing patient prior to making a prognosis or suggesting remedies, the consultative evaluation team must carefully analyze the education or training program prior to offering any consultation. Setting the focus and providing guidelines for the consultative evaluation are tasks required of the program manager and his staff. Also, it is the prime responsibility of the program manager to effectively elicit suggestions for improvement from the team, determine the viability of such suggestions, and facilitate the utilization of the team's input.

The consultative team evaluation can provide unique evaluative input that is excluded by all other types of evaluation activities. Following is a discussion of several purposes for conducting a consultative team evaluation. They are not exhaustive, however, and the reader should not limit his purposes to those.

To Provide Expertise Otherwise Unavailable To the Program or Institution

The use of the consultative team evaluation approach allows for the selection of individuals with expertise that complements that of the institutional or program staff. Consultative team members may be aware of programs which have worked for other institutions under similar circumstances. If an institution wishes to evaluate its administrative structure, it can invite several specialists in organizational development to view the existing structure and its operation and to make subsequent recommendations for its improvement. The consultative team evaluation by these organizational development specialists may turn up alternatives that are not obvious to current staff.

To Identify Program Components Which Are Deficient

Possibly the most important purpose of a consultative team evaluation is the identification of deficient program components and activities. Only when these areas are identified can action be prescribed for improvement. A consultative evaluation team comprising representatives of a number of groups will provide alternative views of what types of situations represent program deficiencies. Evaluation teams from inside the institution may be too close to be objective about these deficiencies.

To Help Update and Insure the Relevance of Programs and Their Components

Whether made up of internal or external personnel, a consultative team can contribute to program accountability. Educational institutions are accountable to the outside world, and consultative team evaluation is the best way to insure that educational programs are relevant. Team members can filter their observations through their personal background and experience, making recommendations and suggestions concerning how the institution can best meet the needs of the students, their future employers, and others to whom the institution is accountable.

To Provide an Outside View of the Program and Its Components

Often, individuals intimately involved in day-to-day activity are so closely associated with the *process* that they may overlook obvious deficiencies of the activity itself. It is therefore useful to gain an *external view and judgment* regarding the program or activity. This might involve the observation of the overall organization of a program or department, the observation and analysis of a particular educational segment, or even the observation of equipment used in a particular program. The consultative team evaluation can provide a new perspective which can be useful to the program managers in making needed changes in the program.

To Provide In-service Training for Team Members

One function of the consultative team evaluation is to upgrade educational or training personnel. Through involvement in the evaluation, personnel may encounter instructional techniques, materials, and facilities that will be useful to them in their own programs. In addition, the involvement in an evaluation team allows staff members to become more familiar with the process of evaluation. Experience of this sort can help them evaluate their own teaching practices and program components.

To Facilitate Working Relations of Instructional and Ancillary Personnel

A consultative team made up of internal staff members—instructors, counselors, administrators, and other supportive educational or training staff—can produce many side benefits. The interaction of members of such a team may do much to improve the working relations among the staff. For example, in a public career education program, several staff members of the business education department might cooperate with staff from the home economics department in observing and assessing the former department. Staff members from the two departments will not only have an opportunity to study aspects of the business education program but also to know and understand one another to a greater degree. In an industrial organization, the involvement of the personnel director, supervisory and management personnel, and staff members from other departments can also increase awareness and communication both horizontally between departments and vertically between line and supervisory positions.

To Inform Community Personnel of Program Character

A consultative team comprising representatives of the public community can add a new dimension to the assessment of public educational programs. A more highly educated public, informed of program goals, characteristics, and outcomes, can lend much support to the educational institution. Most community representatives have a vested interest in the educational program, stemming from one of several situations. Their sons or daughters may be students, former students, or future students; citizens may be hiring or working with former occupational students; and all will be taxpayers who, directly or indirectly, are supporting the educational agency financially. In addition, a consultative team evaluation involving community representatives can facilitate communication between educators and the public. Used in this way, the evaluations can provide a vehicle for educational accountability to the public.

To Reinforce Aspects of the Program Which are Beneficial and Outstanding

The consultative evaluation team should also identify exemplary or outstanding characteristics of a course or program. Many evaluation activities overlook the mention of these and focus entirely on deficiencies. However, the commendation of exemplary activities will encourage educational or training personnel to expand their use or, possibly, to manipulate them to offset or overcome the deficient areas. Perhaps an experimental teaching device has dramatically decreased teaching time necessary for one area of instruction. This will encourage the department to retain this device and will allow them to channel more time to the teaching of other areas.

WHO SHOULD SERVE AS CONSULTATIVE EVALUATION PERSONNEL?

The selection of individuals for a consultative evaluation team will vary with the purpose and objectives of the evaluation. If the purpose is the assessment of an instructional segment directed toward sales analysis, team members might be professional sales representatives or sales trainers. On the other hand, if the purpose of the evaluation is the assessment of an entire career education program in a public educational institution, the evaluation team will probably be made up of individuals from a cross-section of educational specialities and occupational areas. Both the purpose and the scope of the evaluation will be key factors in the selection of consultative evaluation personnel. Additional factors are the financial resources of an institution and availability of potential team members. The following groups of individuals are presented as possibilities for inclusion on evaluation teams.

External Technical Specialists or Experts

Technical specialists, when utilized on a consultative evaluation team, can most effectively focus on the assessment of *content* of the instructional program, and it is best to select individuals who possess expertise in the specific area of instruction under study. If a course in computer design is the focus of the evaluation, an electronics engineer or a computer specialist might be a member of the team selected to review, assess, and make recommendations regarding the computer design course. Technical experts can be selected from at least three groups of individuals: industrial specialists, university professors or researchers, and private consultative firm representatives. There may be more possibilities, but these will at least give a springboard for selection. If an industrial organization is selecting an evaluation team, specialists might include members of the firm or its affiliates. If it is a public educational institution, industrial specialists might be selected from community industrial firms. One advantage to the selection of technical specialists from the ranks of public and private universities is that university professors often have allowances for released time for consultation. Firm representatives comprise a relatively new source for consultative team members. Over the past decade there has been a tremendous increase in the number of private consulting firms that have been formed, and these can provide valuable services to the educational or training institution.

Education and Training Professionals

Education and training professionals can focus on a number of aspects of the program under consideration. Because their area of expertise is curriculum and teaching, these individuals can contribute to more intensive analysis of instructional programs and are competent to focus on more specific recommendations regarding the content of instructional programs. In addition, education and training professionals can make evaluative recommendations concerning organization, administration, ancillary service, and other related components.

Education and training professionals can be selected from within or without the institution. Institutional personnel should include instructors from parallel or complementary programs, administrators or supervisors of the program, and ancillary personnel such as placement personnel, guidance and counseling personnel, and instructional materials specialists. External personnel, on the other hand, might include instructors, administrators, and ancillary personnel from neighboring institutions of public education or industry as well as instructional design and teaching methods specialists from universities or private consulting firms. In the case of public educational programs, personnel from the state career education office may be of assistance to the local school and may be available to serve on evaluation teams.

Employers of Graduates

Many institutions would not be able to afford a consultative team made up entirely of outside experts because the cost would be prohibitive. An educational institution would be wise to explore human resources within the community such as advisory committee members and employers from local businesses. Representatives from the business and industrial community who either employ graduates or are familiar with the program to be evaluated can provide specific input to the evaluation concerning the employability of students from a particular program. Their assessment and resulting recommendations for improvement can help ensure the relevance of any vocationally oriented program. These individuals may also have the ability to gather employee performance information concerning a number of individuals who are not even under their direct supervision. Moreover, employers are in the position to assess the compatibility of classroom objectives with what is actually desirable on the job.

Employers of graduates may be useful to both private training and public educational institutions. In the case of private institutions that are affiliated with a large industrial firm, the supervisors or foremen of institutional employees would be considered the employers of graduates. In this case, information is easily collected and evaluated. For the public institutions, follow-up is more difficult. A review of follow-up or placement information for graduates can help to identify employers who have employed several graduates of the program. Other employers may be found among members of the local chamber of commerce, and they are often more than willing to serve on evaluation teams. A third source of employers is a group which is probably more closely associated with public educational institutions—cooperative education employers. Coop employers are those who employ current students on a part-time basis to provide occupational experiences and training. These individuals are excellent candidates, as they have already made a commitment to a career education program and will, in most cases, be willing to serve on evaluation teams.

Former Learners or Graduates

The importance of obtaining evaluative information from former students was emphasized in Chapter 4, which focused on the follow-up of former learners. Student judgments regarding the education they received may also be gained by using students as members of a consultative evaluation team. Oftentimes, former program participants are capable of gathering information from current participants which would otherwise be unobtainable.

Former learners or graduates may be selected either from advanced educational programs or from employing institutions. Advanced community college programs, training programs, or university programs provide excellent sources for locating and obtaining the services of former program participants. Also, employers of graduates are usually willing to release these employees to serve in an evaluative capacity for the training or educational institution. Regardless of the source, former learners can be located by way of follow-up information or through the contact of employers or of program managers in advanced programs.

Citizens

Obviously, many former learners, employers of graduates, education and training professionals or experts may also be citizens of the particular community. However, individuals not belonging to these groups can be very usefully involved in a consultative team evaluation. Parents of current or former students can contribute to the observation and analysis of the educational program. "Private" citizens, while contributing to the improvement of the program, can also help to communicate the program's goals and attainments to the community. In public education, this communication is extremely important, since the educational program is supported by the tax-paying citizenry. Recommendations by educational staff members or by local community leaders, such as the city council, the local chamber of commerce, or local service organizations, may help to guide team selection.

Governing Board and Advisory Council Members

In both private and public training institutions, involvement of governing board members on a consultative team will increase their awareness of the program in question. In many cases this will facilitate subsequent planning, increase board awareness of the needs of a program which may increase board support for requests, and reduce the need for more lengthy documentation. Also, advisory board members, especially in public educational institutions, can best fulfill their role through serving on consultative evaluation teams. Such an experience will allow them to evaluate and advise with more confidence.

ESTABLISHING A FOCUS FOR THE
CONSULTATIVE TEAM EVALUATION

The focus of the consultative team evaluation must be established prior to any team selection or establishment of procedures. The purposes stated in the first section of this chapter can give general direction to the establishment of a focus. A single purpose may be chosen, or a combination may be made. Once the general purpose has been established, the program manager must decide what should be evaluated. If no evaluation has been conducted for some time within the institution, initial activity should be broadly focused, with subsequent refocusing on more specific aspects as the need arises. The program manager may have a general feeling for problem areas. Or, earlier evaluation activity may provide direction for investigation. For example, if student performance results have indicated that one program may be deficient, the program manager might direct a consultative team to focus initially on that program.

The evaluation of a total program should include the assessment of the unity or articulation of all individual programs in achieving the objectives of the total program. Philosophy and objectives, management, planning, research and evaluation, learning resources, and physical facilities are examples of areas that have a direct bearing on the success of the total program. Another important component might be the utilization of both internal and external resources. The above are but suggestions; the specific local situation will dictate the choice of any of these or the identification of additional components.

Evaluations conducted subsequent to a total program evaluation may begin to focus more closely on individual programs. Naturally, these more specific evaluations need not follow a total program evaluation if sufficient information to direct the evaluation is already in existence. An individual program is that portion of an institution's total career or training program offerings which is designed to prepare learners for entry into a particular occupation or cluster of occupations, or to enhance proficiency in that occupation (AVA, 1973).

Evaluation may also focus on other more specific components of the education or training program such as course or instructional segments and supportive or ancillary functions of the institution or program. In addition, certain areas of the institutional program—placement services provided to graduates or the administrative organization of the training institution—may be investigated by the consultative team. Program and course evaluations should be directed at the specifics of the course or program such as: course objectives, relationship of objectives to actual needed competencies (on-the-job), course organization, articulation with other courses, supplies and equipment, learning resources (texts and workbooks, for example), and techniques and instruments used in assessing learner performance.

METHODS FOR UTILIZING CONSULTATIVE
EVALUATION TEAMS

As evaluation team members, consultants must be given precise directions concerning their role and the desired outcome of evaluation activity. Basically, three different approaches to utilizing consultative evaluation teams will be discussed in this chapter: the independent on-site approach, the legalistic approach, and self-study and accreditation approach.

The Independent, On-Site Approach

The independent, on-site approach involves the selection of internal or external individuals who are capable of meeting the particular evaluative need defined in the focus of the evaluation. Individuals for such a team might be drawn from any of the groups described in a previous section of this chapter. The number of team members will be determined by the scope and focus of the evaluation. For example, the evaluation of a course may require only two or three individuals, while an institutional or total program evaluation may require from five to twenty-five individuals.

Regardless of the scope (total program, program, or course), a set of criterion questions should be established which define exactly what is to be evaluated. The team of individuals, in consortium with program or course managers, will have identified the broad areas to be assessed. For example, for a total program the team may have chosen to evaluate the objectives and philosophy, management or administrative organization, learning resources, and the physical plant. For each of these components, the team should formulate criterion questions which define the component and guide them in their data collection. The evaluation of management might begin with the formulation of criterion questions such as the following:

> Is the institution effectively organized to facilitate the instructional process and to fulfill its career education or training objectives?
> Is communication within the administrative structure (both vertical and horizontal) effective?
> Do departments cooperate in conducting the total occupational program? How extensive is cooperation among the administrators?

These criterion questions help delineate each of the particular components under consideration. These questions need not be approached directly during interviews. Each team member should be given latitude to formulate his own key questions, deciding which approach is most appropriate for the individual he is interviewing.

The team member may choose to ask a student different questions than he would the foreman of a local machine shop or an institutional administrator. Moreover, flexibility of this sort releases individual talents and innovations that serve to strengthen the evaluation system. The development of clearly defined plans, understandable to all, and a well-prepared set of criterion questions to guide data collection are essential to any evaluation system. Following the initial planning by the program manager, the actual team activities may be divided into five segments: 1) previsitation activities, 2) team orientation, 3) team exploration, 4) report writing, and 5) presentation of the report.

Previsitation Activities

Previsitation activities should begin with the selection of team members and an individual to lead the evaluation team. Selection of members should be based upon what each individual can contribute to the specific evaluation at hand. Teams may be selected from those groups previously discussed in this chapter, including technical experts and specialists, educational and training professionals, employers of graduates, former learners, citizens, and governing board or advisory board members. Care should be taken to select one individual who is clearly capable of coordinating the team and its corresponding activities. The team leader can be a staff member of the program under consideration, although selection of a nonrelated individual may prevent undue bias in the evaluation of the program.

When potential members are requested to serve on the evaluation team, they should be informed of their exact role and duties in the evaluation and of the financial arrangements to be made. Following the selection and confirmation of individuals, additional information should be communicated to each member. A description of the program to be evaluated, results of previous evaluations, a description of plans for the future, and demographic data related to the program under consideration will help to orient the team members to their task before they arrive on site.

The final phase of the previsitation activity should be the scheduling of all activities. The scheduling of evaluation dates may be accomplished by the program manager prior to the selection of team members, or it may be established by the program manager in consortium with the team itself. In either case, the length of time devoted to the evaluation should be commensurate with the size of the program or component to be evaluated. In most situations no more than two days and no less than half a day should be spent at this task. Even within this time frame, careful planning and utilization of personnel will be necessary. The assignment of specific team members to individual evaluative tasks should receive considerable attention by the team leader and the program manager. If an evaluation team has the task of evaluating the total career education program of a secondary school, it may be necessary to make scheduling arrangements far in advance of the evaluation date. In this case, it would be wise to provide out-of-house team members with as much information as possible prior to the orientation. Analyzing existing data, studying objectives of the program, and thinking over, under, and around criterion questions all take time. Even in-house members will be better equipped if they are given time to digest such materials.

Team Orientation

An orientation of the team by the team leader or program manager is essential when a consultative team evaluation is being conducted by more than two individuals. Scheduling of the orientation session will depend greatly on the type of team and the overall schedule of the evaluation. The orientation session for a team of citizens evaluating a public educational program may be held as long as one or two weeks prior to the actual visitation. For financial reasons, a team of experts brought in from outside the community may require that the orientation be held just prior to the initiation of the visitation.

Important aspects to be covered at the orientation meeting include objectives of the evaluation, objectives of the programs or components that are to be assessed, information already available, and the time frame for the visit. A considerable portion of the orientation must be spent on the identification of components to be evaluated and on the formation of criterion questions (if these have not already been formulated). A detailed discussion should center around the techniques for gathering data. For most on-site consultative team evaluations, such techniques will consist of interview and observation, in addition to the analysis of existing data. Team members must also be briefed on the categories or groups of people that they will interview, the length of interviews in terms of time, and methods for recording interview and observation data.

At this briefing, the program manager should inform team members of the intent of courses, individual programs, or total programs under consideration. Furthermore, any material which will illuminate these objectives should be distributed to the team, if such material has not already been distributed through the mail. Other material, such as follow-up data that will aid the team in its task, should also be made available. This data, along with data gathered through interviews and observations, will enable the team to assess more accurately the outcomes of the program to be evaluated.

Before the briefing session is adjourned, all questions that the team members may have should be answered. Team members should also be reminded of the time schedule for the on-site visit and advised of their specific interviewing and observation schedules, which have been established by the team leader and/or the program manager.

Team Exploration

Team exploration should focus on information pertinent to the component under evaluation. The focus and scope of the evaluation, of course, will determine who is to be interviewed and what is to be observed. Although in the case of a total program or institutional evaluation it would be desirable to involve and interview all those who have contact with the program, in most instances there is not sufficient time. A sampling of individuals involved in and affected by the program can offset time limitations. Figure 6–1 shows an example schedule of an individual who is involved in the evaluation of a total career education program.

Team members should use a notebook or a clipboard to record observations and interview results. In some instances it may be advantageous to print or Xerox lists of the criterion questions, allowing space for the recording of interview responses for each question. Figure 6–2 presents an example recording form for the assessment of an institution's objectives.

Each team member should be allowed sufficient time to record the responses to his interview questions following each interview. Re-

8:30 a.m. - 9:30	Interview a group of students in the Metals Trade Program.
9:45 a.m. - 10:45	Interview Mr. Chance, the personnel manager of Smithson Tool and Die.
11:00 a.m. - 11:45	Interview Sam Small, a recent program completor employed at Smithson Tool and Die.
12:00 noon - 12:30	Lunch at school.
12:45 p.m. - 1:45	Interview Mrs. Robinson, mother of current student in the program.
2:00 p.m. - 2:45	Interview with Mr. Brown, Director of the local state employment office.
3:00 - 5:00	Team meeting (metals trade classroom)
5:00 - 6:30	Dinner.
6:30 - 9:00	Team meeting (metals trade classroom).
9:00 - 10:00	Report findings to staff.

FIGURE 6–1   *Example Team Member Schedule*

OBJECTIVES

Primary Goal:

Determine if objectives are developed in measurable terms and utilized in all levels of instruction.

Interview Tasks:

1. Determine if measurable objectives exist for (a) total program, (b) individual programs, and (c) specific courses.

2. Determine what relationship exists between (a) total program, (b) individual program, and (c) specific course objectives.

3. Determine how often the (a) total program, (b) individual program, and (c) course objectives are reviewed for possible revision.

4. Determine if administration, advisory committees, students and staff members are knowledgeable about total program objectives.

5. Determine who was involved in establishing the total occupational program objectives as stated in the Local District Plan.

6. Determine if program and course objectives are communicated to students.

7. Determine if program management objectives are communicated to all staff members.

FIGURE 6–2   *Recording Form for the Assessment of Objectives (reproduced from "Team Member Handbook," Springfield: State of Illinois, 1974).*

cording following the interviewing has proved more effective than writing during the interview. It is important that the team meet at some time during the first day of the exploration to ensure that each team member is progressing in the right direction and collecting the appropriate information. At this meeting any deviations can be corrected before the full day of interviewing and observation is completed.

Report Writing

The example team member schedule in Figure 6–1 shows the team discussion to begin at 3:00 p.m., following the day's data collection. This session should consist only of team members and should not include any of the education and training personnel from the evaluated institution. Team members should be given the opportunity to discuss their findings privately. Their task during the afternoon and evening sessions is to formulate specific conclusions or answers to the criterion questions and to establish recommendations for those conclusions that indicate deficiencies.

> *Criterion Question:* Is vertical and horizontal communication within the administrative structure effective?
>
> *Conclusion:* Vertical communication within the administrative organization appears to be minimal.

Once conclusions have been agreed upon, recommendations can be drawn which give direction to the educational or training agency for the remedy of identified deficiencies. A recommendation for the above conclusion might be: *Immediate attention should be directed toward the improvement of vertical communication within the administrative structure.*

The team leader should serve as the recorder of the discussion and should direct the team toward its end product, the report. The specific criterion questions can be taken one by one until the report writing is complete. The result should be a series of conclusions similar to the one indicated above, accompanied by recommendations designed to alleviate identified deficiencies. The report format presented in Figure 6–3 was used by one team to present conclusions and recommendations concerning one component of a high school vocational program.

The column in Figure 6–3 entitled "suggested solutions" should be noted. It should be emphasized that this is the most important aspect of the evaluation report and represents the greatest contribution that the consultative evaluation team can provide. Many team evaluations fall short in this respect. That is, often evaluation teams only point up things that are deficient without suggesting means for their remedy. It is in presenting suggested solutions that the consultative team fulfills its appointed task.

For the conclusion and recommendation mentioned above dealing with vertical communication, the following suggested solutions might be provided.

1. A department newsletter should be initiated.
2. Meetings should be held for the expressed purpose of communicating plans, new activities, and the like.
3. The public relations office should become involved in internal communication.

Suggested solutions should be tailored to fit the resources and needs of the program being evaluated.

CONCLUSIONS	RECOMMENDATIONS	SUGGESTED SOLUTIONS

FIGURE 6–3   *Example Format for Report Writing*

Presentation of the Report

The team's findings are summarized in the final report, which should be presented verbally to those individuals responsible for decision making within the educational or training institution. As the team leader personally communicates the conclusions and recommendations to the appropriate staff members, he can make necessary clarifications and provide supporting evidence to the staff. Staff members should be encouraged to discuss and react to the team's conclusions. The purpose of this discussion is to correct any items which are unclear or in error before the report is released in final printed form to the agency program manager and other decision makers.

The time necessary for presenting the report will, of course, be dependent upon the scope of the evaluation and the extensiveness of the evaluation report. It is important, however, that the evaluation report—along with all necessary changes and corrections—be completed prior to the team's exit from the educational or training institution. Experience has shown that it is more effective to complete the report at the time of the evaluation than to take it from the institution and complete it elsewhere, returning it to the institution at a later time.

The above suggested format for the evaluation report is very useful in terms of utilization of the results. Chapter 9 focuses more specifically on the utilization of consultative team evaluation results.

The Legalistic Approach

A second alternative to the consultative team evaluation is the legalistic approach which involves the utilization of two independent evaluation teams who are asked to present opposing cases with regard to an educational or training component. The focus of these teams may be on a single decision, such as, *Should we expand our nurses training program?* or *Is our administrative structure effective?*

In any of these instances, one of the evaluation teams (or individuals) prepares a case in favor of the program or evaluative focus. This team is referred to as the advocate team. The advocate team's counterpart in the legal system is the defense lawyer. The advocate evaluators are given the responsibility for gathering data, making warrants, and organizing arguments into conclusions which support the program or a component under consideration.

The second team, referred to as the dissident team, opposes the proposition or program under consideration and prepares a case against it. Its role is to show that the program is faulty or not needed. This team also builds a case based upon data, warrants, and arguments.

Both teams prepare written reports of their findings and arguments following their collection of data through interviews, observation, and analysis of available information. These reports are presented to the program manager or other key decision maker. In addition, the advocate and dissident teams exchange their reports.

Subsequent to the submission and exchange of reports, the program manager schedules a meeting with the two evaluation teams or their representative leaders. During this meeting, each team's report is presented and each leader is given the opportunity to enumerate and verbally substantiate each of his contentions. At this time, the program manager is afforded the opportunity to cross-examine each party and can ask for supportive evidence. The advocates and dissidents are also allowed to cross-examine each other regarding presented arguments and evidence.

During and following the cross-examination meeting the program manager synthesizes the findings of both teams, drawing his own conclusions based upon the two cases. This evaluation approach differs from our legal and judicial system at this point. The program manager is not required to make judgment between the plaintiff and defendant. Instead, the decision maker is allowed to synthesize findings from each case, gaining insights to make his educational program more effective. Figure 6–4 presents a schematic view of the legalistic approach to evaluation.

Kourilsky (1973) in her discussions of adversary evaluation, as she entitled it, has stated five advantages of this approach:

1. The decision maker tends to receive a wider array of information, mainly because both sides are being presented.
2. The decision maker tends to receive a better quality of evidence.
3. The process diminishes the possibility of unwitting bias.
4. This approach would tend to diminish the "yes-man" syndrome.
5. The adversary relationship tends to expose hidden assumptions.

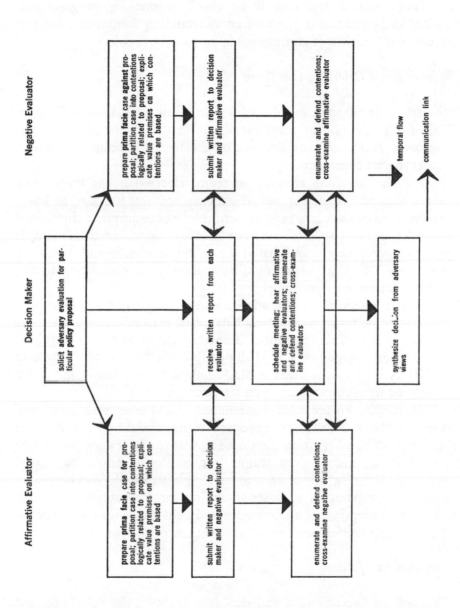

FIGURE 6–4   *Schematic of the Legalistic Approach to Evaluation (reproduced from* Evaluation Comment, *vol. 4, no. 2, June 1973, with the permission of Marilyn Kourilsky and the Center for the Study of Evaluation, UCLA, Los Angeles, California).*

The legalistic approach is an excellent one for program and course assessment and provides an outstanding framework for the effective utilization of consultants in an evaluative role.

Selecting and Orienting the Team

The selection of team members for a legalistic evaluation will differ little from selection of team members for the independent, on-site approach. However, coordination of the legalistic team as a whole merits special consideration.

The first decision required in team selection is the number of teams needed. Obviously, at least two are needed but in some instances more than two may be desirable. For example, a third team could be utilized to cross-examine the two opposing teams and to prepare recommendations based upon the evidence and argument presented. This third team could be composed of internal, external, or a combination of personnel.

In the selection of the advocate and dissident team members, care should be taken to achieve a balance of personnel, expertise, and evaluating skill. This is essential if an accurate picture is to be gained from opposing arguments. If at all possible, each team should include specialists in the same areas so that arguments on each issue will be countered by arguments of equal strength.

To further ensure adequate balance of opposing teams, orientation for the dissident and advocate teams should, if possible, be combined. The orientation should be similar to the session previously described for independent teams, but emphasis should be placed upon the differing role of each team. Emphasis should also be placed upon the preparation of cases including the format for reporting. Also, the blueprint of all procedures should be reviewed, including the reporting conference and subsequent use of the findings.

Preparation of Cases

The task of the advocate and dissident teams is the collection and organization of evidence, the formulation of conclusions, and the establishment of warrants relating the facts to the conclusions.

Data collection on the part of both teams should be facilitated by encouraging the institutional staff to provide both teams with the information they desire. In law cases, for example, clients often give their lawyer only those facts which they regard as favorable to them. However, this can be disastrous in a court trial. The layman is often unable to discriminate between facts that are favorable and unfavorable, important and trivial. In an evaluation, the withholding of information will only lead to a faulty conclusion on the part of the evaluator or a weak conclusion that is shown to be based on inconclusive or hearsay evidence.

To translate data into evaluative conclusions, the evaluator must have a standard against which to measure its significance. This standard may be referred to as the "warrant" for the given conclusion. Consider the following example.

> Information gained from instructors through interviews and observation of class schedules indicate that the time provided for cooperative education classes is inadequate.
>
> 1. The *data* or facts are that "50 minutes per day are allowed for cooperative education."
> 2. The *conclusion* is that "time is inadequate."
> 3. The *warrant* is a state requirement that 90 minutes per day class time be allotted for cooperative courses.

The actual report can assume one of several formats, depending on the needs and wants of the program manager and upon the design of the cross-examination conference. The evaluation report can range from a brief "bill of particulars" to a complete presentation of conclusions, arguments, and supporting evidence.

The less detailed report could include a listing of conclusions such as:

> 1. There is a lack of emphasis on student youth groups.
> 2. The student desire for cooperative education programs exceeds available offerings.
> 3. Training equipment in the meta lurgy laboratory is antiquated.

The conclusions listed above could be extended to provide for a more definitive statement. This type of qualified conclusion includes more evidence than the above three conclusions.

> 1. Based upon interviews with staff and students and a review of organization membership lists, there appears to be a lack of emphasis on student youth groups.
> 2. Student survey data, substantiated by a sampling of interviews and the

Conclusion	Data Source	Warrant
1. Student youth groups are lacking emphasis	1a. Staff 1b. Students 1c. Membership lists	Expert judgment
2. Student desire for cooperative education exceeds available offerings	2a. Student survey 2b. Interviews 2c. Enrollment statistics	Need compared to available
3. Training equipment in metallurgy department is antiquated.	3a. Specification of equipment 3b. Recommended standards	Specs. compared to standard

FIGURE 6–5   *Example of Alternative Format for Presenting Team Findings*

> review of enrollment statistics, indicate a greater desire for cooperative education courses than there are existing opportunities.
> 3. Based upon a comparison of existing metallurgical equipment to specifications provided by the American Society for Metallurgical Engineers, training equipment in the metallurgy laboratory has been deemed out of date.

Obviously these conclusions will be more convincing than the first group, and are most desirable when the report must stand alone.

A third alternative for presenting team findings is presented in Figure 6–5. This form provides a column for stating conclusions, in this case similar to the unqualified conclusion stated above. Here, conclusions are supported by presenting additional information in chart form with a column indicating the source of evidence and a column which presents the warrant.

The Cross-examination Meeting

The purpose of the cross-examination conference is to provide an opportunity for each evaluation team to verbally present its evaluation findings for examination by the team that will do the questioning. Ideally, each team should present the written report of its findings to the program manager prior to the conference. In addition, each team should provide a copy of its report to the opposing team. This exchange will allow everyone involved in the cross-examination conference time to consider each evaluative conclusion.

If only a list of unqualified conclusions is presented in the report, the program manager may ask that each team verbally substantiate its conclusions. However, conclusions lacking sufficient data or factual bases will be readily identified during cross-examination. During the conference the program manager can begin weighing conclusions of one team against the opposing conclusions of the other team. Once a conclusion has been accepted, he may ask the evaluators to provide suggestions for change or improvement—remedies for the identified ailments.

It should be emphasized that the program manager does not act as judge or jury, accepting only one evaluation report as a winner. The manager draws information from each report, incorporating it into one synthesized report. This composite report becomes the report from which directions for improvement and priorities for action can be established.

In some cases it may be beneficial to hold meetings subsequent to the cross-examination meeting and involving the program staff for purposes of synthesizing findings and formulating plans for overcoming the identified deficiencies.

Self-study and Accreditation Approach

The self-study and accreditation approach is similar to the independent, on-site approach in that it requires a team of individuals to review the institution and its programs. Regional accrediting agencies have been in existence for decades, requiring educational institutions to be reviewed on a sequential basis, usually every five or seven years.

As well as being utilized for accreditation purposes, the approach can be used independently by an institution to evaluate and improve its offerings. Private as well as public institutions may find this approach to be useful.

Staff and committee members of the American Vocational Association have formulated an approach for assessing vocational and technical education programs and are in the process of field testing this approach. This chapter section is based heavily on the AVA's efforts. It should be emphasized, however, that this procedure is not rigid and variation in its use is encouraged to better suit the needs of a particular institution or program.

Fundamentally, the self-study accreditation approach involves three steps:

1. An in-depth self-evaluation study.
2. An on-site verification or audit by a team of qualified people from outside the institution.
3. A review by an independent third group, based on evidence in the self-evaluation report and on-site visiting team report.

Two basic instruments have been developed for use in each of these three steps, and each step generates information to be used in the succeeding steps. These two instruments include an institutional form and a program form. The former is intended for use in the evaluation of each program in the institution, while the latter is meant to evaluate factors broader in scope than individual program evaluations. Neither form is complete in itself; each is designed to be used in conjunction with the other. Like most accreditation studies, the self-study provides the real advantage and strength to such an approach. That is, this study can provide staff members with the data upon which to base systematic analysis of institutional and program operations and resources. The self-study also facilitates the staff's working as a team, providing not only an evaluation of their activities but also a means of improving the working relationships among staff members.

The second step of the self-study accreditation approach involves the visitation of an external team to the institution or program. This visiting team has the task of verifying the accuracy of data reported by the institution in its self-evaluation study. Team members try to determine the extent to which reported data give a full and true picture of actual conditions and operations and verify the extent to which outcomes coincide with stated objectives.

The third step of this approach involves the review of team findings and self-study findings, and it helps to synthesize the information from both. By drawing on its broader perspectives, this review group is in a position to improve the evaluative instruments and procedures and is able to resolve any differences of opinion between institutional personnel and on-site personnel. It is also the responsibility of the review team to provide recommendations and suggestions for improving existing deficiencies. This self-study accreditation approach is not intended to be used for grading or comparing institutions. Its primary focus should be the improvement of the institution and its subordinate programs. In other words, this approach can be utilized for purposes much different than those of most accreditation agency evaluations.

The following segments of this section will be devoted to a more detailed discussion of each of the three steps of the self-study accreditation approach to institutional and program evaluation. Most references will be made to the very broad institutional evaluation which involves program evaluation. However, alterations in both the scope and specificity of this approach can easily be made.

The Self-evaluation Study

Prior to the initiation of any self-evaluation activity, the chief school or training administrator should appoint a steering committee to be charged with the overall responsibility for the self-evaluation. In some cases, this administrator will serve in the capacity of a steering committee member. The steering committee should lay out the course of action for the evaluation study, outline a time schedule, orient other members of the institution and community, appoint working committees to conduct different parts of the study, and provide sufficient materials to the committee members. In addition, a primary responsibility of the committee will be the assembly and synthesis of individual committee reports into one final composite report.

In selecting members for self-evaluation teams, it is important to obtain a representative sampling. Members from each program and level within the institution should be included on one of the evaluation teams, as this will facilitate communication of evaluation activities to all staff members. Probably of greater consequence is the fact that those who have been involved in the self-evaluation will be more likely to take action to remedy the deficiencies identified by the evaluation.

In its specific application of the self-study accreditation approach, the AVA (1973) recommends that a committee be appointed for each of the evaluation forms covering both institutional characteristics and each individual program within the institution. Figure 6–6 presents an example of an institutional evaluation form. This example is specifically designed for the assessment of philosophy and objectives of the institution. Both the institutional staff and the

FIGURE 6–6   *Example Institutional Form for Philosophy and Objectives* (*reproduced from* Instruments and Procedures for the Evaluation of Vocational/ Technical Education Institutions and Programs *with the permission of the American Vocational Association, Washington, D.C.*).

PHILOSOPHY AND OBJECTIVES

Vocational/technical education is judged in light of how well it meets its stated objectives, and how well the stated objectives fit the needs of the people to be served. At the institutional level, objectives are concerned with defining the institution's responsibility as to clientele and needs to be served, services to be provided, and occupations to be taught. They grow out of population and labor market need surveys, and are limited by the institution's mandate or charter and available resources.

Characteristic

The vocational/technical education philosophy and objectives of the institution are well-defined and properly stated and used. They adequately reflect the institution's purpose.

Guidelines   *Evaluation*

1. The institution publishes a clear statement of its philosophy and objectives for vocational/technical education.   ____

2. The statement is included in the school's catalog and is distributed to students, school personnel, and the public.   ____

3. The institution's various objectives are consistent and compatible with each other and with the institution's purpose and mandate or charter.   ____

4. The statement of objectives describes the clientele to be served and delineates the school's responsibility for serving component groups such as: ____

    a. Secondary school youth   ____
    b. Postsecondary school youth   ____
    c. Unemployed and under-employed out-of-school youth   ____
    d. Unemployed and under-employed adults   ____
    e. Employed youth and adults   ____
    f. Women/men   ____
    g. The handicapped   ____
    h. The disadvantaged   ____

FIGURE 6–6   *(Continued)*

5. The statement of objectives clearly indicates occupations for which preparation will be offered, level of preparation required for participation, and occupational level to be achieved by satisfactory participation.   ___

6. The statement of vocational/technical education philosophy and objectives describes:

   a. Services to be provided.   ___

   b. The scope of responsibilities of the school, including responsibility for remedial education.   ___

   c. Expected outcomes, including expected social and economic impact.   ___

7. Vocational/technical education objectives are stated in measurable performance terms that lend themselves to specific determination of the degree to which they are being realized in the school.   ___

8. The objectives are stated in such a manner that:

   a. Students and the public can understand them.   ___

   b. They enable potential students to determine whether or not the school's objectives are compatible with the students' own occupational objectives.   ___

   c. They give direction to the institution's vocational/technical education planning and activities.   ___

   d. They enable the public to determine the extent to which the institution can be expected to serve community need.   ___

9. The means through which philosophy and objectives are to be realized are described in the published statement.   ___

10. Objectives are realistic in terms of capability for achieving them; or, conversely, the capability exists for achieving objectives.   ___

11. The statement of objectives clearly differentiates between what the institution realistically expects to do and what it feels ideally it should be doing; it includes an evaluation of what is not being done as well as of what is being done by the school.   ___

12. An objective of vocational/technical education is to prepare individuals for initial employment, to improve the occupational competency of employed individuals, and/or to prepare individuals for a change of occupation.   ___

FIGURE 6–6 *(Continued)*

13. Objectives include provision for:
   a. Taking active steps to bring vocational/technical education services to people who need them. ___
   b. Continuing the education of former students. ___
   c. Discontinuing preparation for occupations in which employment opportunities no longer exist. ___
   d. Maintaining quality control over institutional offerings and services. ___

14. Objectives other than preparation for the world of work are clearly stated and their relationship to occupational preparation objectives indicated. The objectives reflect adequate provision for students who wish concentrated preparation for work. ___

15. The philosophy and objectives indicate a respect for the right of students to set their own occupational objectives and to select those institutional offerings compatible with their own career objectives. ___

16. The statement of philosophy and objectives gives evidence of commitment to vocational/technical education on the part of the governing body and the administrator of the institution. ___

17. Staff, students, and constituency are consulted and involved in developing and revising the statement of philosophy and objectives. ___

18. The statement of philosophy and objectives is examined and revised periodically to keep it accurate and current. ___

19. The statement of philosophy and objectives expresses the institution's intent to measure and to prevent insofar as possible undesirable unplanned outcomes of the vocational/technical education process. ___

visiting team use this and other forms in their review. Figure 6–7 is an example of a program form on the assessment of philosophy and objectives at the program level.

FIGURE 6–7   *Example Program Form for Philosophy and Objectives (repro-duced from* Instruments and Procedures for the Evaluation of Vocational/Technical Education Institutions and Programs *with permission of the American Vocational Association, Washington, D.C.).*

PHILOSOPHY AND OBJECTIVES

A vocational/technical education program is judged in light of how well it meets its stated objectives, and how well the stated objectives fit the needs of the people to be served. At the program level objectives grow out of requirements of the occupation taught and the interests and abilities of students.

Characteristic

The philosophy and objectives of the occupational prepara-tory program are well defined and properly stated and used.

Guidelines   *Evaluation*

1. The vocational/technical education program publishes a clear statement of its philosophy and objectives. ____

2. The statement of philosophy and objectives is distributed to faculty, staff, students and the public and prominently dis-played in places where it will be seen by students and visitors. ____

3. The objectives are consistent and compatible with the institu-tion's vocational/technical education objectives. ____

4. The statement of philosophy and objectives describes:
   a. Clientele to be served ____
   b. Services to be provided ____
   c. The scope of responsibilities of the program ____
   d. Expected outcomes in terms of student performance ____
   e. Entrance requirements in terms of student performance ____

5. The program objectives and requirements are known and under-stood by students prior to entry upon the instruction program. ____

6. Objectives are stated in measurable performance terms that lend themselves to specific determination of the degree to which they are being realized. ____

7. The objectives are stated in such a manner that:
   a. Students and their parents can understand them ____

FIGURE 6–7   *(Continued)*

    b. They enable potential students and their parents to deter-
mine whether or not the program objectives are compatible
with the student's own occupational objectives

    c. They give direction to instruction, planning and related
activities   ___

    d. Employers can determine the extent to which preparation
fits their requirements   ___

8. The means through which philosophy and objectives are realized
are described in the published statement.   ___

9. Objectives are realistic in terms of capability for achieving them;
or, conversely, the capability exists for achieving objectives.   ___

10. An objective of the program is to prepare individuals for initial
employment, or to improve the occupational competency of
employed individuals.   ___

11. The program provides job skills applicable more broadly than to
a specific job with a specific employer.   ___

12. Objectives other than preparation for the world of work are
clearly stated and their relationship to occupational preparation
objectives indicated. The objectives reflect adequate provision
for students who wish concentrated occupational preparation.   ___

13. The philosophy indicates a respect for the right of students to
set their own occupational objectives and a recognition that the
program exists as a service to aid students in achieving their
self-chosen occupational objectives.   ___

14. The statement of objectives is formulated in consultation with
students, former students, staff, the Occupational Advisory
Committee, and others.   ___

15. The statement of philosophy and objectives is kept current.   ___

16. The statement of objectives clearly differentiates between what
the program realistically expects to achieve and what it feels it
should be doing ideally; it includes an evaluation of what is not
being done as well as of what is being done in serving its
constituency and in developing, upgrading, and updating occupational proficiency.   ___

17. The statement of philosophy and objectives expresses the intent
to measure and prevent insofar as possible undesirable unplanned outcomes of the educational process.   ___

The following evaluation code is employed for rating each of the characteristics within these forms:

M = Major improvement needed. Some weakness of crucial nature.

I = Improvement needed. Weaknesses are of a less serious nature than those coded M.

S = Satisfactory; adequate.

E = Excellent; very well done.

NA = Not applicable.

In total, the following institutional evaluation forms are provided by the AVA:

Distinguishing characteristics
Philosophy and objectives
Matching objectives to need
Indicators of success
Delivery systems
Organizations; governing body
Administration
Staff
Finance and business management
General advisory committee
Planning
Research and evaluation
Recruitment and admissions
Guidance and counseling
Placement and follow-up
Student educational records
Student activities
Learning resources
Physical plant

In addition to the above evaluation forms, the AVA also provides a set of forms for each of the *programs* of the institution. This set includes forms for:

Distinguishing characteristics
Philosophy and objectives
Matching objectives to need
Indicators of success
Organization and management
Occupational advisory committee
Program research and evaluation
The teaching-learning process
Curriculum learning resources
Supplies and equipment
Instructional space and facilities

Obviously, if a working committee is to be established for each of these characteristics in every program, one individual may be required to serve on more than one team, but it is possible to combine several of these committees to look at more than one characteristic. It is suggested that committees focusing on the evaluation of institutional characteristics include those most directly concerned with the particular characteristics under study, plus a member of the instructional staff, the administration, the student or learner group, and a general advisory committee member. On individual program evaluation committees it is recommended that the head or director of the program be a member of the team, as well as an instructor, an instructor in a related department, a student or learner representative, and a member of the related advisory committee. It is also often advantageous to include a member of the administrative staff and a former graduate and/or cooperative employer of the program. Committee members should meet once a week or as often as necessary to complete the self-evaluation within a two- or three-month period. In some instances it is desirable to hold periodic meetings at which time committees can report briefly to the entire departmental or institutional staff for reaction and simple communication. This effort helps bring about an exchange of ideas and a coordination of the entire self-evaluation study.

Once individual committee reports have been completed for each of the institutional characteristics and programs, the steering committee or overall committee must consolidate the individual reports. A statement of major strengths and weaknesses must then be made, with an indication of plans for the remedy of the weaknesses and the overall improvement of the institution. The steering committee should present this report to the entire staff of the institution for their reaction. This document becomes very important to each of the staff members as they establish individual and departmental priorities. This report can also serve as a guide for a staff development program. A suggested organizational format for the final self-evaluation report is presented in Figure 6–8.

In summary, the self-evaluation study aspect of the self-study accreditation approach involves 1) appointment of a steering committee, 2) establishment of working committees, 3) completion of institutional and program evaluation forms by working committee members, 4) consolidation of individual reports and the preparation of strengths, weaknesses and plans, and 5) distribution of the report to each staff member within the institution.

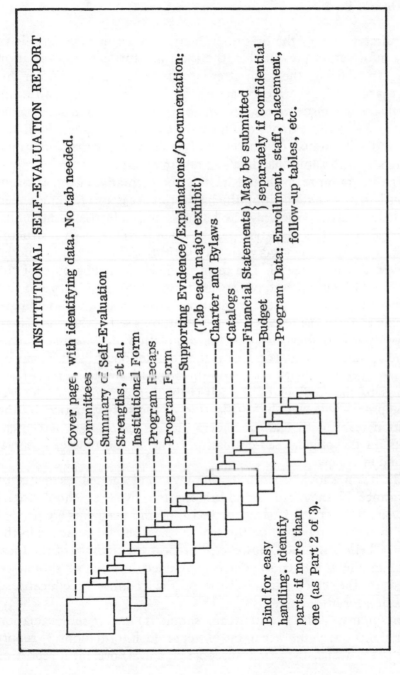

FIGURE 6–8 *Example Organizational Sequence for Self-evaluation Report (reproduced from Instruments and Procedures for the Evaluation of Vocational/ Technical Education Institutions and Programs with permission of the American Vocational Association, Washington, D.C.).*

The On-site Visit

The primary role of the on-site evaluation by an outside team is to verify information presented in the local institution's self-evaluation report. In addition, the team attempts to: 1) determine whether this report accurately represents actual conditions in the institution, 2) evaluate the institution's system for conducting valid self-evaluation, 3) verify the extent to which outcomes correspond with the need and with stated objectives, and 4) supplement the self-evaluation report with additional data and documentation.

The visitation team should include representatives from all occupational areas included within the institution. It is also recommended that individuals representing the business and industrial community be included on this visitation team. When possible, each instructor and staff member involved with the institutional program should be observed and interviewed. The team members and subgroups of the team should focus on each of the institution's characteristics and also on each program within the institution. Team members should have available to them the results of the institution's self-evaluation. There are basically two alternatives to the completion of these instruments by the visitation team. The first is the completion of blank forms by the team members, with a subsequent comparison of visitation team findings to the findings of the self-evaluation committees. The second approach involves the verification of the self-evaluation by the visitation team, with team members making appropriate agreement checks on the original self-evaluation forms at the time of observation and interview.

The team should report its findings, and factual elements of significance if they are found unreported by the school, in its self-evaluation report. If strengths exist, or improvements are needed other than those reported by the school, these should be noted in the report. There is no need, however, to repeat the findings of the local school in the team report. Once completed, the report should be mailed to the chief administrator of the training or educational institution for his review.

In summary, the on-site team should 1) review self-evaluation material, 2) verify the accuracy of reported information, 3) report information which they find unreported, and 4) present a report of findings to the institutional director and the third party review group.

Third Party Review of Findings

The on-site visitation overlaps somewhat with the independent visitation team approach discussed earlier in this chapter. In addition, third party review of findings bears a resemblance to the legalistic evaluation approach. The educational or training institution has considerable latitude in using this step of the self-study accreditation approach to evaluation. Ultimate structure of this third party evaluation will depend on the resources available and the desired outcome of the evaluation sequence. The primary role of this third group is to review the results of the self-evaluation and of the team evaluation and to make recommendations and suggestions for improvement—thus becoming consultative in nature. In a private training institution it is possible to establish a committee of individuals who are knowledgeable of training activities without being directly involved in those programs under consideration. This group of individuals can review the results of a number of program evaluations, observing the strengths and weaknesses of each, and of the composite of evaluations. Based upon this review, the team can make recommendations concerning the directions to be taken.

As in the case of the private training agency, so also can a public educational institution use the third party evaluation. It is also possible to use an external team of individuals for a particular region of the state. For example, a consortium of educators, either in similar programs or in university preparation programs, may be established to review the self-evaluation and team results for a number of schools within a particular region. This would eliminate the necessity to orient a number of review teams to their role and function. In addition, this team could be made up of experts who could recommend activities and solutions they have observed in other institutions.

In other situations, it may be feasible to establish a team of state office personnel to take the responsibility for reviewing local institutional reports and making subsequent recommendations for improvement. However, care should be taken in situations such as this to minimize the punitive connotation which might result. In summary, the review team should 1) analyze the self-evaluation report and the on-site team report, 2) synthesize the findings, and 3) prepare recommendations for improvements.

Regardless of the technique utilized in this approach, it is important in the overall evaluation that the evaluation procedures themselves be closely monitored. This will help to identify weaknesses in the evaluation structure so that changes can be made for subsequent applications of the techniques and overall approach. All of this should contribute to a successful evaluation system.

UTILIZING CONSULTATIVE TEAM RESULTS

As with any form of evaluation, utilization of results is a most crucial feature of the consultative team evaluation. Unlike most evaluations, however, major emphasis of the consultative evaluation is on suggested solutions. With most forms of evaluation, the utilization of evaluation results—the initiation of planned change—is a responsibility which falls clearly on the shoulders of the staff. It is the staff's responsibility to identify possible solutions and to determine what direction will be taken for particular departments, courses, or programs. In a course evaluation, the consultative team provides staff members with alternative plans for change, and it is agreed that the team itself will guide the plans for change. For this reason, it is important that suggested solutions be practical, acceptable to staff, and well-formulated. If suggested solutions are carefully drawn, the evaluator can be certain that the staff will give them due consideration, and he has fulfilled his consultative role.

To formulate viable solutions, the consultative evaluator must be thoroughly familiar with the institution being evaluated. Evaluative conclusions can often be drawn without such close familiarity. These are mere statements of the deficiencies of the program as measured against the evaluator's notion of what is ideal. Suggested solutions, however, must be based on the school's own potential. Solutions must be rooted in a thorough understanding of institutional problems. The consultative team has *not* fulfilled its role if its solutions are not so based—if suggested solutions take into account only the "ideal" approach and not the most reasonable in terms of the school's actual capabilities. For the consultative team evaluation, suggested solutions are the key to utilization of results.

Even if the consultative evaluator is convinced that his solutions are well founded, it is best that he substantiate results to staff in the overall evaluation report. Naturally, the staff will want to be certain that change is necessary and possible if they are to take steps to implement suggestions.

To ensure the utilization of results, the consultative team must be certain that staff is open to their help. No staff will welcome a consultative evaluator who points fingers or places blame on individuals. For this reason, and to clarify evaluation findings, it is wise for the consultative evaluator to hold private conferences with those individuals who will be required to implement changes, unless it is necessary to involve others. It is particularly important that the consultative team supplement written findings with verbal explanation. Solutions are much more difficult to communicate than conclusions. Furthermore it is only reasonable that staff be allowed to react to suggested solutions explaining why they are impractical, if this is the case. If it is shown that suggested solutions are not adequate for a particular institution, it is the evaluator's role to come up with new, more workable suggestions for a remedy.

REFERENCES

Ash, L. C. *Instruments and Procedures for the Evaluation of Vocational/Technical Education.* Washington, D.C.: American Vocational Association, 1972.

Kourilsky, M. "An Adversary Model for Educational Evaluation." *Evaluation Comment,* 1973, vol. 4, no. 2.

Levine, M. "Scientific Method and the Adversary Model: Some Preliminary Suggestions." *Evaluation Comment,* 1973, vol. 4, no. 2.

Stake, R. and Gjerde, C. "An Evaluation of TCITY: The Twin City Institute for Talented Youth." Urbana: Center for Instructional Research and Curriculum Evaluation, University of Illinois, 1971.

Toulmin, S. *The Uses of Argument.* London: Cambridge University Press, 1958.

7

The Evaluation of Education and Training Personnel

WHY EVALUATE EDUCATION AND TRAINING PERSONNEL?

The national trend toward accountability in our public schools and the concern for profit making in private training institutions have brought about a widespread concern for evaluating all aspects of instructional programs. One of the most challenging tasks has been the evaluation of personnel responsible for maintaining and conducting occupational or training programs. Even given the best instructional materials and exceptional physical facilities, a program conducted by an incompetent instructor will at best be marginal. Similarly, the ancillary personnel belonging to an instructional program, e. g., administrators, counselors, or training directors, can have a great effect on the outcome of that program. To ensure that their impact is indeed positive, the evaluation of education and training personnel is a necessary component of any internal evaluation system.

Personnel evaluation is nothing new in business and industry, nor in education. Business organizations continuously evaluate their personnel to increase efficiency in the direction of profit. Public educational institutions, however, have traditionally evaluated their teaching personnel simply to meet local mandates or to support tenure decisions. The focus in education has often been limited to evaluation of first year or nontenured instructors. Since many individuals other than instructors contribute to an educational program, it has been unfortunate that the focus of evaluation has so typically excluded administrators, department heads, training directors, paraprofessionals, and instructional assistants.

Personnel evaluation may be approached from many angles. The position of the evaluator in the educational system will determine to a great extent what methodology he chooses or what approach he takes. Learner or trainee evaluation of the instructor, evaluation by a supervisor or trained observer, evaluation by a colleague or peer, performance testing, and self-evaluation by instructional personnel— each contributes a unique slant which should not be overlooked in the evaluation of an occupational program. At the same time, most evaluations are directed at the answering of specific questions posed by the instructional situation. It is important that the evaluator choose the approach which contributes the most relevant output with the least undue bias. There are many reasons and purposes for evaluating personnel, each of which may require a different approach. Only the most commonly encountered purposes are presented in this chapter.

To Help Improve the Effectiveness of Education and Training Personnel

The professional improvement and development of instructional and ancillary personnel is thought by many to be the primary goal of any staff evaluation procedure (Miller, 1972; Gage, 1959). Personnel evaluation, regardless of the method utilized, should provide information which will illuminate an individual's strengths and exemplary characteristics as well as his weaknesses. When weaknesses are uncovered, the educator or trainer can begin to identify ways and means of remedying his deficiencies. For example, an instructor could review learner ratings of his performance and, based on this review, could conclude that he spends too much instructional time lecturing. Remedial action might be the use of more diverse methods in the classroom. Another, less direct method of improvement might involve review of an instructor's evaluation results by a supervisor, coupled with subsequent recommendation to the instructor for improvement. There are many ways to use evaluative information for improvement. Ultimately, several sources of information should be used and consultation with others encouraged in choosing alternatives. The last section of this chapter provides detailed direction for combining various sources of evaluative information and using these for instructional improvement.

To Help Ensure the Accountability of Education or Training Programs

This purpose or goal of personnel evaluation is probably the broadest of those presented. To ensure the accountability of a program is to ensure that the program is doing what it was intended to do in the most efficient manner possible. Both administrative and instructional personnel in charge of a program have specific responsibilities and functions contributing to the overall efficacy of the program. Personnel evaluation can help to determine if each individual is contributing his fair share to the educational or training endeavor.

To Aid in Decision Making Regarding Tenure and Salary

Tenure decisions are almost universally required in institutions of public education regardless of level. Usually at the close of an individual's second or third year (possibly longer in institutions of higher education) a decision is made regarding the retention of educational personnel. With the increasing activity of teacher organizations affiliated with either the American Federation of Teachers or the National Education Association, pressure has been placed on local school administrators to base tenure decisions on objective and valid evaluation. In most cases, discussion of findings and prescriptions for improvement are required of the administrators.

In some local educational agencies and in most private training institutions, salary advancement is based on performance appraisal. That is, raises are contingent on the job performance of the individual. While salary may not be the only reward for educators and trainers, it is certainly important, and all those involved desire a fair determination of their performance. Therefore, a viable system of evaluating performance is a necessity.

To Help Make Decisions regarding Promotions

Much like merit salary increases, promotions must be based on valid and reliable evaluation. Promotions can be of two types—intradepartmental and interdepartmental. Intradepartmental promotions are those which involve the advancement of an individual within a department, as when an instructor is advanced to a lead instructor or department chairman. Interdepartmental promotions are promotions which involve a move from one department to another or from a department to a higher administrative post. An interdepartmental promotion could involve the promotion of an electronics instructor to an occupational directorship or a principalship.

Promotions are usually made to utilize personnel most efficiently and to reward outstanding performance. Since the propounding of the "Peter Principle," administrators have felt the need to be a great deal more informed about their promotional decisions. It is important, then, that decisions for promotion be based on accurate performance evaluations.

To Aid in Selecting Education and Training Personnel

An aid in the selection of personnel for promotions, evaluation also facilitates the selection of new training and educational personnel. Simulation exercises may be utilized by personnel managers and public school administrators to screen outstanding or potentially outstanding instructors. When used for the selection of teachers, these are called teacher performance tests and will be discussed later in this chapter. The simulated teaching experience, or teacher performance test, holds great promise for the evaluation of existing instructors and the selection of prospective teachers, providing that acceptable criteria are developed to measure teacher competencies.

To Certify Practicing and Prospective Instructional Personnel

The certification boards of many states have attempted, with varying degrees of success, to certify teachers by performance rather than by credentials—on the theory that credentials have proved to be inadequate indicators of teaching expertise. This trend will place an increasing emphasis on teacher evaluation techniques and practices.

It should also bring the certification agencies, university teacher educators, and local educational agency personnel into closer consortium, resulting in better articulated programs.

To Help Enrollees Choose Instructors or Courses

Published evaluations of personnel can help potential enrollees choose between alternative instructors or courses. If evaluations are fair, and if students know what type of classroom situation is conducive to learning for them, this sort of evaluation can work to pair students with their most effective learning atmosphere.

These are all possible purposes of, or goals for, personnel evaluation within instructional programs. Certainly there are more, and there will in many cases be overlap among them. In the establishment of a personnel evaluation system, the purpose and/or goals should be specifically delineated both to guide further activity and to help avoid any misunderstanding or resistance by staff members.

WHO SHOULD BE EVALUATED?

Education and training activities are the function of enterprises or organizations and represent much more than an individual effort. That is, they involve not just a single instructor presenting information but include a number of instructors, supportive personnel, and administrators who should not be overlooked in any personnel evaluation system. This emphasis on all involved personnel, however, has not been the tradition.

The current emphasis on accountability has brought attention to the evaluation of all school personnel, but a survey conducted by the National Education Association in 1971 revealed that more progress is necessary. This extensive study identified only eighty-four school districts which claimed to have formal administrator evaluation systems; of those districts, 75 percent relied on a checklist for the evaluation.

Moreover, ancillary personnel are almost universally excluded by formal evaluation systems. Ancillary personnel include counselors, advisors, library or instructional resource personnel, and paraprofessionals or instructional assistants. It is the authors' contention that all persons involved in the instructional system should be evaluated in some way. In the remainder of this chapter, primary emphasis will be placed on instructor and administrator evaluation. However, much overlap exists in methodology for the evaluation of ancillary personnel.

METHODS FOR EVALUATING EDUCATION AND TRAINING PERSONNEL

Assessment of education and training personnel performance can focus on information which relates to either of two broad classes: 1) observable behavior of the educator or trainer, or 2) results of this behavior as expressed in learner accomplishments. Educators and trainers have been cautioned against overemphasis on each of these classes of evaluative information. However, each has advantages and disadvantages, which will be discussed later in this section. Basically, *behavior* can be observed and recorded by way of three methods: observer ratings, job target evaluation, and self-analysis. With regard to the *consequences* of an instructor's behavior, two broad categories of measurement will be discussed in this chapter: teacher performance testing and contract plans.

Observer Ratings

Observer ratings of teachers have traditionally been limited to supervisory ratings. However, the use of ratings by peers or colleagues is gaining popularity. Even more noticeable is the increased use of ratings by students. It has become increasingly apparent that, because learners observe teachers daily throughout a course or program, they are in an excellent position to judge teacher performance realistically.

Types of Rating Systems

Administrator or Supervisor Ratings. Perhaps the oldest and most traditional approach to instructor evaluation has been the supervisor or administrator evaluation or rating. Administrator or supervisor ratings are usually accomplished during or following a classroom visitation and are based on an individual's observation of a particular teacher in the process of instruction. Such visitation should be planned with care and the supervisor or administrator should use some form of standard rating scale or checklist to make the rating as structured and as reliable as possible. However, just as an incompetent instructor can have a damaging effect on an otherwise excellent educational program, a poor observer can upset an otherwise acceptable evaluation strategy. It should be clear to any evaluator that an instructor should not be judged according to how closely his teaching technique corresponds to the technique formerly used by the administrator or supervisor. Who should visit, how often, and for what purposes, are questions whose answers must be determined for each specific educational or training function. Likewise, the status of the individual being evaluated may determine the "who" and "how often" of the visitation, e. g., a first-year instructor may need to be more closely observed than an experienced instructor.

Regardless of the scheduling of the visitation and the person of the individual who conducts the evaluation, it is essential that a conference be held following each visitation and rating of a particular instructor. This conference should be attended by the evaluator and the person being evaluated. At this conference, the evaluator should communicate his observations and perceptions regarding a particular instructor's performance. This will help the instructor improve his instruction—and the improvement of instruction should be the primary goal of instructional evaluation. Specific rating forms and scales for the evaluation can assume many different formats and will be discussed in a later section of this chapter along with guidelines for constructing them.

Colleague or Peer Rating. Another observational evaluation technique is the rating of instruction by colleagues or peers. This technique involves observation of a particular instructor by one of his peers or associates. The colleague observation and rating usually assumes the same format as that of the administrator and supervisor ratings. Many times the individual instructor may suggest that a particular individual whom he respects observe or sit in on one of his classes or conferences to provide critiques of procedures or activities in the classroom. One of the greatest shortcomings of the colleague observation and rating has been the sparsity of rating scales that remain applicable across all instructors. Usually colleague observation is conducted without the use of such an instrument or scale and, of course, this brings to bear certain points of bias.

The inherent advantage in using both a supervisory and a colleague rating system is in gaining a multiple view of an instructor's activities and techniques. When one considers the primary goal of all colleague evaluation systems—that of improving instruction—it is obvious that the most important result will be the suggestions for improvement. Moreover, any form of evaluation is useful if it helps to substantiate other forms of evaluation. A final advantage of the colleague rating is that this approach to rating minimizes resistance on the part of instructors or faculty members.

Of course, all evaluation methods possess disadvantages as well as advantages. One disadvantage was referred to in discussion of the administrator or supervisory evaluation or rating, that of bias toward one particular instructional technique by the observer. If the observer or rater has found that the discussion technique has worked most effectively for him, he may view another instructor's use of the lecture technique as inappropriate and may overemphasize the discussion technique. Another disadvantage might be the effect of personality conflict. If a particular evaluator is observing an instructor with whom he has had prior disagreements, these conflicts may influence his evaluation of the instructor's teaching activity. Also, with any observational technique or process there is the possibility that an intermediate appraisal will be confused and substituted for an ultimate measure. For example, an ineffective mechanic may be judged to be proficient because of an impressive set of well-maintained tools and knowledgeable talk about his work. Another disadvantage, which is somewhat unique to colleague observation and rating of instruction, is its reciprocity. When one colleague observes another's instructional presentation and rates him highly, the ratee may feel obligated to do the same when it comes his turn to observe the rater.

Odionre (1971) has colorfully labeled two kinds of flaws or

disadvantages of such an observation or rating system. The "halo effect" is the tendency to rate a person highly because of:

1. Past record—good past work tends to carry over into present.
2. Compatibility—those we like we rate higher.
3. Recency—a good job yesterday is valued higher than a good job last week.
4. Blind spot—I don't see defects that are similar to my own.

Odionre's "horn effect" is the tendency to rate people lower because of:

1. Perfectionism—our expectation may be too high; consequently we are disappointed.
2. Contrary—an individual who disagrees too often.
3. Oddball—the maverick or nonconformist.
4. Guilt by association.
5. Dramatic incident—a recent goof can wipe out a year's work.

These factors, of course, are important in considering the development of an instrument and the administration of a faculty or instructor evaluation system.

Learner or Student Rating.   Evaluation of instructors by their learners has been a popular practice for a number of years at all levels of education and training. However, it has been utilized to a greater extent at the university, sales, and management levels. For example, a study conducted by Stecklein (1960) reported that of 800 colleges surveyed, learner ratings were regularly used in nearly 40 percent and an additional 32 percent were considering their use at the time the survey was conducted.

Typically, learner evaluation has been conducted by using questionnaires, checklists, and rating forms which are completed at the end of or following a particular course. Many colleges and training departments have formalized this system and have attempted to control for bias on learner ratings by ensuring anonymity. This has been done by not requiring names to be placed on forms and by ensuring that a particular instructor does not see the actual form. Some colleges have gone so far as to institute a system of teacher evaluation which is managed entirely by students, from the administration and collection to the publishing of results. This practice has been especially evident in large universities.

Published ratings of instructors have been used in some of these cases to aid future enrollees in selection of courses and instructors. However, their greatest advantage may actually be to the instructor by helping him to identify how the learners perceive his instructional abilities, techniques, and activities.

Like the administrator rating and the colleague rating, the learner rating must be based on a well-formulated instrument or question-naire which has undergone considerable field testing and revision. With regard to the administration of the learner evaluation, Ebel (1972) has suggested that the distribution and selection process should be governed by three criteria: objectivity, coverage, and timing. In terms of objectivity, Ebel suggests that some distance should be preserved between the faculty member or instructor whose course is being evaluated and the learners doing the evaluating. Research at the University of Kentucky reported by Kirchner (1969) has shown statistically that learner ratings were significantly higher when the instructor was present at the time of the evaluation. Consequently, it is important that the procedures for distribution and collection of the instruments be standardized.

The second point suggested by Ebel, the extent of coverage, depends on what is sought from the evaluation. An organization-wide evaluation of all instructors would provide for a comparison between and among various discipline areas or occupational areas. If this coverage is desired, the instrument should be general enough to apply to all instructors. On the other hand, if a particular department's faculty is the focus of the evaluation, the instrument could be more specific to the subject matter and laboratory facility.

Ebel's third point concerning timing suggests that it is usually best to provide students the opportunity to complete evaluations prior to termination of the course. If the instrument administered is completed outside of class, the return rate may be adversely affected. Also, this may allow a certain bias to enter in, if those persons motivated to return the instrument share a similar bias. Miller (1972) in his book, *Evaluating Faculty Performance*, suggests that if returns of any one class are below 70 percent, the reliability of results should be questioned.

Miller further suggests that care be taken to prevent the evalua-tive instrument from acquiring a punitive connotation. As mentioned earlier, the learner appraisal of instruction should have as its primary goal the improvement of instructor performance. However, it can contribute to decision making regarding merit increases, promotions, tenure, and other decisions. When this information is used for decision making, it should be supplemented by other ratings and evaluative information.

The advantages of a learner evaluation system appear to outweigh the disadvantages. One major advantage is that learners have had the opportunity to observe continually what they are rating. That is, they have had much more contact with the instructor than any outside observer could ever have. A second advantage is that learner evaluations allow for a large number of ratings and this allows a number of individual biases to be averaged, increasing the likelihood of an accurate representation.

A third advantage lies in the fact that learners seem to take good instruction very seriously. Ratings from a questionnaire answered by 1,603 high school juniors and seniors in 1970 favored those teachers who were demanding and cared about learners as fellow human beings. This runs contrary to the notion that learners give more favorable ratings to those instructors who entertain the class.

The disadvantages to student evaluation of teaching are not easily confirmed. One of the basic ones is the lack of understanding on the part of instructors and administrators with regard to what the student evaluation can provide. For example, most opposition to student ratings seems to be motivated by a deep-seated and pervasive distrust of students. They are often seen as incompetent judges, biased, immature, and arbitrary. Many feel that learners confuse good teaching with showmanship. However, research has shown that students are perceptive and become more so when they realize their opinions are seriously regarded. The idea that students have no right to judge is rapidly losing ground as the concept of academic freedom is extended to include students. Educators are coming to feel that students have the right to bring their interests and opinions to the attention of the teacher and the institution.

Possibly one of the most serious shortcomings of student evaluation of teaching is the inadequacy of the devices or instruments used in these evaluations. These instruments, like all other rating forms and evaluation instruments, have reliability and validity constraints. However, these statistical shortcomings can be overcome by means of adequate preparation and testing.

Another criticism of student evaluation of teaching is rooted in the belief that the good students will rate the class high and the poor students will rate the class low. However, research has shown that class size, rater sex, rater's grade point average, and teacher's sex have little bearing on student ratings of teachers, and most studies indicate that the grade which a student expects to receive in a course is not related to his rating of the teacher. In addition, examination of ratings of elective versus required classes and ratings by majors and nonmajors has proved that these factors do little to bias the rater. Research on the evaluation of college teachers has pointed up only two factors which are significant in terms of student ratings. The first, the rater's class (graduate students versus undergraduate) has apparently produced biases in ratings. Likewise, the teacher's rank (instructor versus assistant professor or associate professor, for instance) appears to make a difference in terms of rating.

Types of Rating Scales

Good (1959, p. 440) has defined a rating scale as "a device used in evaluating products, attitudes, or other characteristics of instructors or learners (the usual form is an evaluation chart carrying suggested points for checking)." The rating scale differs in important respects from other paper and pencil devices. In addition to any limitations imposed by the form itself, ratings are limited by characteristics of the human rater—perception, memory, sensitivity, and accuracy of observation. Guilford, in a 1954 edition of an educational measurement book, groups rating scales into five categories—numerical, graphic, standard, cumulative point, and forced choice—suggesting that this classification is a very loose one. Guilford's excellent treatment of rating scales is anchored in psychological theory and is based on a fairly experimental point of view. Remmers (1963), in *Handbook of Research on Teaching*, has extended Guilford's rating scale analysis by making it more practical for constructing rating scales for teaching. This chapter section, based largely on the work of Remmers, describes six types of rating scales: numerical, graphic, cumulative point, checklist, multiple choice, and forced choice.

Numerical Rating Scales. Numerical rating scales, as the name implies, measure characteristics by assigning numbers to the specific rating categories. For example, an agreement scale such as the following, with a number assigned to each of the five categories, allows for summarization in a total score or a number of subscores.

EXAMPLE ITEM 1

The instructor stimulates people's interest.

1. Strongly agree
2. Agree
3. Uncertain or indifferent
4. Disagree
5. Strongly disagree

With some numerical rating scales, no numbers actually appear on the instrument and numbers are assigned by raters to each category only following the completion of the instrument. An extension of the more simple numerical rating scale includes a further description of the item and a listing of sample evidences to aid the observer in making his particular rating. The following example item presents this type of format.

EXAMPLE ITEM 2

The instructor is fair and impartial.   SA   A   U   D   SD

                                            0   1   2   3   4

Sample evidences

Shows no favoritism or partiality; praise and criticism are based on fact; all criticism constructive; no pets; appraisal of people is fair and reliable; no excessive criticism of individual people; maintains the confidence of learners.

Figure 7–1 presents an example of an experimentally refined numerical scale developed by Ryans (1960). The content of this Classroom Observation Record was determined after considerable empirical investigation and revision. It allows the rater to categorize both learner and instructor behavior on a scale from 1 to 7. The type of scale used in Ryan's instrument can also be adapted to include liking

Teacher Behavior								
Partial	1	2	3	4	5	6	7	Fair
Harsh	1	2	3	4	5	6	7	Kindly
Disorganized	1	2	3	4	5	6	7	Systematic
Inflexible	1	2	3	4	5	6	7	Adaptable

FIGURE 7–1   *Example Items from a Numerical Scale Instrument*

or disliking, approval or disapproval, acceptance or rejection, and the like. These appear to be on a linear continuum, with a zero point at the center or the point of indifference. However, because it is awkward to manipulate negative numbers on rating scales of this sort, in most cases positive numbers are employed. Remmers suggests that extreme categories (categories on the scale which it can be assumed no one will use or respond to) should be omitted. Because numerical scales are easy to construct, to apply, and to process, there has been extensive use of the numerical scale in many instructor or other personnel evaluation forms.

Graphic Rating Scales. The graphic rating item is simply an item stem possessing a straight line with rating categories positioned along the straight line. The scale can assume many different forms, with or without descriptive categories and with or without numbers for the scale units. Example Items 3 and 4 present different scale category descriptions for two similar items.

EXAMPLE ITEM 3

Is the instructor permissive?

Extremely	Rather	Hardly	Somewhat	Not at all

EXAMPLE ITEM 4

To what extent is the teacher permissive?

| Permissive in all situations | Usually permissive, rarely authoritarian | Not dependably permissive; sometimes dictatorial | Usually dictatorial |

These descriptions, of course, could be extended to an even more specific delineation of each category, up to a paragraph for each. Obviously, the more specific one becomes in describing categories, the more consistent will be information from raters. In addition, Example Item 3 would have something of a norm-reference. That is, the rating of an instructor's permissiveness would be based solely on the background and the former observations of the particular rater. On the other hand, the base for Example Item 4 would be more of a criterion-referenced sort.

Graphic items can also be grouped with a number of stems utilizing the same categories for rating. This can be a great advantage in terms of saving space and of preventing the rater from changing his response mode for each item. On many rating scales the line or continuum of a characteristic is divided into unit distances, usually of equal length. Sometimes numbers are even assigned to points along this continuum. This facilitates scoring of the items by simply summing or averaging item responses. Example Items 3 and 4 incorporate a horizontal line, but this is not necessarily required. A vertical line or arrangement can provide more room for descriptive categories, especially when only one rating per page is included. However, space limitations and preferences of raters should be the determining factors in choosing the format of the particular graphic items. Remmers has presented the following nine suggestions for constructing graphic rating scales:

1. The line, whether horizontal or vertical, should be unbroken.
2. The line should be five or six inches long, enough to allow indication of all discrimination of which the rater is capable.
3. The direction of the lines should be the same, i. e., the socially desirable end should be the same for all traits.

4. If several objects are to be rated, the best arrangement of the page is that which rates all of them on one characteristic before proceeding to another characteristic.
5. Guilford (1954) suggests that for unsophisticated raters the good end of the line should come first.
6. Descriptive categories should be as near as possible to the points of the scale they describe.
7. The categories need not be equally spaced.
8. In other than machine scoring, a stencil divided into numbered sections makes a convenient scoring device.
9. Guilford (1954) suggests that segmented lines should not call for any finer discriminations than will be used in scoring.

If a particular educational or training agency possesses an electronic scoring machine or has access to one, it may be advantageous to design numerical or graphic rating scales that can be processed by such machines. This can save a considerable amount of time in scoring and summarizing the individual rating scales though it may negate points 1 and 2.

Cumulated-point Rating Scales. The cumulated-point method of scoring is similar to psychological tests which score items as either 1 or 0. The common form of items for this type of scale include the yes-no and true-false type of item. Example Items 5 and 6 present two forms of the cumulated-point rating scales.

EXAMPLE ITEM 5

This instructor usually gets ideas across—explains things clearly and is easy to understand.

___YES ___NO
(1)   (2)

EXAMPLE ITEM 6

In this class we often use charts, diagrams, maps, specimens, or models.

___YES ___NO
(1)   (2)

An example of an instrument which incorporates fifty questionnaire items of the cumulated-point rating scale type is entitled My Teacher and was constructed by Leeds and Cook (1947). For this or any other dichotomous type of item, each response would have a particular number code. In examples 5 and 6, a "yes" would be scored as 1 and a "no" response would be scored as 0. Response numbers then could simply be summed and cumulated to form a total score as well as subscores if the instrument is so designed.

Checklist. Checklists are simply lists of behaviors or activities which are checked by a rater as being witnessed during a particular observation. Checklists are valuable instruments for determining what an instructor does and can be extended to record even the number of times a particular activity or technique has been utilized. Following is a simple checklist.

EXAMPLE ITEM 7

Handles effectively and efficiently the routine of classroom management. ___

Respects the worth and dignity of the individual learner. ___

Gives careful attention to the physical conditions and appearance of the classroom. ___

Secures good results in teaching. ___

Seeks improved ways of teaching. ___

Uses many devices to enrich the learning process. ___

Makes use of available visual equipment. ___

In addition to recording the existence or frequency of actions, the checklist can also be modified to record the proper sequence or occurrence in time of particular acts or maneuvers as shown below.

EXAMPLE ITEM 8

Use of the Overhead Projector

Position projector ___

Plug projector into receptacle ___

Place sample transparency on projector table	___
Turn on projector	___
Adjust position of machine	___
Focus projector	___
Turn off projector	___
Insert first transparency	___
Turn off projector	___
Turn off projector while changing transparencies	___

Multiple Choice Rating Forms. The familiar multiple choice test item can also be used for rating instructional or other educational personnel. It has been discussed rather thoroughly in other chapters of this book and, basically, incorporates an item stem with a number of alternative choices. Multiple choice items may be of the sentence completion or question and answer type. Example Items 9 and 10 present both types.

EXAMPLE ITEM 9

With respect to knowledge of subject matter, my instructor:
  a. Appears to know the subject matter extremely well.
  b. Seems moderately well informed.
  c. Appears to be poorly informed.
  d. Appears to be very poorly informed.

EXAMPLE ITEM 10

What is your instructor's attitude toward teaching?
  a. He seems to be very enthusiastic about teaching.
  b. He seems to be enthusiastic about teaching.
  c. He seems about average in enthusiasm towards teaching.
  d. He seems indifferent towards teaching.
  e. He does not seem to enjoy teaching.

The multiple choice item can provide valuable teacher evaluation information, but it does pose some problems in scoring results. Traditionally, the multiple choice item in a cognitive achievement test possesses a correct response. However, in the context of teacher evaluation there is no right or wrong answer. For many items, each category can be assigned numbers 1 through 5 or 1 through 7 depending on the number of alternatives. It is also possible to summarize each item by recording the proportion or percentage responding to each category or to each alternative of the item. In this way, the information gathered will indicate to the teacher exactly how the raters responded to particular characteristics. This would be especially true in the use of multiple choice items on a student rating form.

Forced Choice Rating Scales. The forced choice rating scale is much more complex to develop than the aforementioned types of scales. The forced choice scale is basically the presentation of diads, triads, tetrads, or quintads or particular descriptive information from which the respondent or rater must choose one or the best one of those that are presented. The set of possible responses, that is, the diads, triads, and so on, usually contain as many items as there are factors being assessed by way of this type of instrument.

An instrument developed by Cosgrove (1959), designed to obtain diagnostic information about a teacher's performance, is readily adaptable to the needs of an institutional trainer. This instrument contains four factors: a) knowledge and organization of subject matter, b) adequacy of relations with students in class, c) adequacy of plans and procedures in class, and d) enthusiasm in working with students. For each one of these factors, nine specific descriptors were developed. Example items 11 and 12 are drawn from this particular instrument. Each set contains four items, each of which pertains to one of the above factors.

EXAMPLE ITEM 11

Measures:

Set A. ___Always on time for class   (c)
        ___Pleasant in class   (b)
        ___Very sincere when talking with students   (d)
        ___Well read   (a)

EXAMPLE ITEM 12

Measures:

Set B.   ___Contagious enthusiasm for subject   (d)
       ___Does not fill up time with trivial material   (c)
       ___Gives everyone an equal chance   (b)
       ___Makes clear what is expected of students   (a)

The forced choice scale has several advantages. First, it overcomes the rater's tendency to leniency because he is forced to make some kind of judgment. In addition, the distribution of ratings or scores on a forced choice type rating scale is much more realistic than some other rating scale distributions. Another point which can be considered either an advantage or disadvantage is that the results of the forced choice rating scale are meaningful only to the individual instructor being rated. That is, the results simply indicate what the particular teacher possesses as strongest and weakest factors and do not lend themselves to comparison of instructors.

Determining the Content of Rating Scales

One of the major problems with instructor evaluation in general and rating scale development in particular is the fact that no firm definition of a good instructor exists. Teaching techniques are highly individual and those which are effective for one instructor may be much less effective for another. Therefore, it becomes almost impossible to develop an instructor evaluation scale that could be utilized by all regardless of level or subject matter area. It is suggested, however, that those who will be rated should be involved in the development of the specific instruments and the procedures which will be utilized. Obviously the judgment of the person in charge of the instructor evaluation and of persons involved in the development of instruments and procedures will determine what is most appropriate to the purposes of the evaluation system. This will include the choosing of qualities, behaviors, skills, habits, situations, and the like to be evaluated. There are several basic means of determining content to be measured by the teacher evaluation rating scale. Three of these will be discussed in this chapter: systematic conception of teaching, consensus of competent judges, and critical incident technique.

Systematic Conception of Teaching.   Instrument content based on explicit conception of the teaching and learning process was utilized in a series of instruments constructed by Simpson and Brown (1952). They carried out a study of learning and teaching by means of these scales in eight different college level programs. The corresponding scales or major factors of their instruments included: motivational level of students, handling assignments, problem identification, problem selection, problem solution, tryout of solutions, evaluative abilities, record keeping, locating resources, considering learning abilities in selecting resources, opportunities for democratic group discussion, and purposeful reading.

Considerable emphasis in recent times has been placed on the identification of competencies for teachers and also administrators, counselors, and paraprofessionals. This has occurred at varying levels—elementary, secondary and post-secondary—in public education. Competencies possessed by occupational and career education personnel have been identified through several extensive studies (Terry et al., 1971, and Odbert, 1973). These studies, which have identified competencies for administrators, counselors, and varying levels of instructional personnel, provide an excellent starting point for the development of faculty or instructor evaluation forms based on the systematic conception.

Consensus of Competent Judges.   The second means or method for identifying content for instructor evaluation rating scales is the consensus of competent judge technique. As the name implies, this involves analysis and selection by a group of experts of specific traits, competencies, activities, skills, and abilities to be evaluated by way of the instructor evaluation instrument. An example of an instrument which was developed using this technique is the Classroom Behavior Record (Ryans, 1960). Items for this instrument were selected by a group of judges and then were greatly improved through the experimental and statistical refinement of the instrument. Even though this technique has been somewhat popular, it does possess many constraints, for example, experts are often not the on-line personnel who have an accurate knowledge of what is required and necessary for a particular educational position.

Critical Incident Technique.   A third approach to content identification for rating scales is entitled the critical incident technique. Basically, it involves the identification of effective and ineffective teachers by way of systematic observation. This can be accomplished by soliciting the judgments of learners, peers, administrators, and specialists from outside the particular institution. Once the exceptional and poor teachers are identified, the respondents or raters are requested to indicate behaviors which they feel contribute to making each of these teachers either exceptional or poor. These behaviors are categorized, and rating scale items can then be formulated to identify the existence of good or questionable behaviors. Obviously, this method is rather involved and would require considerable expenditure of time and effort to identify content for rating scales. Regardless of the technique utilized in constructing rating forms, emphasis should be placed on revision of the instruments both prior to and pursuant to their use.

Job Target Evaluation

The job target approach to personnel evaluation is not strictly limited to instructional personnel but may be applied to all educational or training personnel. The job target approach has assumed many names including *performance goal procedure, performance evaluation,* and *management-by-objectives.* A 1971 survey conducted by the National Education Association indicated that 25 percent of school systems which evaluate administrators use this approach. One benefit of the method is the improvement of a person's job performance in a congenial atmosphere fostered by a collaborative relationship between the evaluator and the evaluatee on all aspects of the evaluation procedure.

The job target approach should begin with a systemwide collaborative effort to determine and write down (formalize) not only the policies and purposes of the institution or school district but also the broad goals and expected results of each administrative unit and position. This effort can be extended to include each instructional provision. Any subordinate objectives or goals should be articulated within the broad goals as formalized in the goal statement. The focus of job target evaluation is on three questions: 1) What are we trying to accomplish? 2) How well are we doing? and 3) How can we do better? The objectives of this sort of evaluation system usually relate to improving supervision so as to improve performance, planning for individual growth and development, providing information to assist in improving marginal performance, identifying special talents and skills, and protecting both individual and institutional rights when determining dismissals due to substandard performance. This type of personnel evaluation system has proved useful in the industrial sector and is expanding into use in the public education system.

Once broad institutional goals have been set, the job target approach begins with a conference between an individual and his immediate supervisor or superior. In most cases, an instructor will meet his department chairman or his training supervisor. Likewise, the department chairman will probably meet with an assistant principal or with a training director. Together, the subordinate and the supervisor decide which goals are important for the subordinate to achieve in a given time period. In making this decision, they keep in mind the broad objectives for the institution and for the particular position. Identification of goals leads to developing a program of action to improve job performance and setting the schedule within which the activities will be completed. Both individuals review progress in conferences throughout the time period and repeat the same procedure for future and additional performance targets. When there is disagreement on the achievement of a particular objective by the superior and the subordinate, there are several alternatives available—both evaluations can go on file and an appeal made to a higher authority, or the subordinate may be counseled by different supervisors, to mention just two.

One assumption implicit in the job target approach is that the administrator who knows what he wants to accomplish will know how to accomplish it. Obviously, the supervisor can help to identify means of achieving these objectives or goals. It is likewise obvious that this approach has much to offer in terms of individualizing a particular personnel evaluation system. A job target evaluation system could be applied to administrators, counselors, instructors, paraprofessionals, and other educational and training personnel. In addition, it takes into account the specific and varying tasks encountered from one instructor to another. Another advantage is its ease of

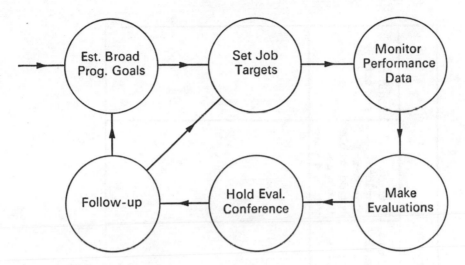

FIGURE 7–2   *Schematic of Job Target Approach (reproduced from* The National Elementary Principal, *1973, 52(5):51–55 and used with permission of the author and The National Association of Elementary School Principals, Arlington, Virginia).*

implementation. Evaluation instruments, for example, can even be as simple as a plain sheet of paper. This represents a radical departure from the rating scale approach described in the prior section of this chapter. Figure 7–2 is a schematic representation of the job target approach to personnel evaluation as presented by Harold Armstrong (1973). Armstrong lists six interrelated steps for job target evaluation: establishing performance objectives, setting job targets, monitoring performance data, conducting evaluations based on performance data, holding evaluation conferences, and conducting the follow-up to the evaluation conference.

Formulating Job Targets

Traditionally, the selection of job targets has been based on informal assessment of prevalent problems or desired outcomes which are rarely written down on paper. Borgen and Davis (1974) have outlined an excellent plan for the preparation of program management objectives, to use their term.

LISTING OF PROBLEMS, PROJECTS, AND OUTCOMES

COLUMN A	COLUMN B		
Projects, problems, outcomes, idea changes, activities that you want to achieve	Essential to complete this year	Desirable to complete this year	Not to complete this year but desirable to complete within 4 years	Could be put off

FIGURE 7–3 *Example Form for Listing Problems, Projects, or Outcomes (reproduced from J. Borgen and D. Davis, Planning, Implementing, and Evaluating Career Preparation Programs, Bloomington: McKnight Publishers, 1974, and used with permission).*

Step 1: Identification of Problems

This plan begins with identifying and listing both problems confronted and project outcomes that the individual educational or training person being evaluated may want to achieve. These project products or outcomes should be listed on a form such as that shown in Figure 7–3. This listing might be based on a number of documents or items including 1) position or job description, 2) institutional evaluation report, 3) student information, 4) budget and cost study reports, and 5) prior personnel evaluation reports. As this list could be almost unlimited, the individual staff member must be selective in choosing those problems or desired outcomes which can be overcome or attained within the specific time and resource limitations. Hence, the second major column of the form in Figure 7–3 has been provided for establishing priorities for each of the listed problems, outcomes, or projects. In this column the individual staff member should check whether a task is essential to complete that year, desirable to complete that year, desirable to complete within the next four years, or capable of being postponed indefinitely.

Step 2: Establish Evaluator Relationships

The next major step in the development of job targets should be the formal assignment of a particular individual to a specific supervisor—either the department chairman or training supervisor. As noted before, department chairmen would most likely report to a training director or a principal or assistant principal. Once these relationships have been established, a meeting should be scheduled between the supervisor and his subordinate. During this meeting, the supervisor should review the list of problems and their priorities and make recommendations for changes in this list. This will ensure that there is agreement between the evaluator and the evaluatee with regard to projected job targets.

Step 3: Orientation Meeting

A third step should involve a meeting of all of those personnel who report to a specific individual. For example, all instructors would meet with their department chairman. The purpose of this meeting

Name _____ Date _____

Title and/or Position _____

CONDITIONS	OUTCOME STATEMENT	CRITERIA			
		Reality Based Results			
Time Period and/or Target Date	Management Responsibility	Minimum Acceptable	Average Expected	Maximum Probable	Unit of Measurement or Formula

FIGURE 7–4 *Example Form for Constructing Quantitative Job Targets reproduced from J. Borgen and D. Davis, Planning, Implementing, and Evaluating Career Preparation Programs, Bloomington: McKnight Publishers, 1974, and used with permission).*

Name _____

Title and/or Position _____

Date _____

CONDITIONS	OUTCOME STATEMENT	CRITERIA
Time Period and/or Target Date	Plans for Change and Problem Solving	Statement Describing Conditions That Will Exist

FIGURE 7–5 *Example Form for Constructing Nonquantitative Job Targets* (reproduced from J. Borgen and D. Davis, Planning, Implementing, and Evaluating Career Preparation Programs, Bloomington: McKnight Publishers, 1974, *and used with permission*).

should be for the supervisor or chairman to orient the staff to the writing of job targets or program management objectives. Although this step will not be necessary once the job target evaluation system has been instituted, considerable attention should be paid initially to writing these objectives. Borgen and Davis (1974) have differentiated between two types of job targets—those that may be evaluated with quantitative indicators and those that must be evaluated with non-quantitative indicators. With either type, the job target should consist of an outcome statement, a conditions statement, and a criteria statement. Figure 7—4 presents a form which can be used in constructing job targets which possess quantitative criteria. The "outcome statement" column is a restatement of the problems, projects, or other outcomes which were identified in Step One and further in Step Two (see Figure 7—3). The "conditions statement" gives the time period or target date of completion. The criteria column indicates, in the case of the quantitative job target, the exact minimum, average, and maximum numbers to be achieved. With the case of job targets which do not possess quantitative indicators, the criteria column would include a short description of the report, action, event, or happening that would show that the outcome has been accomplished or achieved. Figure 7—5 presents a form for preparing job targets that do not have easily measured outcomes and completion times.

The orientation session should provide ample opportunity for each instructor or subordinate to write sample job targets and to gain the supervisor's reaction to the adequacy of the written job target.

Step 4: Job Target Preparation

Step Four should provide the individual instructors or other staff members the opportunity to write performance job targets for each of the problems identified and formalized in Step Two.

Step 5: Review of Targets by Evaluator

Step Five should provide a final review of each staff member's job targets by the supervisor or evaluator. If necessary, a conference can then be held on an individual basis between staff members and supervisors to clarify or to revise any job targets which the supervisor feels are inappropriate or inadequate. Once this review is complete, there should be total agreement between each superior and his subordinates with regard to the targets and the conditions and criteria by which the targets will be evaluated.

The third stage of the cycle (Figure 7-2) would be the next point of reference—monitoring performance data—and involves making the evaluations based upon this data by assessing the criteria section of each job target and comparing actual performance to intended performance. Once performance data has been monitored and evaluations have been made by a superior, a conference should be held (Step Five, Figure 7-2) to discuss the accomplishments and failures of the individual staff member. Recommendations based upon this conference should be agreed upon by both the supervisor and the evaluated person. In many instances it may be valuable to hold such an evaluation conference prior to the end of a particular training period or school year. This would allow the instructor to discuss his preliminary accomplishments and to project whether he is going to accomplish what was intended. This will provide the opportunity for in-process or formative feedback to the educational or training staff member regarding his performance.

Self-evaluation by Educational and Training Personnel

Ideally, instructors would systematically assess and revise their own teaching behavior. Most instructional personnel desire to improve but lack knowledge of self-evaluation procedures and do not possess self-directing learning styles. McNeil and Popham (1973) believe that instructors who have not received training on how to focus on relevant aspects of their work may tend to criticize superficialities— personal mannerisms, appearance, voice, or use of materials. In most such cases, the instructor relies on personal, incidental observations of his own teaching behavior—and of his learners' behavior—which lead occasionally to minor adjustments in teaching procedures. Generally, McNeil and Popham believe, teachers are not likely to change their performance without visible evidence of a discrepancy between what they want to achieve and what they are actually achieving. The burden of proof is best shouldered by a well-conceived program of self-evaluation.

A thoughtful and constructive approach to self-evaluation should

"Used; found valuable"	"Used; found of doubtful or no value"	Original number and item on questionnaire	Might be interested in trying
121	5	(13) Voluntary and continuing colleague discussions or seminars by instructors of a particular course.	43
121	13	(7) Comparative check on your efficiency using one teaching approach vs. your efficiency in using another approach.	36
91	9	(12) Visiting in a colleague's class for the purpose of evaluating and improving your own classes.	44
81	36	(2) Open-ended relatively unstructured written evaluation by students.	37
79	28	(1) Evaluative questionnaires or checklists constructed by the teacher to be filled out by your students.	49
51	6	(3) Yearly written recap of own activities and an assessment of the strong and weak aspects of such activities.	46
49	6	(16) Soliciting the help of administrators or supervisors in evaluating one's own teaching.	29
46	4	(15) Planned meetings with colleagues for the purpose of evaluation of your own and others' teaching.	56
43	16	(6) Published teacher evaluative instruments.	64
32	1	(10) Tape recording or TV recording of regular class sessions and then feedback analysis on your part.	90
32	4	(17) Systematic search in printed resources for diagnostic tools and procedures for self-evaluation.	36
22	5	(14) Regular luncheons to discuss evaluations of own and others' teaching.	41
20	13	(4) Comparative ratings by your students on specified dimensions of your instruction vs. that of other instructors.	59
10	1	(8) Other action research, in addition to that in No. (7) above, to test teaching efficiency. (Please describe on the back of this sheet.)	17
5	2	(9) Cooperating colleague who near the end of a semester or quarter leads a discussion in your class of strong points and weak points of the class with you absent.	45
4	10	(5) Student evaluation committee to provide feedback to the instructor.	63
3	1	(11) Tape recording of an evaluative class session in which strengths and limitations of classes are analyzed. (This discussion to be led by the instructor, by a student, by a panel of students, or by a colleague.)	43

FIGURE 7–6   *Listing of Self-evaluation Activities from a National Survey (reproduced from R. H. Simpson, "Biological Science Instructors' Use of Self-evaluation Tools," the American Biology Teacher, vol. 24, no. 8, 1962).*

involve the use of one or more tools or procedures to help diagnose possible areas for improvement in the teaching-learning situation. Also, administrators or other supportive personnel can utilize systematic introspection to help identify areas of weakness which need improvement. Such systematic analysis of strengths and weaknesses can result in careful planning followed by actual tryout of steps designed to produce an improvement. It can be seen that there is considerable overlap between self-evaluation and the other types of evaluation discussed in this chapter. Obviously, learner and peer ratings, as well as administrator ratings and job target results may be utilized by an individual instructor to improve his performance. In addition, teacher performance tests, which will be discussed in the next section of this chapter, have valuable implications for self-evaluation. Since there is this great overlap, and since many of the self-evaluation techniques are of an informal nature, great detail will not be given to these techniques in this section. Presented instead is a listing of techniques and information relative to their usefulness as perceived by practicing educators.

In a survey conducted by the American Association of Colleges of Teacher Education (Simpson, 1962), an attempt was made to gather information on self-evaluation practices and attitudes. Each of the 245 biological science instructors involved in this study was asked to indicate which of seventeen self-evaluation activities they had utilized and to give a judgment of the value of each. Figure 7–6 presents the list of seventeen self-evaluation strategies in rank order according to use. In addition to the seventeen tools or strategies which were presented in this survey, further approaches were solicited from the respondents. These resulting strategies included: 1) instructor's written assessment of his own teaching, 2) assessment of learner achievement during and pursuant to instruction, 3) assessment by colleagues, 4) adaptation from business or industrial evaluation procedures, and 5) assessment by learner feedback. This survey provides valuable suggestions for self-evaluation in a local setting.

Observer ratings, job target evaluation, and self-analysis, then, are evaluative methods which focus on the behavior of the instructor. At least two techniques have utility in measuring the *consequences* of an instructor's action or behavior. *Teacher performance testing* and *contracting* will be discussed in this section.

Teacher Performance Testing

This technique was developed by James Popham for use in public educational institutions but is readily adaptable to any instructional or training program. It is predicated on the assumption that the teacher's chief reason for existence is to bring about a beneficial change in behavior of learners, including modifications in learner's knowledge, attitudes, and skills. Fundamentally, a teacher performance test is a short-term instructional activity in which the instructor is presented with an objective and given time to plan and present a lesson to a group of naive learners. Following the presentation, the students are assessed with regard to the objective.

The teaching performance test assesses the instructor's ability to accomplish prespecified changes in learners, using whatever instructional procedure or tactic the teacher wishes.

Popham (1973) describes two main roles that this test may assume: *instructional improvement* and *skill assessment.* For instructional improvement, the teacher performance test can show a teacher how to improve at instructing learners. For skill assessment, the teacher performance test can identify weak and strong teachers as an aid to assigning them or making other administrative decisions. To initiate self-improvement, Popham recommends the use of the teaching performance test in small groups of teachers. An in-service improvement program can be organized around short-term tests in a particular subject matter area such as data processing. At weekly meetings, the group might observe one participating instructor taking his turn at instructing a small group of learners, perhaps for fifteen or twenty minutes. Based on the results of the post-test of the learners involved, the group could exchange views regarding how the lesson might be improved and what features of the lesson appeared to be most effective. This type of activity can be beneficial to both the individual doing the instructing and to the group of observers. A slight alteration in this process might involve the observers as actual learners, with the particular instructor presenting an adult lesson. It should be emphasized that when initiated in the context of self-improvement, teacher performance testing should remain absolutely nonpunitive in nature.

Regardless of the role which teacher performance tests assume, Popham has delineated four basic steps for the teaching performance test.

Step 1: The Instructor Is Given the Objective and Necessary Background Information

The instructor must begin with a clear statement regarding the objective of the particular lesson. This objective must be stated in measurable terms and often a sample test item should be presented so that the instructor or the person being evaluated knows exactly what will be expected of his students. Background information might be a two- or a three-page narrative regarding the subject matter under consideration. For example, if a particular teacher had the task of presenting the components of an IBM computer card, the brief description in an IBM manual might be presented for background information.

Step 2: The Teacher Plans the Lesson

The second step begins with the teacher's planning a lesson designed to achieve the objective. Usually only a brief period of time is necessary. Also, the time utilized for the lesson itself may be brief. Experience has proved performance tests to be successful for instructional periods as short as ten minutes or as long as two weeks. For example, an instructor might be allowed two hours to prepare for a fifteen-minute lesson. The choice of material and technique should be left entirely to the individual teacher, who will know what best suits his particular wants and needs.

Step 3: The Teacher Conducts the Lesson

During this step, the teacher presents the lesson to learners who have been identified as naive to the subject matter under consideration. These learners should be drawn from a good cross section of student types, and care should be taken to avoid a situation where the sample of students is naive to the subject matter because of special status, for example, a group of seniors who have not yet taken senior business math because they have been previously identified as slow learners. Such a choice would affect the results of the teaching performance test, as results would actually measure only the teacher's ability to teach a group of slow learners and not a class of normal students. A good cross section is best insured by identifying as large a group of "naive" students as possible and taking a random sample from this larger group. The size of the sample group can vary from just a handful to a large class.

Step 4: The Learners are Post-tested

At the end of the lesson the learners' achievement is measured against the objective. If the lesson focused on identifying the components of an IBM keypunch card, the post-test would measure the learner's comprehension of those components. In addition to obtaining a cognitive measure of achievement, Popham recommends that the evaluator also assess the learner's interest in the lesson at the time.

Popham has stated that there are at least five attributes which an effective teacher performance test should possess:

1. Objectives must be measurable and attainable in the time available.
2. Objectives should be unfamiliar to the learner but should not seem absurd.
3. Background information for the teacher should be adequate but brief.
4. The post-test should be congruent with the objectives and easy to administer.
5. The test must be capable of discriminating among teachers.

With the limited description of teacher performance tests presented in this chapter, the reader should be able to construct a usable test, and continued use of the tests should aid in their improvement and revision. For additional information on such tests, the reader is referred to *Evaluating Instruction* (1973) by James Popham. Popham also markets teacher performance tests commercially through Instructional Appraisal Services, Box 24821, Los Angeles, California 90024.

Although teacher performance tests are ideally suited to the goal of improving instruction, they may also be used for skill assessment to find out which teachers are superior and which are inferior with respect to particular competencies. In other words, it would be valuable for an administrator to know who possesses superior ability to bring about prespecified behaviors in students. In the case of skill assessment, there is the underlying assumption that comparisons among teachers are required and, therefore, it is necessary to set up either large or small groups of learners so that the relative instructional skill of teachers in both situations may be appraised. Popham specifically recommends five common procedures which should be utilized regardless of the use made of the results of teacher performance tests. He extends this list to seven for improvement purposes and to nine for skill assessment. The five procedures which are common to both instructional improvement and skill assessment are:

1. Allow sufficient planning time for the teacher.
2. Use naive but teachable learners.
3. Use small or large groups of learners.

4. Consider use of item-sampling post-tests.
5. Routinely assess learner affect.

For instructional improvement, Popham suggests that clinical observers should: 1) conduct instructional analyses based upon learner performance, and 2) provide opportunities for the replanning and reteaching of unsuccessful lessons. For skill assessment, the following procedures are recommended:

1. All relevant conditions should be comparable for each teacher.
2. Learners should be assigned to teachers randomly.
3. More than one performance test should be completed by each teacher.
4. Test security should be preserved.

By utilizing teacher performance tests, the instructional skill of faculty members can be greatly improved. Additionally, school and training institutions can monitor the skill of their instructional personnel.

Of course, as do any other personnel evaluation techniques, teacher performance tests possess several constraints. An obvious constraint is the time available. In most cases, teacher performance testing will require that the individual teacher be involved extracurricularly, contributing additional time prior to or following the school day. This, of course, may pose a problem in many public educational agencies. Another constraint is that teacher performance tests are only a simulation of an individual's actual performance. For example, a particular teacher may do extremely well on a teaching performance test due to excellent planning and very conscientious effort, while in the actual classroom situation he does not take sufficient time to plan and does not possess such a conscientious attitude. The fact that the skill being assessed by a teaching performance test is only instructional skill can also be a constraint. Teachers and training personnel may have a number of responsibilities and competency requirements in addition to the instructional responsibility. This should be taken into consideration as judgments are made.

Contract Plans Which Focus on Student Achievement

McNeil (1971, 1973) has developed an alternative for assessing teacher competence which involves the use of contract plans based on student achievement or gain. The contract plan can be used for either improvement or decision making and begins with the development of a carefully selected set of objectives for a particular group of students. Supervisors and teachers must agree on what will constitute evidence that the teacher has been successful in changing the skills, competencies, or attitudes of the students. Such an agreement, or contract, is prepared prior to a teacher's instruction of the group. Following instruction, evidence is collected to determine how well the students have achieved the prespecified objectives and to identify any unanticipated outcomes.

A contract may involve peers as well as supervisors in the task of helping an individual instructor improve. For instance, a group of peers may be scheduled to observe a particular instructor during the instructional act. At this time, observers have the opportunity to record student-teacher interaction as well as other classroom activities. When considered in light of the student results, these observations become valuable feedback to the evaluated instructor.

Contract plans may be expanded to suit long-term as well as short-term teaching periods. Teachers may set objectives for end-of-quarter or end-of-semester student performance, for which each individual teacher will be held accountable. End-of-quarter or end-of-semester results might then be reported to program administrators as one factor to be considered in teacher evaluation. Throughout the quarter the teacher may set shorter term objectives, either daily or hourly, to be controlled by smaller or short-term contracts. These shorter term contracts could be evaluated and negotiated with peers. The peers could then provide formative feedback to the individual teachers which could aid them in achieving their longer term objectives as well. Used in this way, the short-term contract could be of no use to the administrators but would be of primary concern to the individual instructor. It would be the longer term end-of-course or end-of-semester results which would be utilized by the program administrator.

Regardless of its scope or purpose, the contracting plan should be based on a four-phase framework or cycle. The first phase—the preobservational conference—should be held for selecting instructional intents and for clarifying the role of the observer. The second phase—observation—involves the recording of the teaching activities. The third phase is termed analysis and strategy and is devoted to interpreting the facts and data collected during observation. The final and fourth phase is the post-observational conference where there is an assessment by both teacher and supervisor of the results from the lesson. This conference is utilized for establishing subsequent teaching plans, including new objectives and changed teaching strategies where necessary.

Step 1: The Preobservational Conference

The preobservational conference between the instructor and those who will observe should occur at least one day in advance of the lesson. This is necessitated by the fact that objectives may change with new insights gained during the meeting. The observer may include the principal, training director, consultant, peer or colleague, or another type of supervisor. The primary purpose of the preobservational conference is to ensure that all are agreed on instructional intent and on procedures by which evidence will be gathered to show if the intents are met. Specifically, this evidence is a measure of what learners are able to do after instruction that they could not do previously. It is important that the preobservational conference clarify the role of the observer to the teacher or instructor. The instructor should be well aware that if the goal is to be self-improvement, the observer will be there to help him and will have no responsibility to report to a higher authority. On the other hand, if the function or role of the contract is accountability, this should be made known to an instructor during this preobservational conference. To summarize, the preobservational conference should cover:

1. Agreement on what the teacher intends to achieve.
2. Agreement on plans for collecting evidence on whether learners have or have not reached the objectives.
3. Agreement on the role the supervisor will play during observation.

Step 2: Observation

The observation phase should focus on the collection of information and data relating to the particular teacher's performance. These should not be ratings or judgments of actual performance but instead should be a record of what happened in the classroom. Ideally, the observer should record all instances of pupil-teacher interaction as well as the techniques and mannerisms utilized by the instructor. A videotape of the lesson is an excellent method of recording, but if limitations prevent the use of such elaborate equipment, it is necessary for individual observers to accurately record information on classroom transactions. Most observations are recorded by means of written and mental notes on the part of the observer. One shortcoming of such records is that they often focus on what is said at the expense of what is seen, and nonverbal behavior such as expressions and so on cannot be reexamined and analyzed.

The observational phase should also include the collection of evidence regarding both changes in students and student achievement of intended outcomes. The collection of evidence should be accomplished through the use of instruments that best match the objectives being assessed. These instruments should not be limited to paper and pencil tests simply because they are easy to administer. The achievement of many objectives can be assessed through situational testing, simulation, performance tests, special attitude scales, and many others. The prospective user of a contracting plan system should refer to Buros (1965), Oppenheim (1966), and Shaw and Wright (1968) for examples of various types of measuring devices. In addition, instructors should be encouraged to develop their own assessment instruments. Chapter 3 of this book should be consulted for this purpose. In summary, the observational phase should include three characteristics:

1. More stress on recording what can be seen and heard than on making a judgment.
2. More focus on learner response and actions initiated by learner.
3. Evidence of changes in learners (as agreed upon in the preobservational conference) is collected.

Step 3: Analysis and Strategy

The analysis session should begin with a look at student results. If the objectives were not achieved by the students, the analysis should focus on why they were not, with suggestions for new teaching procedures to be used in the future. If the objectives were achieved by students, the analysis might indicate characteristics which made the lesson successful, or new directions to be taken in subsequent lessons. The lesson presented should be described to the evaluated teacher by the observer. The observer will need to employ a broad theory base very cautiously in formulating suggestions for the evaluated teacher. Following the specific delineation of the teaching act given by the observer, generalizations should be drawn relative to specific pedagogical factors. McNeil (1973) lists a number of factors which may be useful in analyzing instruction with corresponding kinds of observational data. The observation phase should conclude with the planning of the post-observational conference, the observers collaborating to determine how observational data and suggestions for improvement will be presented to the evaluated instructor. Questions of strategy include: Will we share the data and analyses with the teacher and let him draw his own implications and formulate new objectives and procedures for himself? Do we want the teacher to provide any additional data or to tell us his own feelings about the lessons? Why? How can we be sure that the teacher hears the information we believe important for him to have? These are but several questions which must be considered prior to the post-observational conference.

In summary, four steps should be considered in the analysis and strategy phase:

1. Results of the lesson are compared with previously stated, desired results.
2. The lesson is analyzed, and a number of instructional factors and principles are considered, such as the principle of appropriate practice.
3. Generalizations are formed from supporting data (no generalization is permitted without data to back it up).
4. A plan for conducting the post-observational conference is formed. For example, responsibility is given to team members for sharing data and inferences with the teacher; attention is given to the teacher's own expectations from the team; allowance is made for the teacher's own analysis of the lesson.

Step 4: Post-observational Conference

During the course of the post-observational conference, the teacher should be given opportunities to hear all points of view about the teaching act under consideration. These opinions should reflect judgments based on concrete observations. The validity of the points of view will be tested in the classroom as the teacher agrees to follow suggestions to note the effects of these suggestions on the pupils. The teacher should leave the post-observational conference with new objectives he wants to achieve, new instructional procedures to try out, and plans for checking the results that follow implementation. In summary, the post-observational conference should consider the following four points:

1. The focus is on results attained versus results desired.
2. New objectives are derived from results, data, and inferences made during observation.
3. New teaching strategies are considered.
4. The teacher indicates that strategies will be acted upon and validated in subsequent lessons.

The contracting plan approach has been applied in a number of school systems. One example was the Newport, California, system. Here, participants attended two, two and one-half hour sessions for the purpose of acquiring requisite competencies for the contracting plan. The sessions involved both instruction and formulation of behavioral objectives. During the following two months, teachers formed teams and engaged in what was called performance cycles. Three colleagues from each building and one person from outside the building constituted the team. Each member of the team had opportunities to play the roles of teacher, observer, analyst, and strategist.

These teams followed the four steps or phases previously described. When performance cycles or contract periods were terminated, participants attended large group sessions where televised lessons and instructional problems were presented, affording the participants the opportunity of demonstrating their ability to use the tools necessary for successful operation of the appraisal model. Results indicated that most teachers found the pilot study a worthwhile and stimulating experience. Teachers felt that their teaching had been strengthened to the benefit of their students. The technique was also felt to have helped identify those teachers who had a problem of direction—who did not know what they were trying to accomplish. Similarly, the procedures permitted participants to identify those teachers who had formulated objectives of great importance both to the particular learner and to the society which the school served.

COORDINATING THE PERSONNEL EVALUATION SYSTEM

The implementation of a system for the evaluation of education and training personnel will require a considerable allocation of resources, primarily personnel resources. The total array of professional activities, with teaching in the forefront, should be considered in the design of such a system. Such an array may not be fairly evaluated through the use of only one evaluative input or measure. At the same time, one systematic and reliable procedure is better than any number of casual and highly subjective ones. In this chapter, five basic evaluative techniques have been discussed: observer ratings, job target evaluation, self-evaluation, teacher performance testing, and contract plans. The most traditional of these techniques is probably the observer ratings, though under this category the student rating of teaching has only recently become popular. Additionally, the other techniques are only lately being adopted as feasible approaches to personnel evaluation in public and private education. The use of these methods is greatly encouraged, and it is emphasized that an eclectic strategy should be built, utilizing two or more of these techniques in the evaluation of education and training personnel.

In the implementation of a faculty evaluation system, it is obvious that no one strategy would work in all situations or institutions, but there are some general guidelines that should be followed in instituting such a system.

Step 1: Obtain Administrative Support

To be effective, a personnel evaluation system requires the support of the chief academic officer in public education and the chief training officer in a private institution, and it is necessary that these individuals be well informed and knowledgeable about the instructional evaluation plans. In some settings, the administrative officer may be the individual who is heading the personnel evaluation system; in others, it may be an individual under his command.

Step 2: Develop Procedures and Instruments

This step should begin with the formulation of an overall plan which delineates each of the components of the system and defines their relationships. For example, if a particular institution or a department of an institution chose to initiate both a student rating system and a job target evaluation system, these then should be specifically defined. In addition, the use to be made of the results of each component of the system should be carefully defined. The instruments or data-gathering forms should also undergo a careful preparatory procedure. When possible, a number of individuals should be involved in this planning stage, as involvement will hopefully alleviate some of the resistance to the evaluation system by those being evaluated.

Step 3: Trial Run of Procedures and Instruments

A trial run of the procedures on a limited scale can accomplish two things. First, it can help to ease personnel into the evaluation system. Because of past experience with poor evaluation procedures, many educational and training personnel view any type of evaluation as a threat. The trial run can help personnel become aware of what the system is and what it can do for them. Secondly, the trial run can help to improve the procedures and instruments which are utilized in the system. By initiating the system on a limited basis, careful attention can be paid to the problem areas or weak points in the system as well as deficiencies in the instruments, rating forms, or other formal components of the system.

Step 4: Revise Procedures and Instruments

Based on the input gained during the trial run of the procedures and instruments, changes should be made to overcome the problems identified. This may involve changes in the sequencing of activities and the orientation to the system as well as specific changes in the instrument or observation forms utilized. It may be advantageous to gain feedback from those involved in the trial run by way of a formal questionnaire or a simple interview.

Step 5: Anticipate and Deal with Resistance Points

Resistance of the staff can hopefully be sampled during the trial run of the system and then should be carefully analyzed and steps taken to overcome it. If the function of the evaluation system is staff improvement, this should be emphasized to the staff. On the other hand, if the function of the evaluation is skill assessment, this then should be made known to each of the faculty members who will be involved in the system. Misuse of results is another common concern among faculty members, and in some cases this fear is well founded, so care must be taken by program administrators that staff members know the exact use to which results will be put.

Step 6: Allow for Formative Improvement of the System

After the system is in full operation, a considerable amount of time and effort should be allowed for revision and monitoring. Problem areas in procedure and instrumentation should be identified and remedied. If this step is accomplished following several cycles of use, the system can become a viable approach to the improvement of educational personnel performance in addition to aiding in decision making.

UTILIZING RESULTS

The utilization of results of the personnel evaluation probably entails the most difficult decisions of any form of evaluation. It is not the authors' position to set priorities concerning what types of evaluative information should weigh most heavily in the ultimate analysis. For the assessment of teacher performance (process), student performance and learner rating results (product) are likely to give the most accurate and representative picture. Student questionnaires provide a reasonably objective measure of "process." Although colleague observation can provide excellent input to process evaluation of personnel, it is best used as a consultative strategy. Student performance and learner rating results may be used to identify the problem; such measures as colleague observation are useful means of explaining the problem, identifying causes, and identifying possible remedies.

For bestowal of tenure, other factors will also be considered. This sort of decision should always be based on further knowledge of student-oriented factors and augmented by factors such as instructor attitude, participation in staff activities, and general cooperation with the administration, governing board, or colleagues (if these factors apply to the organizational structure of the institution).

Personnel evaluation leading to promotion will depend heavily on the rank of the individual and on the responsibilities of the anticipated position. Criteria for such promotion may resemble criteria for bestowal of tenure or may be oriented more toward learner performance. On the other hand, if a promotion to an advisory position concerned with teaching methods is being considered, student performance results will weigh heavily in any decision.

Decisions concerning salary increases will be most heavily weighted by student performance results. The instructor who achieves maximum results from a group of students undoubtedly deserves appropriate consideration for a salary increase. Other factors may also be important depending upon the character of the decision situation.

Ultimately the utilization of results for improvement is a responsibility that rests with the individual instructor, and there are measures that may be taken to encourage their proper use. Knowing student performance results is essential if instructors are to feel that recommended changes in teaching methods are worth implementing. "Process" measures should always be augmented by student performance results, and the instructor should be provided with a detailed analysis of these results by the evaluator.

For most forms of evaluation it is recommended that results be disseminated and a general meeting held involving all concerned staff. For personnel evaluation, this is not always a viable solution. To begin with, it is questionable whether other staff can be considered to be "concerned." The conference or meeting with the evaluator should be confidential and private. This should encourage the acceptance of suggestions and will ultimately affect the utilization of results.

Once again, utilization of personnel evaluation results for purposes of tenure, promotion, and so on will vary with organizational policy and with the structure of the organization. The only guideline that will obtain in all cases is to make assessments as accurately and judiciously as possible.

REFERENCES

Armstrong, H. R. "Performance Evaluation." *The National Elementary Principal,* 1973, LII(5):51–55.

Borgen, J. and Davis, D. *Planning, Implementing, and Evaluating Career Preparation Programs.* Bloomington, Illinois: McKnight Publishers, 1974.

Buros, O. K. *The Sixth Mental Measurements Yearbook.* Highland Park, New Jersey: The Gryphon Press, 1965.

Cosgrove, D. J. "Diagnostic Rating of Teacher Performance." *Journal of Educational Psychology,* 1959, 50:200–204.

Eble, K. E. *Professors as Teachers.* San Francisco: Jossey-Bass, 1972.

Gage, N. L. "Ends and Means in Appraising College Teaching." In W. J. McKeachie (ed.) *The Appraisal of Teaching in Large Universities.* Ann Arbor: University of Michigan, 1959.

Good, C. V. *Dictionary of Education* (2nd ed.) New York: McGraw-Hill, 1959.

Guilford, J. P. *Psychometric Methods* (2nd ed.) New York: McGraw-Hill, 1954.

Kirchner, R. P. "A Control Factor in Teacher Evaluation by Students." Unpublished research paper, University of Kentucky, 1969.

Leeds, C. H. and Cook, W. W. "The Construction and Differential Value of a Scale for Determining Teacher-Pupil Attitudes." *Journal of Experimental Education,* 1947, 16:149–159.

McNeil, J. D. *Toward Accountable Teachers: Their Appraisal and Improvement.* New York: Holt, Rinehart and Winston, Inc., 1971.

McNeil, J. D. and Popham, W. J. "The Assessment of Teacher Competence." In Travers, R. M. (ed.) *Second Handbook of Research on Teaching.* Chicago: Rand McNally, 1973.

Miller, R. I. *Evaluating Faculty Performance.* San Francisco: Jossey-Bass, Inc., 1972.

Odbert, J. T. "Career Education Competencies." A presentation at the American Vocational Association Convention, Atlanta, Georgia, 1973.

Oppenheim, A. W. *Questionnaire Design and Attitude Measurement.* New York: Basic Books, Inc., 1966.

Pharis, W. L. "The Evaluation of School Principals." *The National Elementary Principal,* 1973, 52(5).

Popham, W. J. *Evaluating Instruction.* Englewood Cliffs, New Jersey: Prentice-Hall, Inc., 1973.

Remmers, H. H. "Rating Methods in Research on Teaching." In Gage, N. L. (ed.) *Handbook of Research in Teaching.* Chicago: Rand McNally, 1963.

Ryans, D. G. *Characteristics of Teachers.* Washington, D.C.: American Council on Education, 1960.

Shaw, M. E. and Wright, J. M. *Scales For the Measurement of Attitudes.* New York: McGraw-Hill, 1967.

Stecklein, J. E. "Colleges and Universities—Programs: Evaluation." In Harris, C. W. (ed.), *Encyclopedia of Educational Research.* (3rd ed.) New York: Macmillan, 1960.

Simpson, R. H. and Brown, E. S. *College Learning and Teaching.* Urbana: Bureau of Research and Service, University of Illinois, 1952.

Simpson, R. H. "Biological Science Instructors' Use of Self-evaluation Tools." *The American Biology Teacher,* 1962, vol. 24, no. 8.

Terry, D. R., Thompson, R. L., and Evans, R. N. *Competencies for Teachers: Vocational Education Shows the Way.* Urbana: University of Illinois, 1971.

8

Cost
Analysis
Evaluation

Cost analysis evaluation is the least developed and most thoroughly complicated form of evaluation to be encountered by the educator or trainer. There are good reasons for the relative immaturity of cost analysis evaluation. The best reason is that it is a formidable undertaking. Answers are never absolute; figures are never totally correct; benefits are never complete. So why bother? We should bother because we have everything to gain. Current evaluation of costs is so inadequate, so underdeveloped, that every piece of information we can gain, every cost we can identify, helps us to make the necessarily subjective decisions that are our responsibility as educators and trainers to make.

Since most organizations, whether public or private, function and operate within budgetary constraints, decisions must be made which maximize the return on any expenditure. Also, for any educational or training outcome, costs must be minimized.

In industry, where profit making is the primary motive, decision makers use cost analysis to choose production methods which produce the desired product with the least expense. Even the methods utilized by government agencies for the comparison of costs to benefits rely on a good deal of estimation. Costs for education and training programs are *sometimes* obscure, but benefits can *never* be expressed in purely financial terms. This means that education and training personnel must do a great deal of work if they wish to establish the accountability of their efforts.

Benefits of education are closer to observation by the public than most governmental projects and the public is thus in a better position to be critical of educational endeavors. After all, many benefits or outcomes of an educational program are intangible and, therefore, dollar values cannot be attached. But many of these intangibles can be observed by the public: learner attitude, involvement, and so on. Publication and communication of cost analysis data to the public will most likely have little impact, as the burden for utilization of these results really falls upon education and training decision makers.

But improved programs based upon costs and increasing benefits will ultimately be felt by the public as they observe a better educated or trained product—the learner.

Cost analysis can be categorized into one of two types: cost benefit or cost effectiveness. Both of these types of cost analysis require similar computation of costs and benefits. The two are distinguished by the use to be made of resulting data. Cost-benefit analysis involves the ascertainment of costs and benefits of a single program for purposes of improving the relationship or ratio between the costs and benefits. Cost effectiveness analysis requires identification of costs and benefits for more than one program. This chapter will focus on the identification of costs and benefits and will consider cost-benefit analysis and cost effectiveness analysis individually.

WHY CONDUCT A COST ANALYSIS EVALUATION?

It would be easy if all cars were alike. Buying a car would then be like buying apples (if all apples were alike). Benefits would all be measured in cars—costs presumably in dollars. If Joe found that he could buy car A from one dealer for $2,000 and that his same $2,000 covered only half the cost of car B at Shady Dealers, Inc., then unless Joe is something less than half-witted, he will choose the first car from the first dealer. This would be a form of cost effectiveness analysis.

With cars being what they are today, cost analysis is a much more complicated business. Cost analysis of a car involves more than just an analysis of the number of cars for your dollar. Today, to determine his choice of a car, the buyer will want to consider several benefits: gas mileage, availability of parts, resale value—all benefits that may be related to cost. With these simplest of considerations, one might expect to derive a concrete cost-benefit ratio. Yet savings accrued from superior mileage may be offset by a mishap requiring the owner to buy hard-to-get or expensive parts. How does one determine the probability of such a mishap? Most buyers do not. But even this is a form of evaluation—most buyers feel that the likelihood of such an event is small and have actually made an educated guess about the likelihood.

Already, however, we have found serious limitations to the determination of a cost-benefit relationship, limitations that are prohibitive to the most conscientious buyer. Still more subjective considerations complicate the decision-making process. Personal considerations such as style, comfort, and status raise the decision-making process to a much more complex level. The importance of these considerations is not questioned, yet they call for the employment of subjective rather than objective judgment.

We have just seen that when choosing between cars or educational and training programs, there are several levels of judgment we have to make. Three levels of cost efficiency analysis are: 1) The objective judgment, 2) The educated guess, and 3) The subjective judgment.

The determination of costs most nearly constitutes an *objective judgment.* There are problems to be encountered in the determination of costs alone. For instance, it is difficult to gain agreement on what costs to allocate to specific instructional programs. But we can be objective about these costs.

The *subjective judgment* is not always easily made. These sorts of judgments are often so well integrated with our view of the world that we forget to consider them judgments at all. In education, a quite common subjective judgment is that it is better to teach some things than to leave students to learn them by trial and error. In the car business, an equally common subjective judgment is that it is preferable to spend a great deal of money on a car rather than to spend a great deal of time walking to work.

The *educated guess* is the naturally occurring hybrid between the objective judgment and the subjective. It is also the most familiar decision-making process around. The important thing about making an educated guess is to have the best information possible—to have an accurate *objective* assessment of the situation before you make more subjective judgments.

Going back to the discussion of cars A and B, the issue here is strictly cost analysis, and there is really little room for *subjective judgment* on strict cost analysis. Yet many times programs nearly as similar as cars A and B in terms of resulting benefits are chosen in this way. When applied to an *objective* question such as the question of cost, a subjective judgment is called whimsical or chance judgment, and one thing we as educators cannot justify is the choice of programs by whim or by chance. This chapter focuses on the improvement of programs based upon a more objective use of cost and benefit information. Following are some specific reasons for conducting a cost analysis evaluation in education.

To Justify Resource Allocation Decisions

Naturally, when administrators or program managers develop the budget, they will want to know which programs provide the most benefits for the least cost. Morcover, allocations are more likely to be made to the program for which costs and benefits have been identified than for the program for which no costs or benefits have been projected. Just as investors usually rely on information concerning historical performance of stocks and potential of companies, controllers of education and training programs rely on historical performance of programs.

To Promote Better Utilization of Facilities

Although costs for most programs are heaviest in the area of staff, facilities can constitute a considerable expense. In some cases, it will be found that the sharing of facilities reduces the nominal costs for two programs, and available facilities can be stretched to accommodate new programs at little extra cost. The savings possible from the sharing of expenses will show up in a carefully executed cost analysis evaluation.

To Determine Optimum Staff or Manpower Assignments

Since staff costs constitute a sizeable portion of the program budget, achieving optimum utilization of qualified staff members is an important undertaking. For many courses it may be true that the employment of paraprofessionals or instructional assistants will reduce these costs. For example, should it be found that a program in health occupations requires only a half-time professional and can accommodate a half-time assistant, this program would be preferred to an alternative program which requires the full-time services of a professional instructor.

To Determine Optimum Scheduling or Sequencing

Cost analysis may identify scheduling or sequencing patterns that make the most efficient use of the resources at hand. If two courses are offered at the same time—and will attract enrollees of the same type—these programs should be rescheduled. Similarly, it is important to find the optimum schedule for sequencing courses so that the greatest number of students may obtain the greatest benefit from each course.

To Determine Optimum Load for a Particular Program

Many times costs for a program are excessive for one class size and perfectly reasonable for another. In some cases an increase in class size will call for an additional staff member or an assistant, thus dramatically increasing the cost per pupil or instruction hour for the program. Other times it will be advisable to increase the student load or to combine classes to lower the cost per student. Expenses per individual student may make it inadvisable to continue a program which has a limited number of enrollees.

To Decrease Costs of High-cost/Low-incidence Programs

Should it be discovered that a program which serves few students incurs disproportionate expenditures, these costs may be reduced by seeking alternatives. The school may wish to extend an invitation to other schools to share the facilities, benefits, and costs of the program, to the benefit of both schools. Alternatively, it may be advisable to offer extension courses in lieu of the existing program. At any rate, discovering such high-cost/low-incidence programs may lead to the discovery of more suitable alternatives.

To Determine the Advisability of Financing the Development of a New Program

Although in some cases initial costs for implementing a program may appear prohibitive, cost analysis evaluation may support the implementation of a particular program by identifying long-term savings that will underwrite the initial investment. In other cases, cost analysis evaluation may show that implementing a new program is inadvisable, that the costs of implementing a new program, piloting the program, and developing materials will not prove worthwhile in the long run.

To Compare Alternative Programs

Often an institution or training agency will have to choose between two alternative programs, both of which look very similar on the surface. Cost effectiveness analysis will uncover methods for discriminating between these programs and making intelligent choices. Decisions of more limited scope, regarding the choice of competing instructional materials, equipment, and techniques, can also be facilitated by cost analysis.

To Provide Fiscal Accountability

It is nearly always to the advantage of the program in question to keep accurate records of the benefits which have been related to costs. Accountability will make the defense of a program possible in the face of unenlightened criticism.

DETERMINING COSTS

In education and training, the determination of costs need not be considered a mere prelude to cost-benefit or cost effectiveness analysis. By identifying and projecting costs, the program manager can more accurately estimate costs for new programs. Cost estimates are essential to the formulation of departmental or institutional budgets and can justify requests for financial support from state and federal funding agencies. Cost analysis involving the use of this cost information can provide even further benefit to the educational or training institution by meeting one or more of the purposes discussed previously.

The determination of costs is by no means a simple undertaking. To determine the cost of a single program involves many questions of considerable delicacy. There may be great difficulty in gaining agreement on what costs should be allocated to specific instructional programs even if benefits can be defined in measurable terms.

There are many ways in which to break down program costs, any of which may help the evaluator to gain insight into the relative merits of programs. One useful distinction between program costs is the distinction between program development and program operation expenses. Program development expenses are most typically short term. These are costs which relate to the implementation of programs and are not ongoing. Ordinarily they do not vary according to student enrollment. Examples of program development and operation costs are enumerated below:

Program Development Costs	*Program Operation Costs*
Printing costs	Instructor
Ancillary media costs	Building costs
Programming costs	Administrative costs
Design costs	Materials and supplies costs
Packaging costs	Insurance costs
Evaluation costs	Maintenance costs
Implementation costs	

Costs of program operation are variable costs which relate to the number of students enrolled, the number of students that can be accommodated by an instructor or given classroom space, and so on. Distinction between developmental and operation costs will prove useful in determining the cost of a program or the relative costs of two programs. Because they are indepedent of other variables, program development costs should be calculated first.

Program Development Costs

Program development costs are most commonly computed for a new course or program. The types of costs are extremely difficult to anticipate. Dependent upon your program's idiosyncracies, these will be yours alone to identify and to assess. All that the authors can do is to provide you with an example format for identifying types of program development costs. Most of the applications of calculated costs will be made clear in the cost-benefit section of this chapter. Following is a breakdown of program development expenses that may be included in the cost calculation.

Authoring Expense

Authoring expenses are fees paid to an individual for the development of instructional materials. If an individual external to the educational or training institution is utilized as an author, the fee may be an hourly, daily, or contracted fee. On the other hand, if an internal staff member is given released time for authoring, the percentage of his salary proportionate to his released time should be calculated.

Pilot Learners' Reimbursement

Often, a sample group will be asked to react to specific characteristics of new material such as clarity or organization prior to its final revision. If instruction is to be piloted, it may be necessary to pay those learners who will test the material. This cost will vary considerably depending on the availability and age of the audience. In some cases, volunteers or *captive* classes can be utilized at no cost.

Content Advisor Honorarium

Many program development activities involve an expert content advisor from a university or industrial firm. The time and effort required to complete the task will determine the fee to be paid. Usually, experts will work at a daily rate or for a contracted fee for completing the job.

Material Costs

Material costs are those costs for supplementary instructional devices such as slides, tapes, games, or simulation devices.

Layout/Design Costs

These costs are a function of graphic layout and design work. They may be related to printed matter or may include visual aides such as overhead transparencies, slides, and posters. The preparation of figures or diagrams to be included in workbooks or instructor guides are commonly recognized as belonging to this category.

Typing or Typesetting Costs

The preparation of material or copy to be reproduced will involve typing or typesetting costs. Typing, whether done by a regularly employed typist or by an additional person, is usually figured at an hourly rate.

Reproduction Costs

Expenses which are incurred as a function of printing, binding, slide duplication, tape duplication, and the like are included in this category. Items which are relevant to costs include quality and color of paper, packaging, cover stock, number of pages, slides, illustrations, total number of products to be published, type of printing used, and so on.

Administrative Costs

Costs related to the planning, organizing, and monitoring of developmental activity from its proposal to completion are considered to be administrative costs. Usually, a percentage of salary or a daily rate is charged against development for these costs.

Evaluation Costs

Costs incurred in the evaluation of the developmental activities and the resulting product are charged to this category. Evaluation costs include staff time, external expert fees (for review) and similar expenses. The cost categories presented above are related to the developmental activity of an instructional product. Additional developmental costs might include staff time for cost analysis and planning meetings, travel costs for visits to existing programs, and expenses for conferences with experts.

Again, these costs will not apply to every program, and some programs may involve additional developmental expenses which have not been covered here. Based on the previous breakdown of costs, Figure 8–1 provides an estimation of developmental costs compiled for one instructional product. This breakdown should give the evaluator an idea of what sorts of expenses to look for.

Time plays an important part in the developmental costs per program. To accurately assess the developmental costs per program per *year* (as you will want to do when comparing two programs which vary in duration as well as in substance), you will have to allocate developmental costs across the projected number of years that program will be effective. Thus, in the unlikely event that Program A with its developmental cost of $1,123 was to run for fifteen years, while Program B with an initial cost of $1,000 was to run for ten years, then Program A would be the most desirable in terms of developmental expense.

The reader will quickly discern that projecting the duration of a program is no small part of his task in this case. When making this sort of decision, the evaluator will be guided by his knowledge of his own district, its plans, and the circumstances surrounding the implementation of each alternative program. If a needs assessment or a student follow-up has been conducted in his district, he may be able to determine the projected length of a program. Again, he may be guided by such information as the fact that an entire building will be replaced within ten years and, therefore, the developmental costs of one program should be applied to no more than ten years. The

```
Authoring Expense

    Author — 6 days @ $75/day              $450.00
    Programmer — 10 hrs. @ $7.50/hr.         75.00

Pilot Learners

    10 subjects @ $3.00/hour (1 hour)        30.00

Content Advisor

    1 day @ $75.00/day                       75.00

Materials

    2 single concept loop films — $40.00     80.00
    1 film strip with audio — $68.00         68.00

Layout/Design

    10 hours @ $12.50/hour                   125.00

Typing

    20 hours @ $3.00/hour                     60.00

Manager's Expense

    Planning, organizing, monitoring,
    and controlling — 2 days @ $80/day       160.00

Total Expense for Product                  $1123.00
```

FIGURE 8–1   *Estimate of Developmental Costs for One Instructional Product* (*reproduced from* Formative Instructional Product Evaluation: Instruments and Strategies *by Tom E. Lawson with permission of Educational Technology Publications, Englewood Cliffs, New Jersey, 1974).*

developmental costs of another program (say, one which relies more heavily on operational expenditures) can easily be expected to run for twenty years. The authors must, once more, express their regrets for leaving you at this juncture. At the point where these sorts of individual problems arise, you are very much on your own.

Program Operation Expenses

Program operation expenses are those which vary from one year to the next and are often dependent upon student enrollment, that is, they are often derived from per student, per class cost figures. Although program development costs may be allocated to students, they generally do not vary according to the number of students served or the number of classes offered. The exception in this case is the category of allocated costs. These, although they bear little real relationship to the number of students or the number of classes, will vary in *nominal* value according to these numbers.

Program operation expenses for a completed program are most easily determined. Program operation expenses for a proposed program are projected from figures determined from previous piloting or implementation. Costs for a program which has been neither piloted nor operated previously can only be estimated.

To determine program operation expenses for a completed program, one simply reexamines the records (hopefully there are records) of expenditures. In such a case, it is not unlikely that the evaluator will discover his own breakdown of program operation expenses; categories will become apparent as he computes expended funds.

Taking our example breakdown of program operation expenses, we can see that many expenses can be identified as per student, per course, per program, or per organization.

Program Operation Expense	Per Student	Per Course	Per Program	Per Organization
Instructor costs		x	x	x
Building costs			x	x
Administrative costs			x	x
Materials and supplies costs	x	x	x	x
Insurance costs				x
Maintenance costs				x
Depreciation costs			x	x

If projecting the costs of reinstating a program, the evaluator will want to know:

a1.   What costs are computed on the basis of the number of students enrolled?
a2.   How many students will be enrolled?
b1.   What costs are computed on the basis of the number of sections offered?
b2.   How many sections will be offered?
c1.   What costs are computed on the basis of the number of courses offered?
c2.   How many courses will be offered?
d1.   What costs are computed on the basis of the number of programs offered?
d2.   How many programs will be offered?
e1.   What costs will be allocated to programs, courses, sections, and students?
e2.   Is it necessary to compute allocated costs?

These are often difficult questions to answer. Costs determined on the basis of student enrollment normally include such things as materials and supplies. For some programs, e. g., those involving highly individualized instruction, it will be necessary to compute instructor costs on a per student basis. It is best not to include most allocated costs initially; it may turn out that some allocated costs will not have to be computed.

Costs computed on the basis of the number of sections offered will normally be limited to instructor costs. But individual circumstances may make it likely that enrollment costs or some similar administrative costs will be computed per program. Some programs may require special scheduling procedures which increase administrative costs. Again, however, it is more likely that enrollment costs will be computed as allocated costs and that these should be left out of these initial calculations.

Instructor Costs

Instructor costs may be determined per individual student, per course, or per program. Per course or per program costs may be subdivided and computed per student in each course or program.

The utility of analyzing per student instruction costs is very limited. However, to compare the efficiency of one organization with that of another, it may be useful to calculate the average cost per student for instruction. To determine such costs for a total program, one simply adds the total salaries of all instructors and divides by the total number of students served by the program.

More likely to be of use is a calculation of the instructor cost per student per individual program. Again, the simplest calculation of this sort involves the addition of the number of instructor salaries. Should one instructor be a participant in more than one program, cross-program calculations should be made on the basis of time spent working in each program. If an instructor teaches one hour in Program A and four hours in Program B, then 20 percent of his salary should be allocated to Program A and 80 percent to Program B. Unless more than one instructor teaches an individual course, instructor costs per student per course involve multiplication of the instructor's salary by the percentage time spent teaching that course. This figure is then divided by the number of students enrolled in the course.

Simple calculation of instructor cost per course is done similarly. The hours spent teaching that course are divided by the total number of working hours. This percentage is multiplied by the instructor's total salary to produce the instructor cost per course.

To calculate instructional cost per student in a particular program, the instructional cost per program is divided by the number of students participating in that program. Similarly, the instructional cost per course, when divided by the number of students enrolled in the course, yields the cost per student per course.

Material and Supply Costs

Materials and supplies are recurring costs, expended each year by students and staff on a per student or per course, per year basis. A preliminary estimate of supplies for a proposed program can be made by a pilot test of that program. For a program that has been in existence for some time, it is best to calculate average yearly costs over a period of time, then calculate the average yearly cost per student. This cost may be assigned to the projected number of students for the following year, or it may be assigned to a course rather than to individual students.

Building and Maintenance Costs

It is fortunate for the cost analyst that it is seldom necessary to compute building and maintenance costs in the comparative analysis of programs. These costs are normally allocated across disciplinary lines and the total cost per institution is normally unchanged regardless of the program that is implemented.

In fact, the unnecessary computation of building costs may lead to misrepresentation of the actual benefits of a program. Take the following example. In a case where Program A has been subdivided into two *new* programs—Programs A1 and A2—careless computation of costs could indicate that the subdivided programs cost more than they would in actual dollars. Although Program A and Programs A1 and A2 will accomplish similar objectives and require the same operational expenditures, if Programs A1 and A2 were each given one share of allocated building costs, it will appear that Programs A1 and A2 are the more expensive programs. In fact, these two alternatives cost the same.

Administrative Costs

Administrative costs are those costs which are incurred in the coordination, supervision, monitoring, and evaluation of the program or programs of the education or training institution. These costs are usually fixed by salary, and it is often difficult to assign differential amounts to individual programs. Thus, it is common practice to divide total administrative costs by the number of programs. If a particular annual emphasis is on one program, it may be necessary to allocate an increased administration cost to that program for the year. This allocation, in most instances, will represent an estimate.

DETERMINING BENEFITS

While most education and training costs are direct and tangible, most benefits derived from their effective utilization are indirect and often intangible. For example, although the cost of conducting an extensive managerial development program is easily determined, the determination of increased profits, increased manager morale, and other similar benefits of the program is quite complicated. Among other things, benefits must be assigned to *someone* or *something* and in the business of education and training, the evaluator is hard put to determine whether a benefit to industry (public or private economy) constitutes a benefit to the individual recipients of a program or to society in general. Although the determination of costs is never as simple as the computation of dollars spent by an institution or program during a given year, we have tried to limit the judgmental aspects of cost computation. However, with benefit computation, the evaluator must often rely on projections, estimates, and secondary measurements in formulating judgments of benefits.

Just as with costs, no system for determining benefits will cover all the possibilities of an education or training program; but the categories presented below may help to provide a springboard into benefit analysis. Benefits accruable from an occupational program may be classified as economic benefits, noneconomic benefits, and intermediate benefits.

Economic Benefits

Identifiable Benefits

Identifiable benefits are the tangible results produced as a function of executing a program and can be classified as, say, student behavior change as related to specific job skills which have marketable value, attitudinal changes of employer as demonstrated by effective interpersonal communication skills facilitated through a transaction analysis program, and so on. An example of an identifiable benefit is the preparation of a number of watch repair students for *productive* jobs and lives. The preparation of 300 watch repair students in *any* context is identifiable. Whether or not it is a benefit depends on whether or not 300 watch repair students will be able to find jobs within the community. Consequently, the determination of tangible benefits is dependent on the collection of information from a number of sources: the student follow-up, the employer follow-up, a job need survey, and a manpower study. Other sources of information should be identified for each specific situation. Once you have determined that the preparation of these students *is* a benefit, then you can proceed to determine the cost per student.

Target Benefits

Target benefits are projected or anticipated benefits of a proposed program. These benefits are derived from a preliminary estimate of benefits made by a pilot test or from benefits identified by other schools that have conducted similar programs. An example of a target benefit is a projected 2 percent increase in dollar sales for a given sales training program, or a 5 percent increase in manpower estimated for a manpower development program.

The distinction made between identifiable benefits and target benefits is primarily operational and is not absolute. Identifiable benefits are not necessarily those secured by a completed program. Should a nearly identical program be implemented two years in a row, then one would consider the benefits anticipated from the reinstitution of this program for a third year to be identifiable benefits. The distinction, then, is more of degree of certainty than anything else. Since target benefits are less reliably calculated, they should be used only in the absence of identifiable benefits in the determination of costs for a particular program.

Economic benefits related to an instructional program may also be classified according to benefactors: the individual, industry, or

	Benefactor		
	Individual	Industry	Society
Identifiable			
Target			

FIGURE 8–2   *Classes of Economic Education and Training Benefits*

society. The distinction between identifiable and target benefits will prove useful in the analysis of each of these classes. Figure 8–2 portrays this three-dimensional classification for economic benefits.

Benefits to Individuals

An individual may choose to enroll in a post-secondary or community college program to upgrade his skill in a job or to prepare for another job. To do this he may have to resign from his current job or sacrifice part of his leisure time to take instruction. He will also be required to pay tuition and other enrollment fees. These factors all represent costs to the individual for participation in the instructional program. Economic and noneconomic benefits of the program should be evident for such an investment. These benefits are many and include such outcomes as increased salary, job satisfaction, an improved self image, more leisure time, and possibly increased efficiency as a purchaser for the company. Example economic benefits to be gained by the individual from a training program are presented below:

Before Training	After Training
Salary—$600/mo.	$800/mo.
Job status—printer	Printing supervisor
Unhappy	Happy
Made purchases without review	Saved company money in purchasing

These benefits represent both economic and noneconomic benefits to the individual.

Benefits to Business and Industry

Public and career education and private training programs both aid in building a qualified labor force for business and industry. The focus of all internal training programs for private corporations is on the preparation of potential employees or upgrading of current staff to increase corporate profit. Public career education programs do not have this specific focus, but they often serve the needs of industry as they strive to meet individual and societal needs. Increases in the proficiency of individual workers will ultimately mean an increase in profit for industry. Additional aids to profit might include: a lower rate of personnel turnover, an increase in available manpower for certain positions, an increase in staff morale, and a decrease in absenteeism among staff. Benefits within this category are much easier to quantify for internal training programs, because there are fewer variables and increases in profits may be traced directly to the training program. Public training programs are at a disadvantage in this respect; they do not have access to the financial records for each organization that employs graduates. Below is a presentation of several economic benefits to an industrial firm.

Results following training program

2% increase in sales	= $56,000.00
10% lower staff turnover resulting in 30% savings in training costs	= 9,000.00
6% decrease in absenteeism resulting in .05% savings	= 10,000.00

Benefits to Society

The taxpaying public, whose tax dollars are being allocated to public career and occupational education programs, is most concerned with meeting the career development needs of individuals. The ultimate concern is that everyone will be prepared for a productive life in society. Federal and state legislators have directed millions of dollars to career preparation programs to meet, in part, the needs of our society. Benefits which accrue from an education program might be indicated by a decrease in the unemployment rate—this indicating a better prepared citizenry. Additonally, increases in productivity of business and industrial institutions and the increase in the incomes of individuals both have a positive effect on the taxation system of states and the nation. That is, as profit increases (both individual and corporate) so does the tax base. With an increased tax base, other problems of our society and concerns of our legislative body can be addressed. Another benefit to society which education is capable of providing is a decrease in public aid roles and the consequential decrease in public aid budgets. Obviously, societal benefits are much more difficult to measure and quantify into dollar amounts than individual and business and industry benefits. Also, it is difficult to attribute societal changes to specific occupational programs. However, this does not say that this class of benefits should be overlooked. These benefits should more appropriately be monitored on a regional, state, and national basis to aid in overall assessment and cost analysis with regard to federal, state, and regional planning and funding. Below are example societal benefits which may have been affected by the institution of a community college in a particular city.

Societal Changes from 1980 to 1982, Mudville, California

1.2% decrease in unemployment (compared to a 2% national increase)

6.0% decrease in public aid budget for city

Noneconomic Benefits

Although noneconomic benefits for a particular course or program may be easily enumerated, it is not a simple task to compare such subjective benefits. Examples of noneconomic benefits include:

    Job satisfaction
    Learner attitude
    Instructor or staff morale
    Community (tolerance, attitude, etc.)

In many instances, noneconomic benefits are just as important or more important than economic benefits. Some programs are designed specifically to change attitudes or remedy social problems. Drug education programs in the public schools are an example of programs with noneconomic value. Some programs that are superior in terms of economic returns may produce undesirable noneconomic outcomes which prevent their implementation. For example, a program which utilizes television tapes may prove offensive to students and staff alike. Or, staff members may object to a course that incorporates rigidly programmed instruction because it limits the exercise of their personal and professional judgment. In other cases, community support of one program (say, a home-based nursing program) may be less than for another, less expensive nursing program conducted outside of the district.

Decisions which weigh economic versus noneconomic factors are extremely delicate, and before deciding in favor of noneconomic considerations, the evaluator should have *all* economic facts in hand. Not only will this simplify his own decision, but it may have more far-reaching effects. Because these benefits are so highly subjective, it is best not to make such decisions alone. By presenting the facts to the community, school personnel, or the learners or trainees, the evaluator may avoid much grief and may even be surprised by the willingness of the population to sacrifice "style, comfort, and status" for more practical considerations.

Intermediate Benefits

Intermediate benefits are those benefits which can be measured between the time a program is initiated and the time when economic benefits are realized. It is usually difficult to attach specific dollar values to intermediate benefits and thus impossible to compute any type of cost-benefit ratio. However, intermediate benefits are probably the most accessible indicators for analyzing existing programs and choosing among alternatives. In most instances they represent product evaluation results such as those measured by learner assessment, the follow-up survey, and the employer survey and usually reflect the attainment of course and program objectives. For example, an objective of a program might be the placement of 80 percent of its graduates in jobs directly related to the preparation program. The subsequent determination that 86 percent of the graduates were placed represents an intermediate benefit. It is intermediate to the ultimate economic benefits—individual, industrial, and societal. Likewise, intermediate measures of benefit may be made during instruction or upon completion of instruction.

Intermediate measures can be considered as belonging to one of three categories which parallel those described in Chapter 3. These categories include formative, summative, and ultimate measures.

Formative Measures of Benefit

Measures of benefit that are made during the educational or training act are considered formative measures. These measures may represent unit or segment tests given to learners for each week or month of instruction. Formative measures are generally based upon prespec-

Secretarial Science Program

Part A: Budget

	Total	Per Student
Equipment costs	$ 3,000	$ 25.00
Facility costs	1,000	8.33
Instructor costs	24,000	200.00
Material costs	1,600	13.33

Part B: Benefits

	% Achieving Objectives
Objective 16: Each student will be able to type 60 wpm.	89%
Objective 17: Each student will demonstrate familiarity with output function of magnetic card Selectric typewriter (MCST).	93%

FIGURE 8-3   *Example Segment of an Accountability Report*

ified goals and may involve cognitive, affective, psychomotor, or perceptual behaviors. The primary use to be made of formative measures in cost analysis is in assessing small segments of the instructional program or in assessing alternative methods or instructional products utilized for specific aspects of the program. For example, if a teaching machine is being used in teaching law terminology in a business management program, formative measures of benefit would be useful in assessing the cost effectiveness of the teaching machine compared to a more traditional method of instruction.

Summative Measures of Benefit

Summative measures of benefits measure the success of a program in meeting its intended outcomes or objectives. Like formative measures, these measures focus on behaviors, but summative measures are applied after instruction has been completed and are used only indirectly for improvement. Achievement tests, work sample tests, attitude scales, situational tests, and mock interviews are examples of devices which can be used to assess the benefits of instructional programs. These measures are most often utilized to portray program outcomes in light of program expenditures and are useful in illustrating program accountability and in making program comparisons. For example, a program manager may display program costs, indicating the degree to which each program objective has been achieved. Figure 8–3 presents a segment of an accountability report.

Similar benefit information can be utilized to make program comparisons. For example, if two different programs had similar objectives, both the input of costs and the percentage achievement of objectives could be compared to aid in future choice of programs by instructional staff.

Ultimate Measures of Benefit

Ultimate measures of benefit are measures of post-program performance. Ultimate benefits are real life or job related and come the closest to economic benefits. For example, one type of ultimate measure is a rating of an individual's performance on the job by one of his supervisors. If an individual was trained to be a parts manager in an automotive firm and has acquired a job as a service manager in an automotive firm, this similarity between desired and acquired positions represents a positive benefit of the program to both the individual and to industry.

COST-BENEFIT ANALYSIS

The application of cost-benefit analysis to the evaluation of program-level education and training activities involves the comparison of quantifiable program benefits to program costs. Benefits refer to the results, effectiveness, or outcomes of any given program. For instance, if a community is in need of trained biomedical technicians, and 85 percent of the program graduates passed their State Board exam and obtained employment, this represents a quantifiable outcome attesting to the benefit of the program. Further, as a basis for evaluating the creditability of continued expenditures to train technicians, this outcome could be compared with the total cost per learner for training.

Consider the following example: Assume twenty learners were enrolled in an auto mechanic service program and the total costs incurred for the period of their enrollment was $18,000. In addition, assume that two stated program outcomes were as follows: 1) 75 percent of the learners will be employed in an auto mechanics position commensurate with their training, determined through a follow-up survey one year after graduation, and 2) During a given year, the total instructional cost per learner will not exceed $1,100.

Upon completion of a follow-up survey, the costs for the auto mechanics program were calculated on total number employed and on individual learner program costs. On the basis of this information, the following was obtained: 1) Total cost per learner enrolled = $900/learner ($18,000 ÷ 20 = $900). 2) The follow-up survey indicated that only 60 percent (12) of the learners were gainfully employed. Thus, on this basis, the *actual* cost for learner employed would be $1,500 ($18,000 ÷ 12 = $1,500).

To ascertain the cost of the auto mechanics program then, one would have to compare the number of learners gainfully employed and the cost per learner to the previously specified program outcome. For the previous example, neither the placement objective of 75 percent was attained nor was the planned cost per learner, which was exceeded by $600. Thus, this program did not effectively attain the prespecified program benefits. The question, *Is the benefit of twelve additional auto mechanics worth the investment?* can only be answered by contrasting the need for and cost of developing individuals for other occupations to the foregoing reported costs for auto mechanics.

Cost-benefit indices such as the one illustrated above can be determined for all education or training programs within an institution to justify the elimination of marginal programs. In addition, cost-benefit analysis can provide information with which to identify programs which need to be revised or upgraded. In some cases, the comparison of costs to benefits can identify the need to more closely evaluate specific programs or to reallocate resources to improve deficient programs.

To facilitate the analysis of costs corresponding to program benefits, Borgen and Davis (1974) have outlined a commendable strategy for compiling data for the cost-benefit evaluation of education and training programs.

Step 1: Analyze and formulate program outcomes (benefits). These outcome statements should specify the results anticipated as a function of program implementation. A number of publications are available to aid in the development of measurable objectives.

Step 2: Review program outcomes with occupational advisory committee or divisional management. This step will ensure that program outcomes correlate to benefits desired by the divisional management, community, or representatives of the target group.

Step 3: Determine data and records that should be utilized for intermittant cost-benefit evaluation. In cooperation and consultation with administrators, cost accountants, and other appropriate individuals, maintain information and cost records for periodic cost-benefit evaluation.

Step 4: Formulate a method to record data. For the data suggested in Step Two, develop a technique for effectively reporting information concerning program outcomes.

```
                    Program:  Electronics Technician

Program Development                    Per Year        Per Student-Per Year

      1.  Authoring expenses          _____        _____
      2.  Pilot learner reimbursement _____        _____
      3.  Content advisor honorarium  _____        _____
      4.  Material cost               _____        _____
      5.  Layout design cost          _____        _____
      6.  Typing and typesetting costs_____        _____
      7.  Reproduction costs          _____        _____
      8.  Administrative costs        _____        _____
      9.  Evaluation costs            _____        _____
     10.  Meeting costs               _____        _____
     11.  Travel costs                _____        _____
     12.  Other_____             _____        _____

          Total                       _____        _____


Program Operations

      1.  Instructor costs            _____        _____
      2.  Material and supply costs   _____        _____
      3.  Building and maintenance
                            costs     _____        _____
      4.  Administrative costs        _____        _____
      5.  Other _____            _____        _____

          Total                       _____        _____


Additional Costs

      1.                              _____        _____
      2.                              _____        _____

          Grand Total                 _____        _____
```

FIGURE 8–4   *Example Cost Display Form*

Step 5: Formulate a form for calculating program costs.   Develop a strategy which can be used to systematically compute the following types of program costs: 1) program development and 2) program operation. An example of a form which includes the above program costs categories is shown in Figure 8–4.

Step 6: Compile benefit data.   In accordance with the specifications

```
Benefits--Program:  Electronics Technician

Intermediate Benefits

                                     Desired Level     Actual Achievement

  1.  Cognitive achievement

  2.  Psychomotor achievement

  3.  Attitude

  4.  Number placed

  5.  Relatedness of placement

  6.  Employer ratings--general

  7.  Employer ratings--specific skills

  8.  Other_____

Economic Benefits

  1.  Increases in salary

  2.  Increased productivity

  3.  Personnel turnover rate

  4.  Change in absenteeism

  5.  Unemployment rate

Non-economic

  1.  Job satisfaction

  2.  Increase job status
```

FIGURE 8–5   *Example Benefit Display Form*

written in program outcome statements, compile the benefit information.

Step 7: Calculate a cost-benefit profile. For a given program, compute a cost-benefit profile. The form in Figure 8–4 can be utilized to
display costs for each program, and represents the cost side of a
cost-benefit profile. A second form, or a second half of the Figure
8–4 form should be developed. This form should reflect benefit
categories which will parallel the statements of intent or objectives
which were formulated in Step One. Your specific form might look
something like the one presented in Figure 8–5.

Step 8: Determine situations for decision making. Employ the cost-benefit profiles calculated in Step Seven in appropriate decision-making situations. Some of the possibilities include:

1. Determining optimum student load for a program.
2. Justifying resources allocation decisions.
3. Promoting better utilization of resources.
4. Determining optimum staff and manpower assignments.
5. Identifying marginal programs which should be deleted or upgraded.
6. Identifying cost-saving measures for high-cost programs.

COST EFFECTIVENESS ANALYSIS

Cost effectiveness evaluation is used to assist in selecting among alternative courses, programs, teaching methods, or materials. In many personnel functions and career education programs, decisions must be made regarding numerous projects which yield similar results. Cost effectiveness evaluation facilitates the allocation of resources to the most worthy of several alternatives. This cost evaluation technique is designed to aid in identifying those projects which yield the optimum benefit or outcome for specified costs. Essentially, cost effectiveness evaluation differs from cost-benefit analysis in that the latter focuses on the analysis of individual programs while cost effectiveness analysis compares items with identical goals. The evaluator must have both cost and outcome data unique to each project in order to make viable comparisons between projects. With this information, the evaluator can estimate which project will maximize benefits or return on investment.

In cost effectiveness evaluation, then, we attempt to ascertain the worth or value of alternative career education or training endeavors. If costs for two alternative programs are the same, cost effectiveness evaluation will deal only with a comparison of the benefits of the different projects. If not, cost effectiveness will involve the assignment of costs to each alternative. Cost effectiveness analysis requires that the evaluator first identify costs of all alternative projects and then determine the associated benefits. Once these steps have been completed, the evaluator can attempt to choose the alternative that yields the largest benefit for a given cost or incurs the least cost for a specified level of benefits (Alkin, 1972).

One of the major criteria for pure cost effectiveness analysis is that both the cost and benefits be specified in *net economic units.* However, as previously discussed, net economic benefits are often difficult to ascertain, especially for public education programs. It is, therefore, necessary to utilize intermediate measures of benefit. In most instances, this poses no real problem since most program objectives are stated in intermediate terms. Cost effectiveness evaluation can be conducted at either the program development or program operations level.

Program Development Cost Effectiveness Analysis

Cost effectiveness evaluation of a developed instructional product or set or materials may be used to compare a proposed program with the conventional mode of education or training or to compare two new instructional products.

In the following example (Figure 8–6) assume that the learner being trained earns $110.00 per week, and that using an instructional product for *three days* will increase the learner's performance to meet that of a learner with *two and one-half weeks* of experience, utilizing the conventional method of instruction. Further, it is necessary to compensate for the instructor's* time (salary) in assisting in the training process. In this example, it is estimated that the instruction reduces approximately 25 percent of the efficiency of the instructor or demands two out of a total of eight working hours per day.

Assuming that $261.00 is saved for each learner trained with the instructional product, the cost of developing the instructional product can be depreciated by adhering to the following equation:

$$\frac{\text{Developmental cost of product}}{\text{Savings for Learner}} = \text{Total numbers of learners necessary to recover cost of instructional product.}$$

* An instructor in this example is an experienced job incumbent.

	Cost of Conventional Instruction			Cost of Instructional Product	
Learner	$2\frac{1}{2}$ weeks @ \$110.00 per week	\$275.00	Learner	3 days @ \$110.00 per week	\$66.00
Instructor	Loss of 25% efficiency for $2\frac{1}{2}$ weeks @ \$110.00 per week	68.75	Instructor	Loss of 25% efficiency for 3 days @ \$110.00 per week	16.50
		\$343.75			\$82.50

Cost for conventional instruction--\$343.75

Cost for instructional product -- 82.50

Savings per learner --\$261.25

FIGURE 8–6 *Example Cost Effectiveness Schedule*

or

$$\frac{\$1,123.00}{\$261.00} = \text{Approximately five learners}$$

Thus, effectiveness or savings for utilizing this product is realized after the fifth learner and pays for itself threefold with an estimated twenty learners per year. In this example, results were the constant while cost of the program was a variable. A decision in favor of using the instructional product over traditional methodology is strongly indicated. There may be situations where existing resources (budget, personnel) are constant and products or methods are compared to choose the one which produces the most positive result. This represents just another way of looking at costs and benefits of alternative approaches.

Program Cost Effectiveness Analysis

Given an array of program alternatives, the evaluator must develop a strategy to be used in selecting career education and training programs. In business and industrial situations, for example, programs must be chosen which enhance performance and productivity and improve profits. In this manner, resources (money, time, instructor, or physical facilities) can be appropriately allocated only to those programs that have a significant impact on career facilitation, employability, revenue, and profits.

In public educational institutions, decisions must be made with regard to conducting an in-house program, making contractual joint agreements with neighboring schools, or contracting with a private agency or community college to offer the desired program. In either of the cases—training or education—seldom do parallel programs exist within the same institution. That is, programs with identical goals are not commonplace within one education or training agency. Therefore, it becomes necessary to search out alternatives which exist elsewhere or to run pilot or test versions of more than one program to aid in decision making.

Let us consider an example situation in which cost effectiveness analysis was applied. This particular situation involved the selection of a cosmetology program by a secondary level area vocational center. The need for such a program had been documented by a student demand or interest survey and a job supply and demand survey. The program manager did not believe the small number of students (fifteen) would justify the purchase of equipment and employment of additional staff, so he sought to identify alternatives. Two alternatives for cosmetology training were identified: a community college program and a private training agency within the community.

The program manager of the area center explored the costs per student for each of the programs and also considered additional costs such as special administrative costs and costs for transporting students from area center to the place of training. Examples of these costs are presented below.

Program: Cosmetology

Costs per student/ per year	Smith School of Beauty Culture	Allantown Community College
Tuition	$600.00	$525.00
Fees	$100.00	$115.00
Transportation	0	$145.00
Administrative (coordination)	$ 12.00	$ 12.00
Total	$712.00	$797.00

This example cost display shows the private training agency to be less expensive than the community college program. The primary contribution to this difference is transportation expense. Although tuition and fees combined are less expensive at the community college, this saving is offset by transportation costs. There may be other costs associated with the two programs but by displaying all known costs, comparison is facilitated.

A logical next step in comparing the two cosmetology programs is the delineation of benefits for each program. Much of the benefit identification process will be dependent upon the amount of student evaluation that the training agencies have done in the past. One index of benefit which should be easy to obtain is a report of state board exams for program graduates. This may reflect the percentage of passing scores or it may provide average scores. This will provide a standardized measure for both programs—an intermediate measure of benefit. Other measures of benefit will depend upon the degree to which the two training agencies have followed up their graduates and whether or not they have surveyed supervisors and employers of graduates. The example benefit display below presents just some of the benefits which may be accessible for programs.

Program: Cosmetology

Benefits	Smith School of Beauty Culture	Allantown Community College
State Board Exam	Ave. 80/100	Ave. 86/100
Placement of Graduates	95%	86%
Average Salary of Graduates	620/mo.	600/mo.
Job Satisfaction	High	Average
Employer Rating	High	Average

The comparison of two programs based upon benefits is more difficult than comparing costs, since we have no monetarily expressed intermediate measures. Given the benefit picture in column 1 of the above display, some subjectivity must enter into the decision of which is most advantageous. But higher employer ratings and higher ratings of job satisfaction are probably better indicators of program success than are state board examination scores. If this interpretation is made, it can be concluded that the private agency's program is superior in terms of benefits. Also, by relating benefits to cost, the private program would be the area center manager's most logical choice.

The problem of decision making could have been further complicated if the most beneficial program had been the most expensive. If this had been the case, then more information would be required to determine if the higher benefits were worth the higher expenditures required.

The previous example has involved the comparison of two external programs. A comparison could be made between an existing internal program and an external program. This type of comparison would require a more detailed analysis of internal costs such as those suggested by the cost-benefit section of this chapter. Once all costs are computed, then comparisons can be made in a manner similar to the comparison of the two cosmetology programs.

Used within training programs for private corporations, cost effectiveness analysis lends itself to more precise consideration of economic benefits. This fact has led to a somewhat better defined methodology for training programs. One such system for cost effectiveness evaluation is included here. This framework was first implemented at Xerox in 1971 as part of a long-range manpower planning strategy to formulate budget proposals for personnel functions throughout the organization (Cheek, 1973). The key procedural stages include the following:

1. Identify and describe each occupational or training and development program, whether ongoing or proposed.
2. In business and industrial settings, determine those programs which have a legal requirⁱ nent for special consideration.
3. Evaluate all programs on the basis of the following criteria: a) present status, b) implementation feasibility, c) net economic benefits, and d) economic risks of not selecting a program.

When education and training personnel are asked to review their program requirements and to specify the programs that are offered or needed, it is first necessary for them to review the present and projected operating budget. Second, they must identify and indicate ways in which the major programs affect the funding and cost accounting situation of the institution or organization. And third, they must indicate programs that could viably increase employability or performance and prevent major program risks and unnecessary costs.

At this point, we will examine the procedural stages of Xerox's program cost effectiveness strategy described by Cheek (1973).

Stage 1: Identify and Describe

As a first step, each instructor who has responsibility for a particular occupational or training program must describe his offering—whether proposed or ongoing. The program's objectives, implementation strategy, target population, and any other critical factors that might have a bearing on the program's viability are specified. Figure 8–7 illustrates a form which can be used in the evaluation for all programs. It contains example information on a job enrichment program which will be discussed throughout this chapter section.

In completing this form, it is advantageous to use the individual

Exhibit I. Program evaluation form

1. Define and describe the program.	**PROGRAM NAME:** Service Force Job Enrichment Program Program No. 16

DESCRIPTION   (objectives, target population, implementation schedule):

To extend the job enrichment program for the service force —
as piloted in Spring Falls, Avon Hills, and Maplewood branches
— to all branches between 1972 and 1976.

2. Identify and segregate legally required efforts.

☐ Yes   ☒ No

3. Evaluate feasibility:
(a) State-of-the-art implications.
(b) Ease of implementation.
(c) Net economic benefits...

STATE OF THE ART	☒ High	☐ Medium	☐ Low
EASE OF IMPLEMENTATION	☐ High	☐ Medium	☒ Low
ECONOMIC BENEFITS	☒ High	☐ Medium	☐ Low

	Potential revenue impact	Probability of occurrence	Probable gross benefit (cost)
Identifiable benefits:			
Reduction in service force turnover of 1 point.	$ 450,000	.2	$ 90,000
Extension of 1.2 point reduction in absenteeism, as demonstrated in pilot project.	$ 2,132,500	.8	$ 1,706,000
Extension of 5% increase in service force productivity, as demonstrated in initial efforts.	$85,500,000	.1	$ 8,550,000
Total benefits	$88,082,500	.12	$10,346,000
Tangible costs to Xerox of acting: Group personnel staff time to develop program, and line management time to implement program in all branches.	($ 472,950)	.9	$ 425,655
Total costs	($ 472,950)	.9	$ 425,655
Probable net benefits (cost)			$ 9,920,345

- -

...and intangibles.   **Intangible benefits**

Increased morale in service force, with improved customer
service and satisfaction.

"Contagious effect" of job enrichment to other groups, e.g.,
sales and clericals.

Improved service manager development with concurrent sharpening
of their motivational skills. As an extreme example, one
manager at Avon Hills increased his team's productivity 70%.

(d) Economic risks.

ECONOMIC RISKS	☒ High	☐ Medium	☐ Low

Possible consequences of not acting:
Continued escalation of service costs as a percent of revenue.

ASSUMPTIONS AND OTHER CONSIDERATIONS:

Cost estimates assume 4.4 man years of group staff time, .26 man
years of branch manager time, and 15.8 man years of service manager
time to implement program in a population of 1,053 service managers.

Benefit estimates assume elimination of 3 days absenteeism per
month for each of 1,053 service teams, favorable productivity, and that
turnover experience in pilot branches can be cascaded to all branches.

FIGURE 8–7   *Example Program Evaluation Form (reproduced from* Harvard Business Review, *vol. 51, no. 3, May-June 1973, with the permission of Logan M. Cheek and* Harvard Business Review, *Boston, Massachusetts).*

responsible for managing entire department effort as well as instructors of specific programs. The instructor is usually the most knowledgeable about the program's technical features, objectives, and target population characteristics as well as probable scheduling problems. In contrast, the department head or manager can provide information regarding manpower needs and trends, performance deficiencies, and job turnover, in addition to cost economics relevant to each program.

Stage 2: Identify Legal Requirements

In business and industrial organizations, it is required by law that resources be appropriated to special programs. In the past decade, many manpower bills and rulings have been enacted in such areas as labor and industrial relations, nondiscriminatory hiring practices, and wage controls. As the traditional economic goal of corporate organizations is enlarged to include social priorities, such legal mandates will ostensibly increase in the next several years.

The job enrichment effort shown in Figure 8–7 is not a legal requirement. However, other programs in the areas of minority employment and labor relations clearly constitute legal necessities. As Cheek suggests, these programs rarely offer any net economic benefits and are thus intangible in character. Because of the potential legal issues, and the subsequent impact on the occupational image, these programs should be treated separately from other programs and given the highest priority for funding. Once legally required programs have been identified and described, the next step is that of the feasibility evaluation.

Stage 3: Evaluate the Feasibility of Programs

To evaluate the feasibility of any program, several distinct areas must be included:

Determine the present status of the program (needs assessment) as to whether the necessary competencies are available.

Ascertain the feasibility or ease of implementing the program within administrative and personnel functions (will they support and execute the program?)

Determine the cost effectiveness or net economic benefits of the program.

Identify the risks (economic) for not instituting the program.

Evaluation	A. Present Status Criteria	B. Ease of Implementation Criteria
High	▸ Program appears simple ▸ Manpower available in organization ▸ Training or educational facilities available	▸ Implementing program requires little effort to influence a change in staff attitudes and in organizational policies, structure and training or educational environment ▸ Implementing program does not suggest a radical departure from conventional organizational practices
Medium	▸ Program appears complex ▸ Manpower not available in organization but available outside ▸ Training or educational facilities not available but elsewhere available	▸ Moderate effort required for implementing program to effect change in staff attitudes, organization policies, structure and training or educational environment ▸ Implementing program suggests some departure from organizational practices
Low	▸ Program involves new or unfamiliar effort ▸ Personnel not available on staff or outside organization ▸ Facilities and equipment not readily available	▸ Substantial effort required to implement a program to effect a change in line with attitudes, organizational policies, structure and training or educational environment ▸ Implementing program implies a radical departure from traditional organizational practices

FIGURE 8–8   *Criteria for Evaluating the Feasibility of Programs (reproduced from* Harvard Business Review *with the permission of Logan M. Cheek and Harvard Business Review,* Boston, Massachusetts).

Present Status. In order to resolve this area, one must make an in-depth appraisal of the program's technical limitations and the expertise available within existing faculty and training personnel necessary to overcome these limitations. Reexamination of Figure 8–7 of the job enrichment program indicates that qualified expertise was readily available within the ranks of current staff. In this instance, therefore, present status would be evaluated as *high.* For comparative purposes, the technical feasibility of all proposed programs must be regularly evaluated against identical criteria. Part A of Figure 8–8 illustrates criteria for evaluating the feasibility of alternative programs.

Implementation Feasibility. This area is the most important aspect of cost effectiveness evaluation. In most instances, it includes such factors as supervisory attitudes, managerial styles, corporate and administrative structure, and organizational policies. When proposed programs are in new content or performance areas, these factors are somewhat difficult to change.

Cooperation and acceptance are necessary requirements for the successful implementation of proposed programs. In the job enrichment program, for example, Cheek (1973) evaluated the ease-of-implementation factor as *low* because of resistance to an earlier prototype or pilot program (see Figure 8–7).

As to evaluating the *present status,* consistent criteria must be employed when assessing the ease or feasibility of implementing the program. These criteria are indicated in Part B of Figure 8–8.

Net Economic Benefits. It is at this step of the evaluation that cost-benefit analysis is applied to determining the cost effectiveness of alternative programs. In Figure 8–7, potential benefits and costs are identified for the job enrichment program. Also, an estimation is made as to the occurrence of each cost and benefit in addition to the probable dollar input of the program. For the job enrichment effort, the pilot program gave Cheek and his associates economic data concerning its influence on productivity, employee absenteeism, and job turnover.

When pilot program data are available, and when it is difficult to estimate probable benefits linked with the alternative programs, benefits can be estimated by one of two techniques discussed earlier in this chapter section: 1) identifiable benefits, and 2) target benefits.

It should be noted that the benefits specified for the job enrichment program in Figure 8–7 are identifiable benefits. As previously mentioned, these were based on the pilot program and therefore assure that the benefits of the pilot effort could be projected to total program results. Also, intangible benefits and risks are specified in this step.

Cost and Economic Risks. The final stage of the feasibility evaluation is to consider the economic risk of not instituting the proposed program. For instance, failure to reevaluate a sales organization's preemployment interview selection procedures could result in the recruitment of less competent sales representatives.

Exhibit III. Decision table for determining program feasibility

Step 1. Evaluate feasibility and economic benefits/risks.

Using predefined standards, separately evaluate each program's state-of-the-art implications, ease of implementation, net economic benefits, and economic risks of not acting. The Service Force Job Enrichment Program was evaluated (see Exhibit I) as follows:

State of the art	–	High
Ease of implementation	–	Low
Net economic benefits	–	High
Economic risks	–	High

Step 2. Compare technical (state-of-the-art) with operational (ease-of-implementation) feasibility.

1. The "high" state-of-the-art evaluation . . . is matched against "low" ease of implementation.

State of the art	Ease of implementation		
	HIGH	MEDIUM	LOW
HIGH	Very desirable	Very desirable	Marginally desirable
MEDIUM	Very desirable	Moderately desirable	Marginally desirable
LOW	Marginally desirable	Marginally desirable	Not worthwhile

Step 3. Compare Step 2 evaluation with net economic benefits.

2. Results of this evaluation are compared to "high" net economic benefits.

Step 2 evaluation	Net economic benefits		
	HIGH	MEDIUM	LOW
Very desirable	Very desirable	Moderately desirable	Marginally desirable
Moderately desirable	Very desirable	Moderately desirable	Marginally desirable
Marginally desirable	Marginally desirable	Marginally desirable	Not worthwhile

Step 4. Compare Step 3 evaluation with economic risks to determine overall feasibility.

3. Results of this evaluation are matched against "high" risks . . .

4. . . . to determine overall feasibility category of "moderately desirable."

Step 3 evaluation	Economic risks		
	HIGH	MEDIUM	LOW
Very desirable	Very desirable	Moderately desirable	Moderately desirable
Moderately desirable	Moderately desirable	Moderately desirable	Marginally desirable
Marginally desirable	Moderately desirable	Marginally desirable	Not worthwhile

FIGURE 8–9   *Example Decision Table for Determining Program Feasibility (reproduced from* Harvard Business Review *with the permission of Logan M. Cheek and* Harvard Business Review, *Boston, Massachusetts).*

Stage 4: Specify and Assign Resources

Once each program has been evaluated on its unique human resource development merits, an overall cost effectiveness evaluation must be conducted. Figure 8–9 illustrates a method for attaining this comparative assessment.

Cheek's decision table allows each program to be classified into one of the four feasibility categories: 1) very desirable, 2) moderately desirable, 3) marginally desirable, or 4) not worthwhile. It should be noted, moreover, that the table is designed so that a high rating on any factor will be a substantial factor in the selection of the program. A low rating on any factor, however, could eliminate the program from being chosen. Figure 8–9, for example, indicates that even though the job enrichment program was assessed *high* on three of the four feasibility criteria, the single *low* assessment (for implementation feasibility) caused an overall feasibility evaluation of only *moderately desirable.*

Further, a program's priorities schedule can be used for ranking all programs once they have been classified in accordance with the foregoing scheme. As shown in Figure 8–10, the legally required programs appear at the top of the program priorities schedule. In relation to their purported economic benefits, other programs are rated within the category. (As indicated, the job enrichment program is ranked third following the legally mandated programs.) The programs which are evaluated *not worthwhile* are listed at the bottom of the schedule.

For effectively specifying and assigning resources among alternative programs, the program priorities schedule serves as a viable technique. But according to Cheek, to be used effectively, program evaluators must undertake four specific actions:

1. Trim marginal programs.
2. Allocate and deploy staff resources toward the most worthwhile projects.
3. Assess all new programs and rearrange priorities as necessary.
4. Monitor progress.

The foregoing method for evaluating the cost effectiveness of alternative education or training programs facilitates the assignment and deployment of resources (costs) to those programs which demonstrate the greatest benefits and return on investment. What is

Exhibit IV. Program priorities schedule

ACTION PROGRAM	Priority	Timing 1972	1973	1974	1975	1976	1977	Net annual dollar benefit	Cost/benefit ratio (1:n)
LEGALLY REQUIRED PROGRAMS									
Labor Relations Strategy	x							($ 619)	n/a
Protect Right to Select Employees	x							($ 86)	n/a
Continue Validation of Selection Tests	x							$35,000	78.17
Redesign Personnel Data System	x							$ 273	1.78
Develop Part-Time Female Employment Approaches	x							$ 227	4.16
VERY DESIRABLE PROGRAMS									
Restructuring Service Force	1							$14,608	9.6
Service College Coop Program	2								2.74
MODERATELY DESIRABLE PROGRAMS									
Service Job Enrichment	3							$ 9,920	24.3
Assessment Center	4							$ 4,946	15.40
Education & Training Center	5							$ 4,780	3.57
Clerical Selection Program	6							$ 1,799	19.94
Develop College Campus as Primary Employment Source	7							$ 834	2.06
Interfunctional Moves & Fast Track Program	8							$ 679	7.54
Selection Standards for New Sales/Tech. Rep. Types	9							$ 520	11.6
Improve Economics of Field Employment Operations	10							$ 472	1.42
Build Better Technical Recruiting/Selection Capability	11							$ 222	2.48
Monitor Sales & Tech. Rep. Selection Tests	12							$ 211	9.05
MARGINAL BUT DESIRABLE PROGRAMS									
Implement Executive Search Function	13							$ 177	1.67
Refine Career Path Guides	14							$ 110	1.75
Continue National Trend Attitude Surveys	15							$ 107	1.33
Reevaluate Overall Organization Approach	16							$ 93	2.37
NOT WORTHWHILE									
Executive Retreat	x							($ 450)	n/a
Corporate Jet	x							($ 769)	n/a
Savings Plan	x							($ 75)	n/a

Left-margin annotations:

1. Legally required efforts come first . . .
2. . . . then, other programs are ranked by overall feasibility category . . .
3. . . . and within feasibility category by net benefits.
4. Priorities are indicated here.
5. Starting from the lowest priority program, marginal efforts may be trimmed as required by the budget.
6. In any case, these programs are eliminated.

Legend:
||||||| Program and design development
▬▬ Program Implementation

FIGURE 8–10   *Example Program Priorities Schedule (reproduced from* Harvard Business Review *with the permission of Logan M. Cheek and* Harvard Business Review, *Boston, Massachusetts).*

more, this process motivates educational and training evaluators to objectively appraise their programs' acclaimed benefits and to evaluate the plausibility of attaining them. This technique will help foster the move away from the intuition and institutional politics too often symptomatic of resource allocation and budgeting decisions.

LIMITATIONS OF COST ANALYSIS EVALUATION

When one is engaged in the process of ascertaining either the cost benefit or cost effectiveness of a program or instructional unit, it is wise and often necessary to consider several methodological limitations associated with a cost analysis evaluation.

Johnson and Dietrich (1971), for example, recognize the following problems characteristic of cost identification.

1. *Costs are infrequently linear.* Many program and instructional expenses are fixed over narrow ranges whereas others are dependent upon enrollment, material costs, and other factors.
2. *Cost records and data are inadequate.* For the majority of organizations, expense categories are not in sufficient detail to afford accurate cost accounting.
3. *Relevant costs are unavailable.* The concept of opportunity costs is important in considering how resources are utilized.
4. *Cost data on projects are unreliable.* The methods of collecting on various instructional and program functions are as varied as the definitions of those functions.

Borgen and Davis (1974) cite two major shortcomings with the identification of benefits: 1) Many program outcomes cannot be readily quantified and 2) benefits such as income gain are difficult to attribute solely to an education program.

These foregoing cost analysis programs should be explored in reference to their limiting influence on the evaluative process. When appropriately managed, however, they will not severely diminish the extensiveness and worthiness of the cost analysis evaluation. While this chapter by no means presents all of the information that has been compiled and written on cost analysis evaluation, it has attempted to explain several methodologies in sufficient detail to give the evaluator new insight into strategic approaches in this area.

REFERENCES

Alkin, M. C. "Towards an Evaluation Model: Systems Approach." Taylor, P. and Cowley, D. (eds.), *Readings in Curriculum Evaluation*. Dubuque, Iowa: Brown Publishers, 1972, pp. 110–116.

Borgen, J. A. and Davis, D. E. *Planning, Implementing, and Evaluating Career Preparation Programs*. Bloomington, Illinois: McKnight, 1974, pp. 8–9.

Cheek, L. M. "Cost Effectiveness Comes to the Personnel Function." *Harvard Business Review*, 1973, 51(3):99–104.

Johnson, F. G. and Dietrich, D. E. *Cost Analysis of Instructional Technology to Improve Learning: An Evaluation of Instructional Technology*. Tickton, S. G. (ed.) New York: R. R. Bowler Company, 1971, pp. 965–975.

Lawson, T. E. *Formative Instructional Product Evaluation Instruments and Strategies*. Englewood Cliffs, New Jersey: Educational Technology Publications, 1974, p. 118.

9

Utilizing Evaluation Results for Planning and Improvement

AN OVERVIEW OF EDUCATIONAL CHANGE

Chapter 2 outlines six limitations traditionally associated with evaluation efforts. All six can be tied to the failure to adequately utilize evaluation in an efficient way. The utilization of evaluation results represents, by far, the most important part of evaluation. Even the best conceived and executed evaluation plan and the most carefully drawn judgments are futile if evaluation results are never used. To ensure utilization of results, the evaluator must do more than simply duplicate and disseminate data to interested parties. Once results are judged, conclusions drawn, and decisions made, action must be taken in a rational manner to implement those changes which have been indicated by the evaluation. The material presented in this chapter is based heavily on the work of Havelock (1970) and the hundreds of individuals who contributed to his work.

It might very well be said that the sole purpose of evaluation is to facilitate the planning and execution of change. Similarly, in most cases where change has been intentionally implemented, evaluation has been the cause. Much of the evaluation and its related planning and decision making has been very informal. It is also the case that informal approach to evaluation has meant an informal or haphazard approach to change. This is why thorough evaluation has become a nationwide priority in a time when planning ahead is of the essence.

The most simple response to an identified need or problem is to ignore it. Responses such as *Let it pass,* or *These things run in cycles* are common masks for attitudes of indifference. Responses such as these are the most marked indicators of poor evaluation. *These things run in cycles* is a stock conclusion based on foggy evidence—a weak evaluation. When educators can comfortably counter an evaluator's evidence with a response of this sort, it is clear that the strength of the evaluator's own case is insufficient.

The simple reflex is a response to a *disturbance*—a problem which has reached such proportions as to no longer allow for indifference on the part of the educator. Once again, should the evaluator encounter this sort of response, he can be certain that he has not done his job properly. The following example sets the scene for a simple reflex response:

> An occupational instructor has been lecturing from the book for three months, and his students appear to be bored to tears. Some of them snore in class, to the extent that the others cannot hear and have walked out of the room. Still others have gone to complain to counselors and parents. Furthermore, the class enrollment has dropped to three students.

For a simple reflex then, the *disturbance* would be outlined something like this:

THE DISTURBANCE: students snore in class

students have *boycotted class* and complained to counselors

in the end, class enrollment has dropped to three students

This sort of disturbance elicits a response from the evaluator or the educator. The response is described in the S-R model as an *Activity Designed to Remedy.* Such an activity might be the following:

THE ACTIVITY DESIGNED TO REMEDY: The instructor plays pop music in accompaniment to his lecture.

Such an activity may have an effect or no effect. Examples of effect or no effect might be these:

EFFECT OR NO EFFECT: the students sit and continue to sleep. (no effect)

the students appear to be listening, class enrollment increases to thirty students. (effect)

the students begin to dance and continue to ignore the instructor's teaching. (new disturbance)

Figure 9–1 presents a schematic of the simple reflex model.

Again, should the evaluator encounter a simple reflex response in an educational setting, he will be sure to conclude that evaluation is

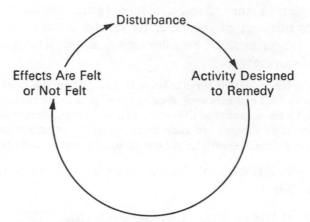

FIGURE 9–1   *Schematic of the Simple Reflex Change Model*

poor. Reflex response is planning by means of trial and error evaluation. First of all, the disturbance is usually brought to light by a crisis rather than by systematic inquiry or assessment. With the previous example, trainee boredom was voiced by trainees overtly. Furthermore, no visible evaluation was conducted to choose alternative strategies or activities to remedy the situation. Rather than employing several *input* evaluation activities, the instructor arbitrarily chose pop music as a remedy. Then, in the case of our example, the instructor attempted to determine intuitively whether the attitude of trainees had changed. He made no attempt to systematically sample student opinion. It is possible that the students were not listening but were only more content to sit quietly when he applied his new method.

Problems of much greater magnitude can easily be precipitated by a simple reflex response approach to education. Teacher strikes, rioting, and boycotts, for instance, are often the result of this type of approach to evaluation. These are all crises precipitated by a reflex approach to overcoming problems.

A third approach to identifying and overcoming a need or problem is termed rational problem solving. This approach begins with the identification of a problem, involves four distinct steps of responsive activity, and culminates with the assessment of success of the activity in overcoming the problem. Figure 9–2 includes each of the components included in the rational model of educational change.

The rational approach to problem solving incorporates systematic assessment, or evaluation, at many levels. The model begins with a decision situation. The classroom, department, building, institution, region, state, or the nation may be identified as decision levels. Of course, most locally directed decision situations focus on one or more of the first four.

All of the evaluation techniques discussed in Chapters 3 through 8 of this text focus on the delineation of evaluation questions and involvement of staff and external personnel in the collection and presentation of evaluative information. A number of different techniques have been specified, including student assessment, follow-up of former students, the survey of employers, the consultative team evaluation, evaluation of education and training personnel, and the cost related study. Each of these activities has something specific to contribute to improving the education or training program. Results from all of the activities, when combined, provide the basis for more intensive investigation of any program. The broader the range of information from which to draw interpretations, the more accurate a

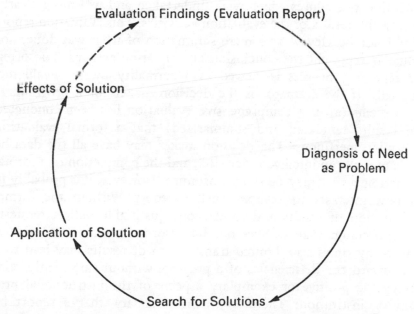

FIGURE 9–2   *Schematic of the Rational Model of Educational Change*

picture will be rendered by the evaluation. The technique chapters presented earlier provide answers to rather specific questions such as: *How do students feel about the sales training program in question?* (survey of current students); *How well are students prepared for employment on the job?* (employer survey); *Do students find employment in the field for which they have been trained?* (student follow-up).

Combination and synthesis of answers to these more specific questions may yield answers to much broader questions such as, *How effective is the sales training program in training individuals for entry level skills in sales positions?* However, for all evaluation information to be utilized by staff in major decisions, it is necessary that conclusions from each form of evaluation be recorded and collected in a useable and representative format.

PREPARING AN EVALUATION REPORT

A prepared evaluation report will facilitate the communication of evaluation procedures which were undertaken and will more clearly portray the results of the evaluation activities. This evaluation report should not be viewed as a mere summation of what was done, nor should it represent the conclusion of evaluation activity. Too often the reporting process is viewed as a formality by the evaluator, especially if the evaluator is the decision maker for a program. It often seems (after a comprehensive evaluation has been conducted and results tabulated and summarized) that a formal evaluation report is superfluous. The decision maker may have all the data he needs to make an intelligent decision, and the completion of a formal evaluation report may be time consuming. However, it is probably in his best interests to compile such a report. Without the formal presentation of results and conclusions, justifiable budget requests and curriculum changes may not be accorded their due consideration. Many times also, limited transmission of results may lead to a bias toward the deficiencies of a program without sufficiently reinforcing the positive or exemplary aspects of the instructional program or institution. Therefore, it is necessary that a report be prepared and presented in written form to those who may be concerned about the focus of the evaluation and those who may be involved in the program itself.

An evaluation report is the servant of an institution and serves in many different capacities; consequently, the format will vary from institution to institution. However, most institutions should be able to organize activities around the categories of objectives, program description, description of evaluation, and evaluation outcomes, since these are all components of any good evaluation system. Figure 9–3 is a recommended format for a formal evaluation report.

Since any evaluation system should be initiated for a definite purpose, the first section of the evaluation report should contain the objectives of the evaluation. Objectives may resemble those presented at the beginning of each chapter, such as, *to determine the*

   I. Evaluation Objectives
   a. Evaluation purposes or goals
   b. Audiences of report

  II. Program Description
   a. Program goals
   b. Student performance objectives
   c. Description of students
   d. Description of program staff
   e. Description of instructional methods utilized

 III. Description of Evaluation Methodology
   a. Scope of evaluation
   b. Time frame of evaluation
   c. Description of activities utilized
   d. Biasing factors

 IV. Evaluation Outcomes or Results
   a. Results by activity
   b. Results by issue

  V. Evaluation Conclusions
   a. Predetermined decision situations
   b. Exploratory evaluation

FIGURE 9–3   *Example Evaluation Report Outline*

adequacy of ancillary services such as guidance, counseling, and placement, or may be expressed with a statement delineating specific decision situations such as, *Should the guidance program be expanded to include a formal placement service for graduates and dropouts?* Whatever method is chosen should be stated explicitly in the very beginning of the evaluation report to emphasize exactly why the evaluation was undertaken to begin with. Even if objectives have been clearly stated, the report should delineate the audience to whom the report has been addressed. This will clarify the evaluator's notions concerning who is responsible for implementing recommended changes. The reader will then be encouraged to synthesize information and will take a more active role in recommending changes. An evaluation designed to meet the aforementioned objectives and decision situations would probably be directed toward the administrative staff, the guidance and counseling staff, the governing board of the institution, the advisory council (if one exists), and possibly even the instructional staff or other staff members who have had something to do with offering of ancillary services such as guidance, counseling, and placement, on a formal or informal basis within the institution. If the report is not specifically directed to a given group, the evaluation should not include this group, even as a matter of courtesy. This may weaken the more appropriate reader's sense of responsibility as he sees that other identified groups really have had no active role in evaluation.

Another job of the evaluation report is to describe the program or institution under consideration in the evaluation. This description should include both the broad goals and objectives of the program—subject matter included—and the specific student goals or student objectives for the course or program if they are available. In addition, a description of the students or learners enrolled in the course should be given. This description might include the age level, background, overall male/female makeup of the group, and other data. Another component that might be included in the description of the program is the instructional methods utilized in the program, number of staff included, background of the staff members included, and other similar components which may contribute to the success or lack of success of the program.

The third component of the evaluation report should be a description of the evaluation method utilized. This description should indicate the scope and magnitude of the evaluation activities as well as the time frame in which they were conducted. For example, if a follow-up survey made up one of the evaluation activities included in this report, then a description should be given of those involved in conducting the survey as well as the scope of the survey including what students or what former learners were followed up. For example, were all of the learners for a particular school year followed up, or were just those students involved in the electronics technician program followed up? It is also a good idea at this point to give some of the factors which may have contributed to a bias in the evaluation results. For a follow-up study, these might include the failure of 35 percent of the former learners to respond to the survey. The reader of the evaluation report may be interested in this information, as it may influence his interpretation of the results. Specifics of the activity such as the follow-up of nonrespondents, the analysis of the information, and so on should also be described for the reader of the report.

If more than one activity is included in the overall evaluation, a description of each of the activities should be presented with some of the specifics such as those mentioned with regard to the follow-up study. At this point in the report, the evaluation director should include any general statements that he feels will help the reader to better interpret the results. These statements might include an indication of his feeling with regard to the bias in one direction or another of the evaluation results, some of the possible shortcomings of the evaluation, and any other limiting or constraining factors which he believes are inherent in the results. An example of a possible indication of bias might be that the evaluation director believes that a specific item in the questionnaire, pertaining to the adequacy of the counseling department, may not be a true reflection of the counseling department but instead might be student bias about what a counseling department should be or should do. Besides illuminating any biases that may have been incorporated in evaluation procedures, this sort of information will help the reader to understand some of the feelings or biases held by the person who actually compiled the report. It is better to present biases in this manner than by the selection or presentation of results. If the evaluator does have strong feelings on a subject, he should not be afraid to present the facts but should have confidence that the presentation of more information will support rather than weaken his case.

A fourth responsibility of the evaluation report is to present the evaluation outcomes or results including not only the actual responses to the surveys but conclusions drawn by teams, figures and comparisons derived from cost-benefit analyses, and so on.

A decision must be reached by the evaluation or program manager concerning what approach to take in presenting evaluation results. One way is to separate data according to the method by which it was obtained. If a student follow-up, an employer survey, and a student assessment have been conducted as part of an overall evaluation effort, a section might be allotted to the results of each of these activities.

A second method for presenting results requires more attention on the part of the program manager or evaluator. This method breaks evaluation results down according to the types of issues or by key questions they address. For example, if an evaluation study has two major objectives—the assessment of the guidance, counseling, and placement service, and the assessment of student performance—results from all activities (student follow-up, employer survey, and student assessment) can be sorted out according to the major purpose they serve. This will help the audience of the report to compare more easily the information from each activity concerning each issue. Many times such comparisons are very important to the formulation of accurate judgments concerning the overall effect or effectiveness of a program. Again, depending on the specificity of evaluation objectives and on the time and resources available to the program manager, the results can be sorted out according to more specific questions.

This second approach should probably be preferred to the first, if key questions have been carefully developed prior to the initiation of evaluation activity. If decision situations have been clearly defined, this sort of organization will allow the audience of the report to make decisions in less time. This format also will insure that each person's decisions are made on the basis of the same information. Otherwise, some members of the audience may be more likely to overlook some relevant evidence because of a shortage of time or lack of interest.

If decision situations were not clearly defined before the evaluation activities were initiated, the first approach may be preferable. In this case, the audience of the report might be encouraged to look for evidence that indicates a decision situation not previously identified or for questions posed by the information which might indicate further investigation is necessary.

In addition to presenting data that have been gathered through specific instrumentation such as questionnaires, rating scales, and so on, the evaluation report should present general observations and more subjective information gathered by the team. This information may be gathered by means of open-ended questionnaire items contained in surveys, such as the follow-up survey or the employer survey, or they may be in the form of subjective judgments by instructors or administrative structure. Instructors may have information to contribute along with results from their observation of students in the classroom. The observation of instructional staff by administrators or supervisors may yield judgments from the latter which should be incorporated in the evaluation report, i. e., results from student assessment testing may indicate that students are very adequate in terms of the competencies which they possess, yet the administrators or instructional staff members may observe a very poor attitude on the part of the students which was not assessed by a formal measure. Such information will be valuable in terms of evaluating the success of the overall program and should be included when possible. Figure 9–4 presents example evaluation results from a student follow-up survey, an employer survey, and an assessment of student performance. Suggestions for the presentation of results for individual activities have been given in each of the technique chapters.

The preparation of the report covering the first four sections we have discussed to this point can be accomplished by the director of the evaluation or his designee. The last section, which includes judgments and the conclusions drawn by the evaluator on the basis of results from the previous sections, requires much broader input from staff and related personnel. Throughout this text, within each of the technique chapters as well as in the introductory chapters, the involvement of staff in evaluation activities has been emphasized. However, in most cases it is impossible to involve *all* personnel who have some kind of commitment or relationship with the program or

Student Assessment Results

89% of typing program graduates have exhibited a typing speed in excess of 60 words per minute in a timed and controlled testing situation.

Student Follow-up Results

Response to:

	HIGH	AVERAGE	LOW
How would you rate the instruction in typing which you received.	80%	16%	4%

(416 students responding)

Employer Survey Results

Response to:

	HIGH	AVERAGE	LOW
Please rate the typing skill of the individual named above.	65%	30%	5%

FIGURE 9–4   *Example Results from Student Follow-up, Employer Survey, and Student Performance Assessment*

component which is being evaluated. The *utilization* of evaluation results can and should provide for the involvement of all personnel, including instructional, administrative, and ancillary, in the analysis of results and formulation of conclusions and judgments based upon these results. Each staff member should share in the actual formulation of recommendations and identification of solutions. They will most certainly be involved in the implementation of these solutions, and will be more convinced of their role if involved in the analysis of results and formulation of conclusions.

Once the report has been prepared by the director of the evaluation, he should distribute it to the staff who will be involved in the formulation of the latter section of the report—the drawing of conclusions. The staff should then be given the opportunity to individually review results and interpret the findings. Staff members should meet as a group to discuss the findings and try to come to a consensus concerning their interpretation. The size of the involved group will determine the method by which the group will attempt to achieve a consensus. If a program staff is composed of only three or four individuals, these three or four can all be involved in analyzing the entirety of the evaluative findings from several different activities. On the other hand, if a program staff consists of fifteen or twenty individuals, the data should be compressed for group analysis to save time in considering the voluminous amount of information. Another possibility is to concern smaller groups with specific evaluation objectives, providing them with information pertaining to a single objective. Later the total group can receive and react to the judgments of each small group.

DRAWING CONCLUSIONS FROM EVALUATIVE RESULTS

Within each of the preceding technique chapters, a section has been devoted to the utilization of results. Within these sections, examples have been given to portray possible methods for interpreting the results. The formal evaluation report, however, should formalize interpretations which have been made by those involved in the program and communicate these to the reader. As used in this text, *an evaluative conclusion is a statement of judgment which has been based upon the systematic analysis of evaluative information.*

Conclusions drawn from evaluation results may relate to predetermined or exploratory decision situations depending upon the purpose for which the evaluation activities were conducted. In Chapter 2 a great deal of attention was paid to identifying decision situations and planning evaluation activities so as to provide information on which decisions may be based. Conclusions would be based upon a synthesis of information pertinent to the particular decision at hand—the predetermined decision situation. Drawing conclusions, however, is not identical to making the decision. The conclusion represents a judgment by the evaluator which is based upon evaluative data. It is the decision maker's responsibility to consider the conclusion in light of other conclusions and of political and social forces which exist both within and outside the education or training institution.

A second type of conclusion which can be formulated is based less specifically on a predetermined decision situation and is more exploratory in nature. Exploratory evaluation is initiated to explore general concerns or feelings about existing program inadequacy. That is, if a program manager believes a program may be inadequate but has no information on which to base his opinion, he may design and implement an evaluation to identify areas or components of the program which need improvement.

Before they draw a conclusion, the staff should review and discuss all information which is relevant to the particular topic. The staff or other related personnel, such as advisory committee members, should review the first four sections of the evaluation report, focusing most specifically on the fourth section which contains the evaluation results. A meeting should then be scheduled at which the staff will discuss the results and complete section five of the report, the evaluative conclusions. This meeting can be structured by the group leader to fit its normal functioning procedures or it may be organized around the following suggested steps.

Step 1: General Discussion

Start the staff conference with a general overview of the task to be faced and field any questions regarding the procedures that were utilized in gathering the evaluation information. If necessary, clarify the other sections of the evaluation report to the group. Then provide each group member the opportunity to offer comments or general information regarding the evaluation findings.

Step 2: State a Conclusion

Ask each group member to draw one positive conclusion based upon the results. It may seem a waste of time to state positive conclusions regarding exemplary parts of the program when most evaluation focuses on deficiencies. However, there are sound practical and psychological reasons for focusing on the positive side. Psychologically, the consideration of positive program attributes will reassure program staff of the formative nature of the evaluation. Practically, the inclusion of exemplary conclusions in the

evaluation report can lead to the utilization of the strongest capacities and capitalize on the program's strengths to overcome its recognized deficiencies. As each person in the group presents a conclusion,
have that person or a stenographer record the conclusion.

Step 3: Review Initial Conclusions

Have the group leader review each of the conclusions that were
developed in Step Two and give his reactions to the conclusion. This
step will help ensure a consistent format and style for formulating
subsequent conclusions. The following questions are presented to aid
in the analysis of initially developed conclusions.

1. Do you have sufficient evidence to support your conclusion?
2. Does the conclusion reflect the consensus of the group?
3. Is the conclusion compatible with the major goal and purpose of the
   evaluation?
4. Is the statement precise and does it specifically note a characteristic of
   the program?

Step 4: Team Development of Conclusions

As mentioned earlier, the size of the group will dictate the method
utilized in formulating a series of conclusions which relate to the
purposes of the evaluation. If small group divisions are made to
consider only one segment of the evaluation results (such as those
pertaining to a single evaluation objective), the entire group should
be afforded the opportunity to react to all conclusions. This can be
accomplished by designating a leader of each small group to be
responsible for presenting the groups' conclusions verbally. To encourage reaction and discussion by the group, it is good to disseminate conclusions in written form or to present them on an overhead
projector. Conclusions should be revised or accepted intact depending upon the group consensus.

Step 5: Edit Conclusions

The group leader or evaluation director should collect all conclusions
from small group leaders. The leader should review all conclusions

and reword those that are in need of correction. All conclusions should be made parallel in style before they are included in the printed evaluation report.

Step 6: Staff Review of Written Conclusions

Once the leader has edited the conclusions, these should be duplicated and given to staff for their consideration. Staff members should be asked to review the conclusions at their leisure and return the copy to the leader, with comments if any are required, by an established date.

Step 7: Print and Disseminate Report

After final changes are made, the report should be duplicated and disseminated to the appropriate audience. The report may be used internally or it may be disseminated to external parties. Here again, the specific purposes and objectives of the evaluation study will dictate the report audience.

UTILIZING EVALUATIVE CONCLUSIONS IN PLANNING

Conclusions drawn from evaluative findings can be utilized in many ways. The CIPP evaluation model provides one structure for the incorporation of evaluation in decision making. Information concerning student and societal needs, available instructional resources, and the formulation or revision of program or course objectives are all relevant to *context evaluation*. Information contributing to decisions such as choice of programs, materials, equipment, and staff can be classified as relative to *input evaluation*. Similarly, information which is used to assess how an actual program, course, or other educational endeavor was implemented, (was it implemented as originally planned?) is all a part of *process evaluation*. Information and conclusions which pertain to the outcomes of instruction or the education or training agency in general, either intended or unintended outcomes, contribute to *product evaluation.*

These four types of evaluation are inextricably related, and in planning or decision making it is often necessary to utilize more than one of these CIPP components. Consider the case of a nurse's aide training program conducted by one community college. Let us assume the following conclusion was drawn by program staff on the basis of results from an employer survey and a student follow-up survey.

> CONCLUSION: Employer survey results from supervising nurses, and feedback from former students, indicate that laboratory skills of nursing aide graduates are less than adequate.

From this conclusion many inferences can be drawn regarding why the laboratory skills of graduates are not adequate. To plan any corrective or remedial action, it is necessary that the evaluator fully understand the problem. To further define the problem, the following types of questions might be asked.

> CONTEXT EVALUATION: Are our objectives for lab instruction relevant?
>
> Are our students capable of meeting the lab objectives?
>
> Are our facilities for lab instruction adequate?
>
> Are our lab instruction staff members qualified?
>
> Do our lab classes, as planned, incorporate an adequate amount of instructional time?
>
> PROCESS EVALUATION: Were the objectives of our program all covered by instruction?
>
> Was the planned amount of time spent on each of the lab skills?
>
> Do our staff members do an adequate job of teaching?

The answers to many of these questions can be found with a

thorough review of evaluative information gathered previously through one or more of the evaluation activities. It may be necessary to initiate more evaluation activities to further define the problem and its underlying causes. The causes of the deficiency are probably many. However, let us assume there is one primary deficiency—inadequate lab experience and skill on the part of the two lab instructors. The general procedures that we can use to remedy the problem can be applied to almost all problems that we might identify within the educational or training institution.

Acquiring Relevant Resources

A necessary first step is the identification and delineation of available resources. These resources are of two broad classes: implementation resources and planning resources. Implementation resources (time, financial, and personnel) are those which fall within the education or training institution's control and can be channeled to facilitate program changes. Many times, the utilization of these resources will not increase an institution's budget, but more commonly it may be necessary to delete one thing to provide resources for another.

Implementation resources may be identified to aid in planning (perhaps one group of individuals need released time from their current responsibilities to conduct a search for solutions). Resources may also be required to obtain or implement a solution on a trial basis, necessitating a financial expenditure or the temporary reassignment of a staff member. There may also be a need for evaluation following the trial run to determine the success of the venture. In many cases, resources necessary for implementing a solution may also be needed to maintain the solution.

Planning resources are much broader than implementation resources and these may exist either within or external to the education or training institution. They are, in essence, those resources that can be used in identifying possible solutions for identified deficiencies. The actual identification and utilization of planning resources make up a sizeable segment of input evaluations as it is defined within the CIPP framework. There are two stages in acquiring relevant planning resources: 1) the identification of leads to possible solutions, and 2) the homing-in on resources which are specifically related to the actual decision situation. Figure 9—5 pro-

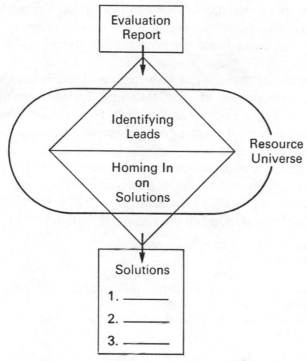

FIGURE 9-5 *The Context of Planning Resource Acquisition*

vides a schematic view of this process which begins with the evaluation report and ends with the selection of a solution.

Moving from top to bottom in Figure 9–5, one can consider the conclusions of the evaluation report, and these items begin to trigger thoughts on where to go for information. The professional experiences of the staff generally provide at least a starting point in the search for relevant information. The common response of *I remember reading (or hearing or seeing) something that pertains to that problem* is often the starting point in the homing-in on possible solutions.

Building and Maintaining Awareness of Possible Solutions

Staff members within an education or training institution have, in most cases, already acquired a bank of information on possible solutions to many problems. The formal training of staff members, in addition to the experiences gained in prior jobs, has made most of them experts in problem solving of this sort. The diversity of staff in terms of background broadens even further the range of expertise available.

One means of maintaining awareness is through newsletters and mass media. Newsletters often contain new development and reports of innovative happenings. Another way to maintain awareness of possible resources is through a personal acquaintance network. Many studies have shown that the most innovative people in any field have numerous contacts and encounters with others outside their system, people who are different from themselves in background, role, perspective, skill, and knowledge (Havelock, 1970). Havelock has suggested ways of maintaining an interpersonal network:

Attendance at professional meetings
Visits to other agencies
Phone calls to outsiders
Interacting with people who are in different roles and different systems whenever the opportunity arises
Maintaining good contacts and a habit of consulting with insiders and colleagues

Brainstorming is a technique which can be used by the group leader and staff members to generate solution ideas. This is probably one of the fastest means of coming up with solutions, and freeing the thinking of staff members. Brainstorming basically involves four steps: 1) preparing the group with background information, 2) setting the stage, 3) establishing and maintaining ground rules, and 4) summarizing and synthesizing the outcomes.

First, the leader should brief everyone concerning the problems at hand. In the example presented earlier, the problem was inadequacy in the staff of the laboratory segment of the nurse's aide program. The group would be told this fact and would be asked to suggest possible ways of overcoming the problem. At this point information on planning and implementing resources would also be presented to the involved staff.

The second step of brainstorming is to set the stage, and this involves the reemphasis of the problem and presentation of several example solutions, to give the staff an idea of what is to be accomplished.

The third step—setting of ground rules—should also be handled by the group leader. Ground rules should allow each participant to suggest anything that comes to mind, regardless of its apparent insignificance. The most important rule is that no initial criticism will be made of any suggestion. Hopefully, this kind of general rule will facilitate free association without any hesitation on the part of the staff. The only comment on ideas by other members of the group should be additions to a previous idea or variations on the same theme. Another important factor at this stage should be the recording of all ideas generated by the group. The *jot board recording* is probably the most useful. This will allow the group to review those suggestions which have been made and will provide a record for later discussion.

The last step of summarizing and synthesizing the results of the brainstorming is really a post-conference type of activity. The group leader can sit down to combine and synthesize some of the suggestions that have been made. Those which have been repeated can be made into one.

A third means of maintaining an awareness of resources involves a knowledge of information systems. The ERIC system, for example, maintains ten clearinghouses for information pertinent to specific specialty areas. One of these centers focuses on career education. Most university libraries maintain a total bank of the ERIC documents on microfiche which are indexed in a monthly publication, *Research in Education*. In addition, many universities offer a computer search service in which the ERIC document files are searched by machine to identify all documents which pertain to a certain topic. By understanding the use of such information systems, the staff of educational and training institutions have a vast source for identifying plausible solutions for identified problems.

Homing In on Specific Solutions

The second phase or step in the acquisition of relevant resources involves the homing in or focusing on aspects within the staff's initial identification of possibilities. The staff should select those solutions which are most relevant to the problems identified by the conclusions of the evaluation report. Much of the procedure involved in the homing in or focusing process can be viewed as common sense. However, there are several procedures which can guide in the overall effort. These procedures or steps are only guides and many may be ignored depending on the specific situation under consideration.

Acquire an Overview from a Comprehensive Written Source. The first step in the homing in strategy is to acquire an overview from a comprehensive written source. It is generally worthwhile to understand or at least gain a feeling for the research development theory and past practice in an area from which you are about to choose a solution. Many times the reading or scanning of a current textbook or research review article can prove fruitful in this first step by defining the scope of the topic, the work that has been done in various places at various times, the level of solid research understanding of the topic, and by providing valuable leads to more detailed sources. This information can provide a better understanding of the area in which you are involved.

Contact at Least One Person Who Has Had Direct Experiences. In most cases you will be able to identify institutions which have had problems similar to those you are experiencing. It can be advantageous to talk with at least one individual from one of these institutions so as to gain information about solutions they have chosen or not chosen, and the reasons for their decisions. This is not to say that solutions can be simply adapted from another situation, but at least a feel for the solution or area of solution will be acquired.

Observe the Solution in a Concrete or Live Form. When possible solutions have been identified as existing within other institutions, it is often advantageous to observe that solution or change as it is being utilized. For example, if one possible solution for the nurse's aide problem has been identified as self-instructional packages for laboratory instruction, and an institution that uses these packages has been identified, it may be worth visiting the institution to view the use of these materials. Visits to other institutions will help to provide answers to questions such as: *Is this solution really working for them? Is it really benefiting them? Will it really work for us?*

Obtain Evaluative Data. Just as evaluative information can be utilized in identifying a problem, this information can be utilized in assessing alternative solutions. If an evaluation of a planned solution has been conducted by another institution, this assessment will undoubtedly be of use to the decision maker.

Pilot-test the Solution. It is often worthwhile to conduct a limited feasibility test of a possible solution. There are three broad categories of measures which can be taken during a feasibility test. The first is benefit. Will the potential solution really do a lot of good if it works? The second is workability. Will the potential solution really work regardless of how much good it is supposed to do? Is it practical for use in this setting at this point in time? The third is diffusibility. Will the solution be accepted by the staff involved regardless of benefit and workability? The following questions can be asked within the framework of these three broad considerations (Havelock, 1970).

1. Potential Benefits
    a) How many people will it help?
    b) How long will it help them?
    c) How much will it help them?
    d) Does it have any negative effects?
2. Workability
    a) Will a proposed solution actually provide the promised benefits?
    b) Will the proposed solution perform reliably?
    c) Can the staff meet the dollar costs and human costs?
    d) Are the costs reasonable in proportion to the expected benefits?
    e) Does the institution have the staff to operate the solution successfully?
    f) Is the solution adequately developed?
3. Diffusibility
    a) Is the solution acceptable?
    b) Can it be demonstrated easily and convincingly?
    c) Can it be tried out on a limited basis before full implementation?
    d) Is it adequately packaged and labeled?

In some cases this step will be impossible. For example, if one of the possible solutions identified is to provide release time for laboratory instructors to work in a local hospital laboratory for three or four hours per day over a six-month period to gain actual occupational experience, this type of solution might be difficult to obtain on a trial basis. But when possible, the trial run is a suggested procedure.

Acquire a Framework for Evaluating the Results of the Trial. If a trial is possible, a framework should be established which allows for the analysis and evaluation of the solution. This might involve testing students following their involvement in the solution activity, sampling staff reaction to the solution, and so on. This evaluation information should be ultimately used to determine whether the solution should be implemented on a full-scale basis. If more than one solution has been piloted, results can be compared to reveal the best possible solution.

Gaining Acceptance by Staff

A very important link in the utilization of evaluation results to bring about change is gaining acceptance of the proposed change by staff. This step of the implementation process is actually the culmination of the review of relevant resources and the selection of a solution. Once a solution is identified, in most education and training situations it cannot be simply mandated or installed by a higher authority. Varying styles of leadership behavior can be utilized to gain staff acceptance of change. Schmidt (1966) describes leadership regarding decision making from an autocratic through a democratic style as follows:

Telling: The leader unilaterally identifies a problem, makes a decision, and tells subordinates what they are required to do.

Persuading: The leader unilaterally makes a decision but instead of telling sets out to persuade the subordinates to accept the decision.

Consulting: The leader, before making a decision, discusses the problem with subordinates giving them a chance to influence the decision before the leader decides.

Joining: The leader works as a group member in identifying a problem and making the decision. The leader in this instance would agree before the group decision to carry out the group's determination.

Delegating: The leader turns the decision making totally over to the group of subordinates. He would agree to support and carry out their decision as long as the decision was related to the boundaries of the problem definition.

It is pretty well accepted that no one of these leadership styles is optimum. Many researchers indicate that an effective leader utilizes each, depending on the situation and the group. Throughout this text, we have emphasized the involvement of those involved in programs in the evaluative effort. However, simply involving staff in the collection of data, formulation of conclusions, and identification of potential solutions may not mean the actual acceptance of the final decision and subsequent implementation of change. The emphasis here is obviously on the democratic end of the leadership style continuum. This is not to imply, however, that some decision and implementation actions would not be most efficiently made by one of the styles of the autocratic end of the continuum—telling, persuading. The effective leader will identify the most facilitative style for each situation and group.

In fostering the acceptance of change, the leader, and in some instances the evaluator, can systematically contribute to the important components of changes. An understanding or an awareness of how individuals accept change may be beneficial in the leading and fostering role. Researchers have identified six phases in the process of accepting and adopting change or innovation:

Awareness: The individual is exposed to the innovation and becomes aware of it. As yet, he has only a passive interest and does not necessarily seek further information.

Interest: The interest stage is characterized by active information seeking about the innovation. Although finding it interesting, the individual has not made a judgment as to the innovation's suitability.

Evaluation: This is a period of mental trial of the innovation. The individual in his own mind applies the innovation to his situation.

Trial: The individual uses the innovation on a small scale in order to determine how it will actually work in his own situation.

Adoption: The results of the trial are weighed and on the basis of post-trial evaluation the decision to adopt or reject is made.

Integration: This involves not only adoption of the change but making it routine as well. It must be integrated into the day-to-day activities of the individual.

These six stages of adoption can be fostered by providing certain information, assistance, or leadership at the various stages. Figure 9-6 indicates some facilitative behaviors. By effectively utilizing

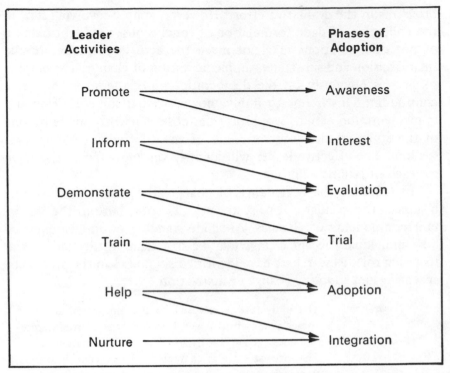

FIGURE 9–6   *Phases of Adoption with Suggested Facilitative Activities*

some of these tools, changes resulting from the utilization of evaluation results can be nurtured and real effects in the education and training program can be felt.

REFERENCES

Havelock, R. G. *A Guide to Innovation in Education.* Ann Arbor: University of Michigan, 1970.

Schmidt, W. H. *The Styles of Leadership.* Washington, D.C.: Leadership Resources, Inc., 1966.

Index